In 2001, Betty Kitchener and Anthony Jorm developed the Mental Health First Aid Training and Research Program in Australia, with the vision of creating "an empowered community providing support to one another in times of mental health problems and mental health crises."

Betty Kitchener and Anthony Jorm have granted permission to the Maryland Department of Health and Mental Hygiene, the Missouri Department of Mental Health, and the National Council for Community Behavioral Healthcare to reproduce and update this copyrighted material for the purposes of improving the mental health knowledge and skills of the United States public in responding to early stage mental illness and mental health crises. This manual, which is part of the overall Mental Health First Aid® USA program, was reproduced and updated with funding provided by the Substance Abuse and Mental Health Services Administration (SAMHSA) Mental Health Transformation State Incentive Grants.

The first aid information in this manual is based on guidelines developed by the Australian Mental Health First Aid Training and Research Program from 2006 to 2008, using the consensus of international expert panels involving mental health consumers, caregivers, and professionals. The following people worked on the development of these guidelines: Claire Kelly, Robyn Langlands, Anna Kingston, and Laura Hart. Further details of the guidelines may be found at http://www.mhfa.com.au/cms/mental-health-first-aid-guidelines-project/.

A range of studies, including randomized controlled trials, have shown that Mental Health First Aid training improves knowledge, reduces stigmatizing attitudes, and increases first aid actions toward people with mental health problems and challenges. [1, 2, 3, 4, 5, 6, 7]

YOUTH MENTAL HEALTH FIRST AID COURSE

This manual is an accompaniment to the Youth Mental Health First Aid® USA training course designed to teach lay people methods of assisting a young person who may be in the early stages of developing a mental health problem or in a mental health crisis. This manual is designed for members of the public who have frequent contact with youth and young adults, such as parents, school staff, sports coaches, and youth workers/volunteers. It is most relevant when it is first apparent to an adult that a youth or young adult is exhibiting signs of emotional, behavioral, or mental health challenges. However, the manual may also provide useful information on how to assist a young person who has had long term mental health challenges or a history of a serious mental disorder.

The *Youth Mental Health First Aid® USA* manual contains information on mental health challenges and disorders in youth and young adults in the United States and incorporates the latest evidence on treatments and services available to them as relevant resources. Throughout this manual, the term *mental health* is used; however, we acknowledge the field's movement toward the term *behavioral health* to encompass mental health and substance use treatments, services, and supports.

The *Youth Mental Health First Aid® USA* manual references youth and young adults or young people, which includes adolescents. The manual uses the term *adolescence* when citing specific research or data and direct quotes and when discussing human development. This population is generally defined as those between the ages of 12 and 18. However, because children develop at different rates, adolescence can start earlier than 12 years of age and can continue through to the mid-20s; thus, this manual could be relevant when helping people who are a little younger or older. For older youth and young adults, behaviors and the resulting first aid responses may look different than those for younger children. When using this manual, first aiders need to use good judgment about whether the information is going to be appropriate for helping a person outside of the age range specified.

The *Youth Mental Health First Aid® USA* manual also addresses the needs of transition age youth, those between ages 18 and 25, because it is during this time that many young people may leave home to be on their own. At this age, some young people may be transitioning out of child service systems, such as child welfare, and into adult service systems. In addition, critical issues of youth rights vary from state to state and from system to system. For example, although most states require minors (those younger than 21 years old) to obtain consent from a parent or guardian before receiving outpatient mental health treatment, in some states, someone who is 15 years old or older may voluntarily apply for hospitalization for mental health services.

In addition to behavioral health challenges, some youth and young adults may have developmental disabilities, and it is especially important for first aiders to be aware of the unique needs of these youth and to treat them with dignity and respect for their individual preferences and needs. *Developmental disabilities* is the umbrella term for a wide variety of disorders acquired before the age of 18, including intellectual disability (formerly called *mental retardation*), epilepsy, and cerebral palsy. Intellectual disability and autism spectrum disorders are addressed in the *Youth Mental Health First Aid® USA* manual, and additional resources are provided.

SOME IMPORTANT NOTES:

The content of this manual is informational in nature and is not intended as a substitute for counseling, medical care, peer support, or treatment of any kind.

The *Youth Mental Health First Aid® USA* manual was not developed for use by youth and young adults themselves. The role of a first aider can be a demanding one, and youth or young adults may or may not have the cognitive or emotional maturity to carry out first aid actions safely. They may try to take on too much, offering counseling to a friend, or may feel trapped and overwhelmed when dealing with issues of confidentiality. However, many young adults who come in contact with youth and other young adults may be very effective as first aiders and should be considered for training.

As acknowledged throughout the *Youth Mental Health First Aid® USA* manual, parents and caregivers play an important role in the mental well-being of their children. Although this manual is intended for a broad range of first aiders, not specifically for parents and caregivers, each section concludes with resources that parents and caregivers may find helpful, as well as how a first aider can support family and caregivers.

This manual is not designed to address specific cultural, racial and ethnic groups; however, cultural considerations are noted, and examples are used to illustrate the importance of addressing cultural and racial differences.

Finally, the *Youth Mental Health First Aid* manual acknowledges that many youth and young adults with mental health challenges have been victims of violence or have experienced trauma.[8, 9] All approaches offered in this manual should be provided in a way that is sensitive to the personal experience of interpersonal violence, including sexual abuse, severe neglect, loss, and the witnessing of violence, terrorism, or disaster.

>> Acknowledgments

The development of *Youth Mental Health First Aid® USA* could not have been accomplished without the significant contributions of many individuals and organizations. First and foremost is to acknowledge the foundational and groundbreaking work of Claire Kelly, Betty Kitchener, and Anthony Jorm for the development of the Australian *Youth Mental Health First Aid* program.

In 2011, the National Technical Assistance Center for Children's Mental Health at Georgetown University drafted the *Youth Mental Health First Aid® USA* manual on behalf of Mental Health First Aid® USA. Special gratitude to Kathy Lazear of the Human Service Collaborative, who, under contract with Georgetown University, was the lead author in the adaptation of the manual, and for the guidance and significant contributions provided by Joan Dodge, Sybil Goldman, and Marisa Irvine of Georgetown University's National Technical Assistance Center for Children's Mental Health. Other Georgetown faculty and staff who contributed their expertise included Kevin Enright, Terri Jackson, Doreen Cavanaugh, Diane Jacobstein, and Vivian Jackson.

Family members and youth were integral partners in the planning, writing, and review of the *Youth Mental Health First Aid* manual. Their efforts ensured that the perspectives of young people and families are reflected throughout and that the manual respects the dignity and strengths of youth and young people. Thanks to Shannon CrossBear, Tyrus Curtis, Jared Jacobs, and Brianne Masselli for providing their initial input and guidance. We are also grateful to Ann Geddes and Jane Walker with the Maryland Coalition of Children and Families, and Maryland Youth M.O.V.E. for their review of the manual.

The following individuals and agencies need to be acknowledged for their contributions and commitment to ensuring that the manual is family driven and youth guided, culturally competent, grounded in good clinical practice, and inclusive of relevant and useful information to guide adults assisting young people with mental health challenges and disorders in the United States. These agencies and individuals include:

• Mental Health First Aid® USA

  > National Council for Community Behavioral Healthcare: Linda Rosenberg, Meena Dayak, Bryan Gibb, Margaret Jaco, and Susan Partain

  > Maryland Department of Health and Mental Hygiene: Daryl Plevy and Al Zachik

  > Mental Health Association of Maryland: Lea Ann Browning-McNee, Lisa Cinelli, Kari Gorkos, and Linda Raines

  > Missouri Department of Mental Health: Patsy Carter and Dottie Mullikin

  > Missouri Institute of Mental Health: Carol Evans and Benton Goon

• National Federation of Families for Children's Mental Health: Sandra Spencer and Theresa King

• Maryland Child and Adolescent Innovations Institute: Michelle Zabel

• Substance Abuse and Mental Health Services Administration, Center for Mental Health Services, Child, Adolescent and Family Branch: Gary Blau

We would like to thank the Stavros Niarchos Foundation for its generous support, which allowed for our curriculum pilot process to occur at minimal expense to both the instructors and the participants in their initial courses.

We especially appreciated the patience and guidance of the individuals who took time to attend the initial course offering in St. Louis in March 2012.

>> Acknowledgments

We are grateful to the following organizations and Mental Health First Aid instructors who graciously provided their time and expertise in testing the new curriculum:

- Altapointe Health Systems (Mobile, AL): Michelle Krulewicz-Dees and Emily Minto-Head

- Aspen Pointe (Colorado Springs, CO): Jason DeaBueno and Sue Readnour

- Community Counseling Centers of Chicago: Shannon Garrison and Sara Lindstrom

- Community Counseling Services (Starkville, MS): Lori Latham and Stephanie Taylor

- Community Partnership of Southern Arizona: Steven Nagle

- Lutheran Social Services (Duluth, MN): Lee Berlinquette

- Madera County Department of Behavioral Health: Debbie DiNoto, Sylvia Romero, and Marizela Terkildsen

- Mental Health Association of Frederick County & Mental Health Association of Maryland: Lea Ann Browning-McNee

- Missouri Institute of Mental Health & Department of Mental Health: Jermine Alberty and Patsy Carter

- Pennsylvania Community Providers Association: Jennifer Bankard

Lastly, thank you to all of the individuals who generously gave their time and input in attending the pilot courses.

The Need for Youth Mental Health First Aid® USA

When I look back on the struggles that I had as a young person and I think of the support that I received, I notice now that some of the assistance was really not helpful. I often felt misunderstood, at a loss for words on how to explain how I was feeling and, honestly, embarrassed to sometimes even ask for help. Back then, when I was younger, mental health was not something we always talked about with our friends, neighbors, coaches or even teachers because if you did there was a fear of being treated differently. Looking back on my experience and understanding my mental health better, I can see where it would have been helpful to have people to talk to that were not always professionals. As a young person you want to fit in and you want to have the same opportunities as others. Now, as a youth advocate, I encourage youth to speak up about their challenges and provide education to adults who want to support youth in a way that is helpful and meaningful.

Mental Health First Aid training is a great resource for anyone who works with youth as it allows a person to learn specific skills that are important during a mental health crisis. Youth may not know how to articulate their needs—I know that at a younger age I couldn't tell someone what to do that would have helped in that moment. Looking back, I can see that now. Help to me was reassuring me that I was safe, was listening to me in a way that didn't make me feel bad or inadequate, but, most importantly, when I did have the courage to ask for help, was someone responding in a way that was helpful not hurtful. I am glad the times are changing and that we are talking more about mental health in the community and offering new ways to support youth during these challenging times.

Youth Mental Health First Aid® USA is perfect because it gives community members, friends, and coaches an opportunity to better understand what mental health is, what some of the common diagnosis are, and how to respond to youth who might be experiencing a crisis. It reduces the misconception many people may have about mental health. What is meaningful is that it gives individuals in our communities the skills to handle a crisis in a way that feels nonjudgmental, safe, and inspires hope for the youth. Youth Mental Health First Aid® USA is a great framework for providing immediate support to the youth and also getting them connected to other professionals and caring adults that can further help in a time of crisis. We all need to ask for help at some point in our life. As young people, we hope that when we do reach out, people are prepared and ready to provide appropriate support and resources. If more people were prepared when I went into a crisis it would never have been called a crisis. It would have been a meaningful conversation about what my needs were in that moment and how the people who were closest to me could support me through it. It is my hope that the training of others in Mental Health First Aid allows them to support youth in the way that I wish I could have been helped.

Brianne Masselli
Director of Training and CQI
THRIVE System of Care, Maine
Youth Development Consultant
Youth M.O.V.E. National

>> Table of Contents

Most definitions of first aid include an iteration of "immediate and temporary help, emergency care, or treatment given to an injured or ill person before professional medical care is available." The goals of *Youth Mental Health First Aid® USA* are twofold—to teach members of the public how to respond in a mental health emergency with youth and young adults and to offer support to a young person who appears to be in emotional distress. By using *Youth Mental Health First Aid®*, individuals coming into contact with youth and young adults can acquire the basic knowledge and skills to respond to a young person in distress.

Mental health status, as with physical health status, affects everyone. In fact, mental health problems are more common than heart disease, lung disease, and cancer combined.[10,11] One in five Americans is estimated to have a diagnosable mental disorder, such as depression, anxiety, or substance use, in any given year, including 13.7 million children.[12, 13] Of those children with a diagnosable disorder, only a third get help from formal mental health care or substance abuse services. First aiders can help address this serious problem by understanding several key concepts woven throughout *Youth Mental Health First Aid® USA*.

The more knowledgeable people are about mental disorders, the less stigma will be associated with these common life challenges. Mental health challenges and disorders can be as disabling as cancer or heart disease in terms of premature death, lost productivity, and increased challenges to having a good quality of life. Not every young person in psychological distress has a mental disorder, but a young person may fall along a continuum of good mental health and mental illness. Many young people with mental health challenges can be helped with early identification as well as early, appropriate support and intervention.

The more aware people are of what effective supports and treatments exist, the more young people will get the appropriate help they need. Eighty–ninety percent of individuals with mental disorders are treatable with an array of services and supports, including different treatment therapies as well as medications. Research has improved practitioners' ability not only to recognize and diagnose mental disorders, but to treat conditions effectively. Increasingly, interventions supporting mental health promotion, substance abuse prevention, and mental health and substance use treatment are evidence based, having been scientifically tested to provide the field with effective approaches for preventing and treating mental and substance use disorders.

The more knowledgeable people are about the signs and symptoms of mental disorders and other mental health challenges, the earlier youth, young adults, and their families will get the help they need. Research has shown that early detection and treatment of mental disorders can have a significant impact on the lives of young people.[14] *Youth Mental Health First Aid® USA* assists first aiders to recognize the signs early, before problems become a full-blown crisis, and respond appropriately.

Youth and young adults face and experience mental health challenges differently than adults. *Youth Mental Health First Aid® USA* was developed because symptoms of the same mental disorders can look different in children and adults. In addition, a number of mental health challenges are more likely to be prevalent in children and young people, such as attention deficit and disruptive behavior disorders, oppositional defiant disorder (ODD), and conduct disorder, which are discussed separately in this manual.

First aiders may not know all of the intricacies of the U.S. health care system, nor are they trained to provide diagnoses; the information provided here is designed to help the first aider assist a person showing symptoms of a mental illness or experiencing a mental health crisis until appropriate professional or other help can be engaged. Youth require the expertise of those who have training and specialized knowledge in child and adolescent issues and a family focus. A family's ability to choose the type and amount of services and supports their child receives is dependent on their income, insurance, or eligibility for public support as well as the availability of services where they live. The U.S. health care system also depends on the efforts of first responders, often emergency medical technicians (EMTs), paramedics, police, and firefighters, who are typically dispatched by a 911 operator to the scene of a crisis situation. All 50 states and the District of Columbia require these first responders to be licensed, but the type and intensity of training in mental health issues vary from community to community.

The importance of being aware of culture, diversity, and the uniqueness of the life experiences of individual youth and families is woven throughout *Youth Mental Health First Aid® USA*. The United States is a diverse country in many ways. In the United States, people's lives are enhanced by the richness of the many racial and ethnic cultures that have been part of the fabric of the country from its beginning to those who have more recently arrived; families who have immigrated as part of a life plan; or those who have abruptly arrived, seeking safety and refuge from war-ravaged areas of the world. Diversity is one of the United States' greatest strengths. Yet, the United States is a country with profound disparities that have an impact on the total health of the country's youth and their families. To be effective, first aiders need to respond in a manner that respects the culture and individuality of youth and their families who they encounter. In addition to adopting an attitude of genuine regard and respect for differences, first aiders must make efforts to increase their knowledge and awareness of factors affecting minority populations (e.g., African Americans, Asian American/Pacific Islanders, Hispanics/Latinos, and Native Americans/Alaska Natives). These factors include: differing worldviews, values, and beliefs; patterns of acculturation, assimilation, and immigration; effects of oppression and ethnic identity; and individual differences within every ethnic and racial group, such as sexual orientation and sexual identity.

The children's mental health field has increasingly focused on what have traditionally been adult concepts of recovery and resilience. According to the President's New Freedom Commission on Mental Health, "Recovery is a process by which people who have mental illness are able to work, learn, and participate fully in their communities. For some individuals, *recovery* is the ability to live a fulfilling and productive life despite a disability. For others, recovery implies the reduction or complete remission of symptoms."[15] *Resilience* refers to the process by which individuals learn to cope and appropriately manage their stress or mental health challenges. Both recovery and resilience rely on the individual to be an active part of the individual's path to wellness. This manual uses terms to support these concepts, such as *family driven* and *youth guided*, when describing types of treatment.[16]

When administering Mental Health First Aid for youth and young adults, the role of family members or other caregivers cannot be overstated. *Youth Mental Health First Aid® USA* defines *family* as the biological or legal parents, siblings, other relatives, foster parents, legal guardians, caregivers, and other primary relationships to the child whether by blood, adoption, legal, or social relationships. *Family* can include any natural, formal, or informal support people identified by the family. It is important to recognize that youth and young adults often turn first to one another in times of crisis and often find themselves in the role of first aiders.

Section 1.1 Mental Health Challenges and Disorders in Youth and Young Adults in the United States expands on the information in this introduction. It is hoped that the *Youth Mental Health First Aid® USA* manual will increase knowledge of mental health challenges in youth and will also give individuals the tools to help when young people in their schools, homes, and communities require first aid for a broad array of mental health challenges, including suicidal thoughts and behaviors, self-injury, panic attacks, reactions to trauma, acute psychosis, substance abuse, and aggressive behaviors.

SECTION 1: Mental Health Challenges and Disorders in Youth

Mental Health Challenges and Disorders in Youth and Young Adults in the United States

What Is Mental Health?

The term *mental health* is defined in different ways. Some definitions emphasize positive psychological well-being, whereas others see it as the absence of mental health problems. For example, the World Health Organization has defined mental health as "a state of well-being in which the individual realizes their own abilities, can cope with the normal stresses of life, can work productively and fruitfully, and is able to make a contribution to their community."[17]

The definition of *mental health* varies across individuals and cultures. Culture influences mental health, mental health challenges and disorders, and mental health services in many ways. Historically, mental health has been seen as a continuum ranging from good mental health to having a mental illness. Recently, an alternative view is to consider a mental health continuum and a mental health problem as coexisting and independent from each other.[18] In other words, someone with a diagnosable mental health problem, such as depression or schizophrenia, can still have a high level of positive mental health, such as social and emotional well-being. However, many people who have no serious or diagnosable mental health challenges or problems may still lack good mental health.[19]

There has been an increasing emphasis on taking a public health approach to children's mental health, which aims to balance the focus on children's mental health problems with a focus on children's positive mental health.[20, 21] This approach not only focuses on treatment, but also includes promotion, prevention, early intervention, and education to improve outcomes and health. This approach includes creating environments that promote and

support optimal mental health as well as building skills that enhance resilience. *Resiliency* can be defined as the capacity of children, youth, and families to successfully overcome life's challenges.

What Are Mental Health Challenges and Mental Disorders?

A variety of terms are used to describe mental health challenges and mental disorders in children, youth, and young adults, such as *serious emotional disorder, emotional and behavioral disorder, extreme emotional distress, psychiatric illness, mental illness, nervous exhaustion, mental breakdown, nervous breakdown,* and *burnout.*

A *mental disorder* or *mental illness* is a diagnosable illness that affects a person's thinking, emotional state, and behavior as well as disrupts the person's ability to work or carry out other daily activities and engage in satisfying personal relationships.[22]

The term *mental illness* is usually used to refer to severe mental health problems in children, youth, and young adults. There are different types of mental disorders, some of which are more common, such as depression and anxiety disorders, and some which are not common, such as schizophrenia and anorexia nervosa.

Mental health challenge is a broader term including both mental disorders (e.g., anxiety disorder, depression, bipolar disorder) and symptoms of mental disorders that may not be severe enough to warrant the diagnosis of a mental disorder (e.g., confused thinking or extreme highs and lows in mood). The Main

Place, a consumer-operated mental health recovery center in Ohio, defines a mental health challenge as

> any disease or condition affecting the brain that influences the way a person thinks, feels, behaves, and/or relates to others and to their surroundings.... Many mental health challenges are caused by a combination of genetic, biological, psychological, and environmental factors.... They are not a result of personal weakness, a character defect or poor upbringing. Recovery from a mental health challenge is not simply a matter of will and self-discipline.[23]

Children and youth with a *serious emotional disturbance* are defined as

> persons from birth up to age 18, who currently or at any time during the past year, have had a diagnosable mental, behavioral, or emotional disorder which substantially interferes with or limits the child's role or functioning in family, school, or community activities.[24]

Adults with a *serious mental illness* are defined by the Substance Abuse and Mental Health Services Administration as

> persons age 18 and over, who currently or at any time during the past year, have had a diagnosable mental, behavioral, or emotional disorder of sufficient duration to meet diagnostic criteria, resulting in functional impairment which substantially interferes with or limits one or more major life activities.[25]

Mental disorders often occur in combination. For example, a person with an anxiety disorder may also develop depression or a person who is depressed may abuse alcohol or other drugs perhaps in an effort to self-medicate. Terms used to describe having more than one mental disorder are *dual diagnosis, comorbidity,* and *co-occurrence.*[26]

The terms generally used throughout *Youth Mental Health First Aid® USA* are a *young person, youth,* or *young adult* with a *mental health challenge* or *mental disorder. Youth Mental Health First Aid® USA* does not cover all the different types of mental health challenges and disorders. The most common and most severe types are covered. However, it is important to note that the guidance in *Youth Mental Health First Aid® USA* may be useful and applied to other mental health challenges that are not covered.

How Common Are Mental Health Challenges and Mental Disorders in Youth and Young Adults?

In 2014, an estimated 43.6 million (18.1 percent) adults 18 or older experienced a mental illness in the past year. Additionally, an estimated 9.8 million adults aged 18 or older in the nation had a serious mental illness in the past year.[27]

The prevalence of mental disorders in children and youth (to the point at which their life is significantly impacted) is also estimated to be approximately 20 percent during a given year.

U.S. YOUTH WITH A MENTAL DISORDER DURING ADOLESCENCE (AGE 13–18)[29]		
	Prevalence (%)	With severe impact (%)
Anxiety disorders	31.9	8.3
Behavior disorders	19.1	9.6
Mood disorders	14.3	11.2
Substance use disorders	11.4	11.4
Overall prevalence with severe impact	22.2	

A number of youth and young adults experience a mental health challenge or disorder that interferes with their development and daily life activities. Some of these mental health challenges are mild and may only last for a short period, and others may last a lifetime. Identifying mental disorders in children, youth, and young adults takes into account their physical, mental, and emotional changes as the young person learns how to cope, adapt, and relate to others and to the world around them.

Facts About Mental Health Disorders in Children and Adolescents

- In 2014, 11.4 % of adolescents aged 12 to 17 years (approximately 2.8 million adolescents) experienced a major depressive episode during the past year.[27] (See *Depression in Young People*)

- Anxiety disorders are among the most common mental health challenges that occur in children and adolescents. (See *Anxiety in Young People*)[30]

- Attention deficit/hyperactivity disorder (ADHD) affects an estimated 4.1 percent of youth ages 9–17. (See *Attention Deficit and Disruptive Behavior Disorders in Young People*)

- Approximately three percent of adolescents in the United States have eating disorders, including anorexia nervosa and bulimia nervosa. (See *Eating Disorders in Young People*)

Unfortunately, many young people with mental disorders do not seek or access any professional help. For example, in 2014, (41.2 percent) of adolescents who experienced a past-year major depressive episode received treatment for depression in the past year.[27] This rate also varies according to the individual's gender, geographic region, past traumatic experiences, health insurance coverage, and overall health.[32] There are many reasons that young people may not access treatment; they may not know they have a mental health problem, youth may feel they will be stigmatized by their peers or family, or they or their family may not know how and where to seek mental or behavioral health care.

Impact of Mental Health Challenges and Mental Disorders

Although mental health challenges and mental disorders can begin in early childhood,[33] mental disorders often manifest themselves in adolescence or early adulthood. In the United States, half of all lifetime cases of mental illness begin by age 14, and there are long delays— sometimes decades—between the onset of symptoms and when people seek treatment.[34] When mental illnesses start at this stage of life, they can affect the young person's education, ability to work and form relationships (including marriage), and they can lead to the use of alcohol and other drugs. These disorders are not always well understood by people who have never experienced a mental health challenge or disorder themselves or lived with a person experiencing a mental health disorder. This is why it is so important to detect problems early and to ensure the person is properly treated and supported. Early identification and treatment of a mental health challenge or disorder can also prevent loss of productivity, high medical costs, and the associated burdens on family members and caregivers.[35]

Mental health challenges and disorders are the leading cause of disability in the United States and Canada.[36, 37] *Disability* refers to the amount of disruption a health problem causes to a person's ability to study, work, look after themselves, and carry on relationships with family and friends. However, because the disability caused by mental health challenges and disorders may not be readily visible to others, people with mental health challenges or disorders can be judged negatively. They may be incorrectly perceived as being attention seeking or not really ill. Others may judge them to be lazy, selfish, or uncooperative, which may be symptoms of the mental disorder. This lack of understanding contributes to the stigma that young people with mental health challenges or disorders can experience. To lessen this stigma, the community's attitude toward mental illness should be fundamentally the same as their approach to physical illness.[38] Young people with mental health challenges also need others to respect and acknowledge their strengths and attributes as well as contributions they make to family, friends, and their community.[39]

Accessing Mental Health Care and the People Who Can Help

Youth and young adults often do not seek professional help on their own because of embarrassment; lack of transportation; a fear that the professional will think negatively about them; and negative attitudes of their peers, family, or friends; or their own negative attitudes. As a result, many times young people will turn to their parents, caregivers, or friends for help.[40] Parents or caregivers may arrange for them to see a professional, and friends and other informal helpers can help educate them about what mental health services and supports are available and how to access them. First aiders can play an important role in encouraging youth and young adults to seek help. A variety of formal health professionals, peer supports and mentors, and informal supports can provide help to a young person with a mental health challenge or disorder.

In the United States, individuals providing mental health services and supports have different names and titles, and the services these professionals can provide may vary from state to state. Below is a brief description of some of the more common formal mental health providers for young people. Among the varied professions listed, it is important to seek individual professionals who have specific expertise in youth and families.

- **Medical doctors, pediatricians, and neurologists** (and other specialists) look for possible physical causes of the mental or behavioral health challenge and can prescribe medication if needed.

- **Psychiatrists** are medical doctors who specialize in the evaluation, diagnosis, and treatment of mental disorders.

- **Psychologists** may provide psychological evaluation, assessment, testing, and treatment but may not prescribe medications.

- **Licensed social workers** are trained to help individuals deal with a variety of mental health and daily living problems to improve overall functioning. States have varying requirements and licensing practices. For example, in some states, only a licensed certified social worker-clinical is able to conduct psychotherapy.

- **Social workers** may have either a bachelor's or master's degree and are helping professionals who focus on both individuals and their environment.

- **Counselors and therapists** provide advice, support, and specific mental health therapy to a person or group of individuals, such as a family. A licensed professional counselor is a counselor with a specific legal license.

- **Nurse practitioners** are registered nurses who have advanced education and clinical master's-level training in a health care specialty area, such as pediatric child health, elder and adult health, psychiatric mental health, women's and newborn health, and school or college health. They recommend medications and areas of treatment, and, in many states, they are allowed to prescribe medications.

- **Peer support providers or specialists** are individuals who have "lived experience" and work to assist others with similar experiences. Such support specialists often have expertise that professional training cannot replicate; however, in recent years, several states and national organizations have developed certification processes to ensure peer support specialists' knowledge and skills meet consistent and high standards of performance. Family peer support providers may be employed in the children's behavioral health field in any state. In addition, a few communities and states are also working to create youth–young adult peer support positions.

In addition to the variety of people who can help, there are also a variety of places where young people can go to get help. Historically, services for children and young adults with mental health challenges were provided either in the office of a mental health center or professional or in a residential facility. The number of alternative and effective home and community-based treatment interventions for children and young adults and their families is growing.[41] Medication is rarely the sole treatment for children and adolescents with mental health challenges and should be combined with appropriate therapy.[42]

During the past 30 years, more and more communities have been implementing a system of care approach to serving children and youth with serious and more complex mental health challenges. A *system* of care is a spectrum of effective, community-based services and supports for children and youth with or at risk for mental health challenges and their families that is organized into a coordinated network, builds meaningful partnerships with families and youth, and addresses their cultural and linguistic need in order to help them function better at home, in school, in the community, and throughout life.

The *wraparound* process is an approach within a system of care to individualize services and supports for a youth and their family bringing together the key agencies and people in a youth and families life to achieve the goals and outcomes determined by the young person and their family.

Care Coordinator, Service Coordinator, and Case Manager

Youth and young adults with complex mental health needs may benefit from the services of a care coordinator. Case managers and service or care coordinators may be one of any number of mental health professionals who organize appropriate services and supports for children and young adults with mental health challenges and their families. Generally, they coordinate mental health, social work, education, health, vocational, transportation, advocacy, respite care, and recreational services, as needed. A youth may have a *plan of care* (also called a *service plan, treatment plan,* or *wraparound plan*) that is specially designed for the individual youth and their family, based on individual strengths and needs. The plan is often developed collaboratively by the case manager or service coordinator with the youth and family. Case managers have an ongoing relationship with other individuals involved in providing care for the youth. A first aider may want to find out from the youth or their family whether they are involved in mental or behavioral health services and if the youth has a care plan and a service coordinator or care manager.

Informal or Natural Helpers and Social Supports

Many young people seek out social support during times of crisis and distress. Social supports and natural helpers may be neighbors, friends, extended family, coworkers, or other people to whom an individual may turn for support, such as family partners, youth workers, respite workers, and some clergy. A strong social support network can provide emotional support, feelings of security, and an increased sense of belonging and self-worth, as well as tangible supports, such as money, transportation, or housekeeping. Informal or natural helpers help to address cultural and language barriers, the shortage of trained mental health professionals, and lack of access to transportation. Informal supports or natural helpers are a key component of a system of care and wraparound approach to serving children, youth, young adults, and their families. Helping young people and their families recognize and build their own social supports is an important role of the first aider.

Self-Help Strategies

There is evidence that self-help strategies, complementary treatments, and lifestyle changes (e.g., exercise, meditation, yoga) can help adults with some mental illnesses,[43] but, in general, there has not been much research on which self-help strategies are effective in assisting youth and young adults.

Some youth and young adults may benefit from self-help strategies of different kinds. Even if strategies do not treat the mental disorder, they may help youth feel better and boost self-esteem. These practices may include more culturally relevant practices and can help young people to pursue overall health and well-being.

Self-help strategies young people may be encouraged to try are those that

>> **Interest them.**
For example, youth and young adults who enjoy media and art may want to try expressing their feelings through their art and may feel that this has some benefits for them.

>> **Encourage a sense of achievement or satisfaction.**
For example, young people may learn a new piece of music or complete a challenging task.

>> **Are social.**
For example, youth and young adults may join a club or make sure to see friends regularly.

>> **Are likely to be safe.**
For example, exercise and massage have positive effects on physical and mental health and few risks. However, youth and young adults with eating disorders or physical illnesses (including obesity) or who have not exercised for a long time should get a doctor's advice before starting an exercise program or massage therapy.

Natural therapies (e.g., aromatherapy, Ayurveda) that have been shown to be safe for adults may not be suitable for youth or young adults because of ongoing physical and brain development.

Health Disparities and Access to Services

The United States is a culturally, racially, and ethnically diverse country. In the 2010 U.S. Census, more than one-third of the U.S. population reported their race and ethnicity as something other than non-Hispanic White alone (i.e., minority). This group increased from

86.9 million to 111.9 million between 2000 and 2010, representing a growth of 29 percent during the decade.[44] Data from the 1990, 2000, and 2010 U.S. Census reveal that the population of Hispanic and Asian children grew by 5.5 million.[45] During the previous 10 years, the greatest growth in number was those children and youth who are multiracial. Similarly, there is great diversity in religious affiliations. The U.S. population, although mostly Christian (at 78 percent), including Protestants, Catholics, and Jehovah's Witnesses, also includes other religions (4.7 percent) such as Judaism, Buddhism, Muslim, and Hinduism.[46] About 16 percent of the U.S. population is not affiliated with any religious tradition.

The United States is also a country of differences within groups, such as income, age, sexual orientation, and gender identity. Each cultural group brings its own beliefs, traditions, and practices to its understanding of mental health, the role of treatment, type of treatment, role of helper, and so forth. Cultural communities can be a source of great strength and resiliency or the origin of emotional distress. This diversity can also lend itself to disparities in all types of health care. Bias, stereotype, stigma, racism, and discrimination may affect access to appropriate and quality mental health services, as well as difficulties in interactions between mental health professionals and children, youth, and their families. (See box to the right for examples of mental health disparities).

Examples of Mental Health Disparities and Disproportionalities[28, 47, 48]

- Hispanics and African Americans report lower risk of having a mental disorder as compared with their white counterparts, but those who become ill tend to have more persistent disorders. Similarly, African Americans were found to have lower rates of lifetime major depression than were their White counterparts living in similar areas, but the rates of major depression in the past year were similar across groups, indicating more persistent illness.

- Asian American/Pacific Islanders are 25 percent as likely as Whites and 50 percent as likely as African Americans and Hispanics to seek outpatient care, and they are less likely than Whites to receive inpatient care. When they do seek care, they are more likely to be misdiagnosed as problem free.

- American Indians/Alaska Natives appear to suffer disproportionately from depression and substance abuse and are overly represented in inpatient care compared with non-Indians and non-Natives, with the exception of private psychiatric hospitals.

- Youth in grades 7–12 who identify as lesbian, gay, or bisexual were more than twice as likely to have attempted suicide than their heterosexual peers.

Racial and ethnic minorities bear a greater burden of unmet health needs and thus suffer a greater loss to their overall health and productivity than their White counterparts. For example, researcher J. T. Gibbs said, "African American youth are more likely than White youth to be identified through the juvenile justice system, they are less likely to undergo a thorough psychological assessment, less likely to receive a psychiatric diagnosis, less likely to obtain therapeutic treatment, and more likely to experience long-term psychological impairments and behavioral and social deficits and dysfunctions."[49] Having knowledgeable, sensitive providers and clinicians will improve the quality and effectiveness of treatment of children who are ethnically, racially, and culturally diverse.

The ease of access to services, as well as the availability of appropriate services also varies from state to state and from community to community. For example, living in a rural or remote area presents unique challenges and opportunities. Services may be scarce, difficult to access, or a long way away. However, other services that may be available include telephone counseling, telemedicine, outreach services, online therapy, and community services. People living in rural and remote areas also often develop strong social networks of informal helpers and can be very creative in using other local resources, such as libraries, local service organizations, faith-based organizations, and schools.[50]

In many communities, it can take days or even weeks to obtain appropriate mental health services. Families may not understand the process of seeking help in the mental health service system or know where and how to access services. The issues associated with health insurance, such as inability to obtain coverage or limits on the duration and scope of services, can also be a deterrent to accessing services. Different rules govern eligibility for access to services and payment in the mental health system in each state. For example, psychologists, psychiatrists, and other mental health professionals vary in the amount they charge. The cost and type of treatment covered will vary depending on individual insurance coverage and state-specific Medicaid guidelines.

Medicaid is health insurance that helps many people who cannot afford medical care pay for some or all of their medical bills. Medicaid is financed and run jointly by the federal and state governments.[51] The Medicaid program does not provide health care services for everyone; a person must qualify for Medicaid. Low income is only one reason for Medicaid eligibility; *eligibility* is based on the young person's status (financial or legal), not the parent's. Also, if someone else's child lives with a family, the child may be eligible even if other family members are not, because the family income and resources will not count for the child. Medicaid is a state-administered program. Each state sets its own guidelines, subject to federal rules and guidelines. States must cover certain services to receive federal funds. Other services are optional and are elected by states.[52]

Legal rights of youth also have an impact on access to care and vary from state to state. In some states, a 14 year old can access substance abuse counseling without parental permission through community or private agencies. Most states require minors (those younger than 21 years old) to get consent from a parent or guardian before receiving outpatient mental health treatment, but, in some states, someone who is 15 years old or older may admit themselves to a hospital for mental health services. Most states that allow minors to access mental health services without parental consent give practitioners discretion about whether to inform the youth's parents about the treatment.

CHAPTER 1.2

Adolescent Development

Adolescence is a time of change and self-discovery, and, although it is different for every individual, there are some things that are common to all youth—the physical, mental, social, and emotional changes that take a young person from childhood to adulthood. Some of the behaviors and changes that occur in adolescence may look like symptoms of mental health disorders. Alternatively, the symptoms of mental health disorders may be masked by these big changes. The changes and stress experienced during adolescence can cause mental health challenges and disorders. Mental health challenges and disorders can have a serious impact on adolescent development. Having an understanding of the changes that occur during adolescence can help adults distinguish whether the young person they are trying to help has a mental health challenge or mental health disorder or is simply experiencing normal, developmental changes.[53]

Definitions of *Adolescence* and *Young Adulthood*

The period of adolescence is defined in many ways. Traditionally, *adolescence* refers to the years when physical development (puberty) occurs, ending when norms of adulthood and sexual maturity are reached.[54] Adolescence largely overlaps with puberty, but other aspects of adolescence are defined by psychosocial and cultural characteristics of development during the teen years. This period varies from culture to culture. In years past, at the point of sexual maturity, young people were expected to be independent and start their own family. Now, adolescence is often described as lasting longer, with young people living with their parents longer, delaying starting their own families, and remaining financially dependent

on their families for a long time. These definitions can be useful in some ways and misleading in others. Brain development, for example, continues at least into the early 20s, meaning that some young people think and behave more like youth than adults until then.

Youth Mental Health First Aid® USA defines adolescence as ranging from age 12 until a young person's 18th birthday; however, the manual also addresses young people up to age 25, because the ages between 18 and 25 have some particular social and legal meanings. These are the ages at which a person is seen by many in society as an adult; they can buy alcohol, vote, and make decisions without needing the approval of a parent or guardian. Young adults ages 18–25 are sometimes referred to as *transition-age youth*. During these years, many young people transition from living at home with their parents or caregivers to being on their own. It is also an age when many young people transition from child services to adult services or to independent living. During these times, for many different reasons, young adults and their families may be navigating all the intricacies involved in these types of transitions.

Changes During Adolescent Development

Adolescent development involves these broad areas: physical, mental, social, and emotional changes.

Physical Changes

Puberty is a time when a young person's body changes from the body of a child to that of an adult. Although the range of normal ages when puberty occurs is wide, it typically begins at age

10 or 11 for girls and at age 12 or 13 for boys. This time of physical change is frequently accompanied by an increase in concern about personal appearance, the surrounding environment, and social acceptance.[55]

Some changes are similar for boys and girls, including an increase in muscle mass and rapid gains in both height and weight. The voice deepens, although this is more pronounced for boys. Pubic hair, facial hair, and body hair begin to grow. Many will have difficulties with pimples or acne. In girls, the main changes are the growth of the breasts and the start of menstrual periods. In boys, lengthening and thickening of the penis begins. For both male and female youth, these changes mean that the body is preparing to produce children, even though in general adolescents are not psychologically or socially ready for parenthood. These changes frequently trigger an increase in sexual thoughts and feelings and may lead to sexual behavior, whether or not the young person is ready for it in other ways.[56]

Mental Changes

Adolescent development also involves changes in the way people think about themselves, others, and the world around them. These changes are the result of a developing brain, life experiences, and education.[57] Children think in concrete ways and tend to accept what they are told. Adults are able to reason, think about abstract concepts, and analyze their own thoughts as well as what others say and do. Adolescence bridges these two ways of thinking.

The part of the brain that is responsible for decision making develops during the course of adolescence. Even if youth usually show good judgment, they may also frequently take risks and make poor decisions, which can be difficult for parents and other adults in their lives to understand. Youth also begin to use more reasoning and logic to solve problems and make decisions, both at school and in their own lives, including thinking about things they see and hear, thinking about their behavior in relationships with others, formulating beliefs, and thinking about consequences and long-term plans. Developing beliefs about the world means thinking about abstract concepts such as right and wrong, the meaning of life, or spiritual or religious beliefs. Such thinking can be accompanied by questioning adults in authority, rules, and social norms; becoming passionate about causes such as animal rights or poverty; and debating topics that are important to them, sometimes becoming intolerant of others' beliefs.

Social Changes

Adolescents are preparing for independence and adulthood, and socially that means turning to friends more than family.[58] Learning to resolve conflict and cope with peer pressure are important.

Youth will begin to ask themselves who they are and who they wish to be, which will include thinking about their future adult roles, desired career, and lifestyle. In developing their identity, many will experiment with different looks and styles, such as changing hair color, clothing styles, and other aspects of appearance. It may also be a period of strengthening or cementing their cultural identity. This is quite normal, even when it is frustrating to the adults in their lives. It is useful to remember that youth are trying out identities to see which one fits best.

Youth learn to manage relationships with others, including romantic relationships. They also begin to understand themselves as sexual beings, without necessarily engaging in sexual relationships. This is also a time when youth begin to notice their sexual identity. Lesbian, gay, bisexual, transgender, and questioning (LGBTQ) youth first become aware of their attractions at an average age of 9–10 years old and first identify as lesbian or gay at an average age of 14–16 years old.[59]

Social changes may be more difficult for adolescent subgroups such as different racial and ethnic groups, LBGTQ, and refugee and immigrant populations. An awareness of the social changes experienced by youth and young adults, especially in a country as diverse as the United States, can help the first aider be culturally appropriate. For example, in Maine, the young people of recently arrived Somali families are adapting to two worlds: their new home and their families' culture.

Emotional Changes

A number of emotional changes occur throughout adolescence.[60] Emotions can be more intense and quick to change. An argument with a friend may quickly result in a screaming match with a vow never to speak to the person again, and a romantic attraction may quickly become infatuation. Emotions develop more quickly, contributing at times to poor decision making. For this reason, youth are more likely to take additional risks, be impulsive, and look for new ways to have fun without considering consequences.

Distinguishing Normal Adolescence from Mental Health Challenges and Disorders

It is sometimes difficult to tell whether a young person is developing or experiencing a mental health challenge or disorder or simply going through normal changes because young people are changing rapidly already, so some of the changes seen in mental health may go unnoticed. Adults, however, are relatively stable, so changes are easier to recognize.[61]

Many symptoms of mental illnesses are similar to parts of normal development.[62] For example, withdrawal is a symptom of many mental illnesses. If the youth is withdrawing from family but spending more time with friends, this is a normal part of growing up. If, however, the youth is withdrawing from everyone, there may be cause for concern. Also, many young people become more private during adolescence, but extreme privacy may be the result of a young person concealing the use of alcohol or drugs, or it may be paranoia, sometimes a symptom of psychosis.

It is important to focus on the impact these changes have on a young person's life. If the young person is struggling with school, avoiding social engagements, or no longer enjoying the things they used to enjoy, it is possible that a mental health problem exists.

Young People with Developmental Disabilities or Autism Spectrum Disorders

The first aider may encounter youth with developmental disabilities, and it is especially important to treat them with dignity and respect.

Developmental disabilities include a wide variety of disorders acquired before age 18, including intellectual disability (formerly called *mental retardation*), autism spectrum disorders, and physical disorders such as vision impairment, epilepsy, and cerebral palsy.

Intellectual disability involves "significant limitations in both intellectual functioning (reasoning, learning, problem solving) and adaptive behavior, which covers a range of everyday social and practical skills."[63] About 85 percent of individuals with intellectual disability can acquire academic skills and be fairly self-sufficient. Others may need more supports.

Youth with *autism spectrum disorders* (autism, Asperger's syndrome, and pervasive developmental disorder) have difficulties with social communication and connection, along with limited interests or repetitive behaviors. Individuals with autism spectrum disorders may have an intellectual disability or be well above average in intelligence. They may or may not have problems understanding language or expressing themselves, but they may also have unusual speech patterns or repeat words or phrases. They may have unusual movements or responses to sounds, sights, and touch or express discomfort with change. Seizures, intense anxiety, and difficulty paying attention are common.

Youth with intellectual or developmental disorders, including autism, are at greater risk of mental health problems, bullying, and traumatic abuse. First aiders should not assume that behavior problems are the result of the developmental disorder, because a mental health disorder or medical problem may also be involved.

Speaking with a young person with a developmental disability may be easier if the first aider

- **Shows respect** by talking to the young person directly, rather than to caregivers.

- **Creates a calm environment** (uses a soft voice, turns off bright lights, turns off music or loud noises, avoids touching the person, uses nonthreatening body language, etc.).

- **Does not interrupt repetitive behaviors** (e.g., rocking, loud talk) if no one is getting hurt; these may be calming for the young person.

- **Uses short phrases, speaks slowly, and gives the person time to answer.** Gives one instruction at a time and uses pictures and gestures. If the young person does not follow requests, they may not understand or may not hear.

- **Avoids leading questions,** because youth may try to give the answer they think you want.

- **Ensures you both understand each other,** but do not pretend you understand if you do not.

- **Prepares the youth for each step of what will happen next.**

For additional resources for an individual with a developmental disability, the first aider can find their state's University Center for Excellence in Developmental Disabilities (www.aucd.org) or Protection and Advocacy Center (www.napas.org). If the young person has an autism spectrum disorder, additional resources may be located through the local chapter of the Autism Society of America (www.autism-society.org). Other resources include

U.S. Department of Health and Human Services, Office on Disability (tips for first responders, various disabilities) www.hhs.gov/od/tips.html#disa

Autism Speaks First Responders Project www.autismspeaks.org/community/family_ services/firstresponders.php

Information on responding to individuals with autism for police, fire, EMTs, and so forth www.myasdf.org/site/about-autism/autism-information-for-emergency-personnel/

Additional Risk Factors During Adolescence

Adolescence is a time of emotional development and emotional vulnerability.[64] Adolescence is when the symptoms of many mental illnesses first appear. Half of all people who ever develop a mental illness will have had their first episode before the age of 14.[65]

Some of the reasons that may put young people at risk include the following:

- **Hormonal changes** may make youth more prone to emotional extremes. Young people, particularly girls, become more prone to depression and anxiety.

- **Orientation toward peers** can lead young people to do things they would not otherwise do, such as experiment with alcohol and other drugs, and can also lead to distress about not fitting in with a desired peer group.

- **Sexual orientation and gender identity** may lead youth who identify as LGBTQ to feel as though they do not fit in and may increase their risk of being bullied or harassed, which can lead to depression.

- **Concerns about appearance** may lead to increased depression, anxiety, and dieting, which may result in the development of an eating disorder.

- **Experimenting with alcohol and other drugs** can lead to a substance use disorder or other mental health challenge or disorder.

- **Increased risk taking behavior** may result in major adverse life events, which may lead to the development of a mental health challenge or disorder. For example, driving drunk may result in trouble with the law, and sexual risk taking may result in pregnancy or sexually transmitted infections.

- **Increased independence** can provoke anxiety in some young people as can the pressure to achieve at school and elsewhere.

- **Involvement in child welfare or juvenile justice or experiencing homelessness or extreme poverty** may lead to the development of mental health challenges.

Impact of Mental Health Challenges on Adolescent Development

Mental health challenges can negatively affect adolescent development in the following ways:

- **Lack of concentration and motivation** can lead to difficulties in cognitive development and educational achievement. Delays in completing education can have long term ramifications. It can be difficult to return to education later in life, and self-esteem, which might be lost because of a failure to complete education on time, can be hard to recover.

- **Withdrawal** from family, friends, and school can delay social development.

- **Use of alcohol and other drugs** can interfere with normal brain development.[66]

- **Dramatic weight loss** can lead to problems with fertility in the long term, because it can interrupt normal menstruation and interfere with normal brain development.

Resiliency & Recovery

It is important to remember that most youth pass through adolescence with relatively little difficulty despite all of these challenges. When youth encounter difficulties, they tend to be quite resilient—to thrive, mature, and increase their competence.

Recovery from mental health and substance use disorders is a "process of change through which an individual achieves improved health, wellness, and quality of life."[67] Recovery refers to both the attitudes and experiences of the individuals receiving care as well as the circumstances, events, policies, and practices that support them. The box below lists the guiding principles of recovery.[68, 69]

Guiding Principles of Recovery

- There are many pathways to recovery.

- Recovery is self-directed and empowering.

- Recovery involves a personal recognition of the need for change and transformation.

- Recovery has cultural dimensions.

- Recovery is holistic.

- Recovery exists on a continuum of improved health and wellness.

- Recovery emerges from hope and gratitude.

- Recovery involves a process of healing and self-redefinition.

- Recovery is supported by peers and allies.

- Recovery involves (re)joining and (re)building a life in the community.

- Recovery is reality.

Protective Factors

Many factors contribute to resiliency. These factors may be called *protective factors*. Protective factors include strong family and social supports and the natural ability of youth and children to adapt to new situations. First aiders have the opportunity to be a part of an environment that is supportive of youth and facilitate early intervention for any developing mental health challenges to help ensure that young people have the chance to enjoy a happy adolescence. Specific protective factors for certain mental health challenges are outlined throughout Section 2, and may include the following:

- Healthy practices

- Good self-esteem

- Good problem solving skills

- Feeling of control in their own life

- Spirituality

- Avoiding alcohol, tobacco, and other drugs

- Consistent home/family routine

- Parental/familial support

- High monitoring of youth's activities

- Regular school attendance and academic performance

- Having a good social support system

- Economic security

- Availability of constructive recreation

- Community bonding

- Feeling close to at least one adult

Mental Health First Aid® for Youth and Young Adults

First aid is the help given to a person who is ill or injured before professional medical treatment can be obtained. First aid aims to

- Preserve life.

- Prevent further harm.

- Promote recovery and resiliency.

- Provide comfort to the person who is ill, injured, or experiencing behavioral or emotional distress.

Mental Health First Aid is the help offered to a person experiencing a mental health challenge, mental disorder, or a mental health crisis. The first aid is given until appropriate professional help is received or until the crisis resolves.

Mental Health First Aid aims to

- Preserve life when a person may be a danger to self or others.

- Prevent the problem from becoming more serious.

- Promote recovery.

- Provide comfort and support.

- Help to identify or guide a person to appropriate resources and supports.

Mental Health First Aid teaches the public how to recognize symptoms of mental health problems, how to offer and provide initial help, and how to guide a person toward appropriate treatments and other supportive help. Mental Health First Aid does not teach people to diagnose or provide therapy.

Why Mental Health First Aid for Youth and Young Adults?

There are many reasons why people who live or work with young people need training in Mental Health First Aid:

- **Mental health challenges and disorders often develop during adolescence,** including depression, anxiety, eating disorders, psychosis, and substance use disorders.[70] Half of all people who will ever experience a mental illness will have had their first episode before age 14.[71]

- **Mental health challenges and disorders are common.** Approximately one in five youth and adolescents experience a mental health challenge.[72] Anyone who has frequent contact with youth and young adults will inevitably interact with some who are experiencing mental health challenges or who have a mental disorder.

- **Youth and young adults may not be well informed** about how to recognize mental health problems and how to get help.[73] They may not know how to seek help or what sort of help is best. Adults can play an important role in getting a young person to help, but adults first need to improve their own knowledge, skills, and attitudes to be able to help.

- **Stigma and discrimination are associated with mental health challenges and disorders.** *Stigma* involves negative attitudes (prejudice), and *discrimination* refers to negative behavior (such as exclusion from social activities). These attitudes and behaviors may hinder youth and young adults with problems from seeking help.[74] They may be ashamed to discuss mental health problems with family, friends, or school staff. They may also be reluctant to seek professional help out of concern about what others will think of them. People with mental health challenges can begin to believe the negative things that others say about them. Better understanding of the experiences of young people with mental health challenges and disorders can reduce prejudice and discrimination.

- **Young people with mental health challenges or mental disorders may not be aware that they need help.** Some mental health challenges or disorders can interfere with rational decision making. A young person can be so distressed that they cannot help themselves. In this situation, parents, caregivers, or other adults close to the young person can facilitate appropriate help.

- **Professional help is not always available.** There are professionals who can help young people with mental health challenges. However, when these sources of help are not available, parents, caregivers, and other adults can offer immediate first aid and assist the young person in getting appropriate professional help and supports.

- **Mental health first aid has been found to be effective.** Several research studies have shown that training in Mental Health First Aid increases knowledge of mental health challenges and gives confidence to individuals to offer help.[75, 76, 77, 78]

The Mental Health First Aid® Action Plan

If you believe a young person is experiencing symptoms of mental illness, you should talk to them about how you can help. Having an action plan can help you do this more effectively. In any first aid course, participants learn an action plan for the best way to help someone who is injured or ill. In regular first aid, the mnemonic used to remember this plan is DRABC(D), which stands for Danger, Response, Airway, Breathing, and Compressions (Defibrillation). The first aider will not always need to take all the actions; it will depend on the condition of the person they are helping. For example, once the first aider determines that the person is fully conscious, the actions of ABC(D) are not needed.

Similarly, the Mental Health First Aid Program provides an action plan on how to help a person in a mental health crisis or with mental health challenges or disorders. Its mnemonic is ALGEE.

YOUTH MENTAL HEALTH FIRST AID® ACTION PLAN	
ACTION A	Assess for risk of suicide or harm
ACTION L	Listen nonjudgmentally
ACTION G	Give reassurance and information
ACTION E	Encourage appropriate professional help
ACTION E	Encourage self-help and other support strategies

normalizing

These actions are not necessarily steps to be followed in a fixed order. They are ordered in this way purely to aid in remembering them. The first aider has to use good judgment about the order and the relevance

of these actions and needs to be flexible and responsive to the person they are helping.

Action A: Assess for Risk of Suicide or Harm

A first aider should look out for any crises and assist in dealing with them.

Possible crises might include the following:

- **The young person may harm themselves** by attempting suicide, using substances to become intoxicated, engaging in non-suicidal self-injury, or attempting to achieve extreme weight loss.

- **The young person experiences extreme distress,** such as a panic attack or a reaction to a traumatic event.

- **The young person's behavior is very disturbing to others** (they become aggressive or lose touch with reality).

If the young person appears to be at risk of harming self or others, the first aider must seek professional help immediately.

Action L: Listen Nonjudgmentally

Listening to the young person is a very important action. When listening, it is important to set aside any judgments made about the young person or their situation and avoid expressing those judgments. Most young people experiencing distressing emotions and thoughts first want an empathetic listener before being offered helpful options and resources. When listening nonjudgmentally, the first aider needs to adopt certain attitudes and use verbal and nonverbal listening skills that

- **Allow the listener to really hear and understand what is being said.**

- **Make it easier for the young person to feel they can talk freely** about their problems without being judged.

- **Respect the youth's culture.**

It is important to listen nonjudgmentally at all times when providing Mental Health First Aid.

Action G: Give Reassurance and Information

Once a young person with a mental health problem feels that they have been heard, it can be easier to offer support and information. *Reassurance* includes emotional support, such as empathizing with how the young person feels and voicing hope, as well as offering practical help with tasks that may seem overwhelming at the moment. Also, the first aider can offer to provide some information about mental health problems.

Action E: Encourage Appropriate Professional Help

Young people with mental health problems will generally get better more quickly and be less likely to have another episode of illness if they get appropriate professional help. However, they may not know about the options available to them. Such options include medication, counseling or psychological therapy, support for family members, assistance with work and educational goals, and assistance with housing. For youth, working with professionals who have child and adolescent expertise is important. A first aider might also be able to help a young person make and keep appointments or assist a parent or caregiver in accessing appropriate help.

Action E: Encourage Self-Help and Other Support Strategies

Encourage the young person to use self-help strategies or to seek the support of their social network of family, friends, and others. First aiders may encourage other significant adults in the young person's life to be supportive and to help identify natural and informal helpers in their community, including peer support groups and peer mentors. Peer supporters—others who have experienced mental health problems—can provide valuable help in the young person's recovery.

IT IS IMPORTANT TO CARE FOR YOURSELF

After providing Mental Health First Aid to a young person who is in distress, you may feel worn out, frustrated, or even angry. You may need to deal with the feelings and reactions you have set aside during the encounter. It can be helpful to find someone to talk to about what has happened, but remember to respect the young person's right to privacy; do not share their name or any personal details that might identify them.

Roles and Responsibilities of Adults When Helping a Youth

Anyone can be a first aider—a teacher, a youth worker, a sports coach, a parent or caregiver, or anyone else who knows the youth well enough to notice that their behavior has changed.

You may have questions regarding helping a young person, particularly with regard to their rights and yours. Some of these questions are answered below.

If I'm helping a young person, and I am not their parent or caregiver, should I contact their parents or caregivers?

Parents play a pivotal role in obtaining any necessary professional help for their children. You will need to consider how best to involve the parents, caregivers, or guardians. In the case of a medical emergency, you need to call for emergency assistance first. If the young person is at risk of suicide or harm (perhaps from alcohol or other drug use), the first aider will need to involve a parent, caregiver, or guardian urgently. Even if the problem is not urgent, it is still best to involve parents and caregivers when possible and as soon as possible. Start by asking the youth if they would like to speak to their parents or caregivers privately or if they would like you, as the first aider, to help. You can offer to talk to their parents or caregivers along with them or by yourself. Parents, caregivers, or guardians may not have a great deal of knowledge about mental health challenges or disorders themselves, and you may be in a position to give them the information they need to get help for their child. This may be information about mental illness or appropriate professional help and how to access it.

If the young person asks you not to involve their parents or caregivers, you need to find out why. In most cases, the young person will say they think their parents or caregivers will not understand, will be angry, cannot afford professional help, or something similar. Most parents or caregivers will do everything they can to help their children. Explaining this can help the young person to overcome their concerns about speaking to a parent or caregiver.

There are situations in which it is not appropriate to contact a parent or caregiver. If a youth reveals an experience of abuse, neglect, or exploitation at home, contacting a parent or caregiver may further endanger the young person. If this is disclosed during your conversation, you may need to contact appropriate authorities. Different states have different laws regarding the reporting of abuse and suspected abuse, including neglect and exposure to violence (See *Appendix 1: Mandatory Reporters of Child Abuse and Neglect: Summary of State Laws*).

If you are unsure whether it is safe or appropriate to approach a young person's parent or caregiver about a possible mental health problem, seek advice from a mental health professional, community mental health center, or a family run advocacy group.

Does the young person have the right to privacy?

Young people have the right to privacy when talking with professionals who are bound to codes of ethical conduct. Although other adults who come into contact with young people may not be bound to these codes, they are a good guide to ethical behavior.

There are limits to confidentiality. If a young person has shared information with you as a first aider and has asked that you keep it confidential, you should do so unless

- You have concerns that the young person is at risk of self-harm or harm to others.

- The young person has disclosed that they are being abused.

- You believe that the young person does not have sufficient maturity to make decisions about privacy.

- As part of your job, you may have guidelines about reporting that override the young person's concern for confidentiality.

If you are not sure whether you should break confidentiality, call your local mental health agency or speak to a colleague.

Even if confidentiality has to be broken, the young person does have the right to privacy, which means that information about their mental health should not be shared with people who do not need to know about it. In a school, for example, the young person's teachers may

need to know, as well as a school counselor or nurse, but information does not need to be shared with the whole staff.

Does the young person have the right to make decisions about their health care?

Young people have the right to be involved in or make decisions about their care. In some states, young people under age 18 have the right to

- **Seek their own health care and make decisions about treatment.** However, if the health professional they speak to does not believe they are mature enough to understand their condition and care, the professional may have to contact the young person's parent or caregiver.

- **Consent to treatment, even if a parent or caregiver does not consent.** If the health professional believes that treatment is in the best interest of the young person and that they are mature enough to understand the treatment and the associated risks, the health professional can act against a parent's or caregiver's wishes. Any conflict may have to be argued in court, and the court will rule in the best interests of the young person.

- **Refuse treatment, even if a parent or caregiver has consented to the treatment.** However, if a health professional or a parent can prove that the young person does not understand the potential consequences of refusing treatment, they can have the young person treated against their wishes.

In an emergency, medical professionals can provide treatment without parental or caregiver consent or the consent of the young person. After age 18, a person has the right to refuse health care or any medical treatment. If a doctor (or anyone else) provides treatment of any kind without proper consent, it is a crime.[79] However, a health professional can seek the support of the courts to treat a person against their will, if the professional believes that there is a risk to others if the treatment is not given or that the person cannot make their own choices.

If I am helping my own child, is there anything else I need to know?

If another adult approaches you with concerns about your child, it is important that you take this seriously. Sometimes a young person seems relaxed and happy at home, and this may lead you to think that the concerns the person is expressing are exaggerated or untrue. However, it may be that at school your child is very anxious or fearful, is socially isolated, or shows other symptoms that are not apparent in the home. It is important that you discuss the concerns with your child and find out whether they feel differently outside of the home.

You might be fearful of discussing symptoms you have noticed with your child because you are worried it will alienate them. For most people, the opportunity to discuss unpleasant feelings can be a huge relief. Let your child know that you will support them to get the help needed. However, do not let the problem become the main focus of your relationship—spend time enjoying each other's company and talking about other things.

It can be emotionally difficult to accept that your child needs mental health care. Some parents feel that they are to blame for their child's mental health challenges or disorders, either because they feel they should have been able to prevent it or perhaps because their own family has a history of mental illness. The reality is that many things contribute to the development of a mental illness. Focus instead on the opportunity to help your child, and if you need it, seek additional support for yourself. The main thing to remember is that you can only do your best.

How to Communicate Effectively With Young People

Providing mental health first aid to a young person can be challenging. Some youth are reluctant to talk with adults about sensitive issues, such as mental health challenges, and others find it difficult to talk about or describe their emotions. Some adults struggle to engage young people in conversations of any kind and will find it even more difficult to talk to youth about sensitive issues. For those adults who find communicating with young people difficult, a number of strategies may help.

>> **Be genuine.**
Young people are very adept at recognizing when an adult is faking it. If you are uncomfortable in a discussion with a young person, admit it. For example, you might say, "This is hard for me to talk about, and perhaps it's difficult for you, too."

>> **Be careful about using slang.**
Use language you are comfortable with. If you try to use slang you are unfamiliar with or not used to, a young person will be able to tell immediately.

>> **Allow for silence.**
Young people may struggle at times to express what they want to say. Interrupting a silent moment may prevent the young person from having adequate time to form their words.

>> **Try different settings for communication to see what works best.**
There is no right setting for tricky conversations, but where you have the conversation might make you or the young person more comfortable. You may find that taking a youth out for a snack offers an opportunity in a different setting to talk about anything they need to. Some adults find it easier to talk to a young person while doing another activity. Others may find that talking to a youth is easier while driving in the car, washing and drying dishes,

or taking a dog for a walk. For someone who works with young people like a teacher or sports coach, talking while playing a sport (kicking a soccer ball around or playing a friendly basketball game) may be more appropriate. Activities that do not require much eye contact can make it easier for the young person to talk, and time-limited activities that have a definite endpoint can be less overwhelming for young people as well. Talk to the young person you are helping to find out what would make them most comfortable.

>> **Do not compare the young person's life with your own experiences from that age.**
Adults often fall into the trap of thinking that young people today have a much easier life. Remember that your parents' generation thought the same thing about you. Saying, "If I had the opportunities at your age that you have today, I would..." is not helpful. The world changes constantly, and new opportunities mean new challenges.

>> **Do not trivialize the young person's feelings.**
Mental illness can occur at any age. Wondering what a young person has to be depressed or anxious about implies that their life experiences are less valid just because of their age.

>> **Do not ask the young person to justify or explain their behavior.**
Young people often act without thinking about the consequences and later realize that they made a mistake. Asking "why" can put young people on the defensive. Asking why they rode down a hill in a shopping cart or threw a party without permission is not as useful as talking about how such behavior could be avoided next time.

>> **Watch your body language.**
This is always important, no matter who you are talking to. However, with a young person, body language needs extra attention because you may be silently communicating that you, as an adult, are the expert. Defensive or authoritarian body language (arms crossed, hands on hips, standing over the young person) will make it very hard to have a useful conversation. If the young person seems relaxed and open, try to match their body language. If the young person appears defensive, make your body language as open as possible by appearing relaxed, keeping your palms out, sitting alongside but angled toward the young person, and keeping your voice calm and low.

>> **Provide positive feedback and look for and acknowledge the youth's strengths.**
Young people are told constantly—by their parents or caregivers, their teachers, and the media—what they are doing wrong. Any positive feedback you provide can help make them more willing to communicate with you. Even something as simple as "I'm glad that you are willing to talk to me about this—it shows a great deal of maturity" can help. Identify the young person's strengths, for example, "You are very organized to be holding down a job in addition to not missing a day of school."

>> **Help them to find the language they are looking for.**
Many young people find it difficult to express their emotions, which can result in their complaining of physical symptoms when the emotional symptoms are what are really bothering them. They may simply shrug their shoulders or say they do not know when asked how they are feeling. You can help them to find the emotional language they need. Offering a few terms to pick from could help, for example, "To me, you don't look very happy. Are you feeling sad, angry, or frustrated?"

Communicating With Young People from Different Cultural Backgrounds

The United States is a culturally, ethnically, and racially diverse country. Culture shapes people's attitudes, beliefs, and behaviors. Young people may find it difficult to talk to an adult from a culture or community different from their own.

If you are assisting a young person with a cultural background different from your own, there can be additional challenges in communication. In some cultures, it is common to describe emotional distress using physical terms rather than emotional terms (e.g., complaints about stomach aches and headaches rather than anxiety or fearfulness). You may find it to be more effective to first establish a warm and trusting relationship with the young person's family, discussing the strengths and interests of the young person, before sharing your concerns about the young person's situation or condition. Gain knowledge of the local services that are effective with and acceptable to members of this person's cultural group before recommending where the young person can go for help.

It is important to know about the different cultural and racial groups in your community and what makes these groups unique without generalizing. For example, when confronted with a mental health challenge, Chinese Americans generally use family and community resources first and mental health services as a last resort.[80] In addition, each family will have different acculturation experiences within each generation that will influence their approach to mental health services. It may be more effective for you to first ask what the young person would want rather than jumping to the conclusion that they want a therapist. Sometimes, a young person will be more comfortable talking to an adult from their own culture than to someone from a different culture.

It is important, however, not to make assumptions about the young person's needs solely on their cultural background. Ask questions about what the young person needs rather than acting on the basis of what you think they need. Ask questions about what has happened to the young person rather than what is wrong with them. Remember that it is more important to make the young person feel comfortable, respected, and cared for than to do all the right things and follow all the rules.

Cultural Safety

A *culturally safe environment* is "an environment, which is safe for people; where there is no assault, challenge or denial of who they are, and what they need. It is about shared respect, shared meaning, shared knowledge and experience, of learning together with dignity, and truly listening."[81]

Practicing cultural safety means

- **Respecting the culture** of the community by using appropriate language and behavior

- **Never doing anything that causes the person to feel shame**

- **Supporting the person's right to make decisions** about seeking culturally based care

Cultural Competence

As noted earlier, there is great cultural diversity within the United States, especially among those under the age of 18. Moreover, everyone is a member of multiple cultural groups, based on race, ethnicity, faith, region of country, type of work, level of education, physical ability or disability status, sexual identity, and so forth. In many ways, every encounter is probably a cross-cultural encounter. Here are a few points to consider in these cross-cultural encounters.

Learn about the young person's culture and concept of mental illness

For example, many Native American/Alaska Native people understand mental health within a broad context of health and well-being that includes concepts of social and emotional functioning. Symptoms of mental illness are understood as part of a person's spirit or personality.[82] If it seems that someone has a problem, they may be described as having a lack of harmony among the spiritual, physical, mental, and emotional forces in their life.[83]

Know what is acceptable, and what is not, in a young person's culture

For some cultural groups, it is important to consider the spiritual context of their behaviors. Sometimes experiences such as seeing spirits or hearing voices of deceased loved ones are embedded in the culture and are misdiagnosed or mislabeled as mental illness. It would not be surprising for someone from a spiritually oriented cultural group such as Native American, Asian/Pacific Islander, African American, or Hispanic to exhibit this behavior and belief. Also, every family or household has a unique family culture. For example, some families have family secrets, and the family's practice may be to never talk about an uncle's past sexual abuse conviction because of shame.

Know what is culturally appropriate communication

When talking to a young person outside your own culture or community, you may need to adjust your usual communication style. The young person may be used to a different level of eye contact or physical space. For example, in some communities, eye contact can be a way to reprimand rather than respect someone, and it could contribute to the young person feeling judged. Similarly, there may be issues of age and gender that get in the way of effective communication. For example, it may not be appropriate in the young person's culture to speak alone with an adult of the opposite sex.

Do not shame the young person, their family, or community

The concept of shame is important in many cultural communities and can be a barrier to seeking help. Failure to practice cultural safety can contribute to the experience of shame. Be aware of the language and behaviors that can trigger the experience of shame in the young person's community. The youth and families of these cultural communities may be reluctant to share their circumstances out of shame.

Use community and family supports

It is important for a first aider to know about both the formal and informal services and supports in a community. Informal supports may be particularly important if access to professional support or mental health services is limited. Encourage the young person to build a social network of personal relationships with people they can trust, respect, and turn to for support or assistance. This person could be a family member, a respected elder of a tribal community, a community liaison, or the neighborhood grandmother.

Be mindful of young people who are immigrants and refugees

Some young people who move to the United States from abroad will be glad to have arrived in this country and will adjust relatively quickly and easily. Others will find the move to the United States difficult because of attachment to their country of origin, loss of family and friends, or difficulties in adjustment. A young person who has come to the United States may have experienced trauma in their country of origin, perhaps because of war, poverty, oppressive government, or separation from a family member who moved to the United States to prepare for the arrival of the rest of the family.[84] Young people in immigrant or refugee families may also experience the same barriers as other cultural groups:

- **Racism and discrimination** that may inhibit a young person from interacting with people from outside their cultural group

- **Language difficulties and inadequate support** for language access to services

- **Lack of awareness and understanding** of the United States' health system

- **High degree of stigma about mental illnesses in their own culture or country of origin**

- **Lack of access to formal services and supports** because of being in the country without legal documentation

- **Lack of knowledge about mental health challenges and disorders**

Many communities have agencies that provide services for specific cultural and ethnic populations. If you live or work in a community with a large migrant or refugee population, it is useful to know about any culturally appropriate services available, particularly those that are tailored to the needs of young people.

Be aware of the possibility of a history of abuse or neglect

Abuse, whether sexual, physical, verbal, or emotional as well as all types of neglect, is a significant risk factor for developing mental health challenges and disorders (See *First Aid for Children and Youth Affected by Traumatic Events* and *First Aid for Young Adults and Adults Affected by Traumatic Events*).

When a young person has been betrayed by an adult in this way, a number of problems are created. The youth may have tried to talk to other adults and been

disbelieved, dismissed, or promised help that they never received. Some young people might be entirely disengaged and distrustful of adults and refuse to talk. Others will seek attachment and affection from every adult they meet, resulting in inappropriate physical intimacy, which can be difficult to cope with.

If you are assisting a young person with this kind of history, be predictable and consistent in your interactions. You need to be firm about what your role as a first aider is and the limitations of your role. If you are going to need to refer the youth to other services, be honest and upfront about this. Show the young person that

- You believe what they have told you about the way they are feeling and experienced.

- What they are sharing is important to you, and you want to help.

- There are adults who can be trusted.

- There are ways to feel and be safe.

If you are helping a young person who discloses that they are being abused and this abuse is not known to any child protection agency, there are steps you need to take to report it. Depending on where you live and what your job is, you may have mandatory reporting responsibilities. In any case, you need to know whom to tell. It may be a government agency or the police. For state guidelines on mandatory reporting, see *Appendix 1: Mandatory Reporters of Child Abuse and Neglect: Summary of State Laws*.

Helpful Resources

FOR YOUTH AND YOUNG ADULTS WITH MENTAL HEALTH CHALLENGES AND MENTAL DISORDERS AND THE ADULTS WHO CARE FOR THEM

Below are resources that may help first aiders learn more about mental health and mental illness in general. Subsequent chapters of this manual will include resources that provide specific information on mental health challenges and disorders as well as relevant services and supports.

WEBSITES

American Academy of Child & Adolescent Psychiatry

www.aacap.org

The American Academy of Child and Adolescent Psychiatry is a membership based organization, composed of more than 7,500 child and adolescent psychiatrists and other interested physicians. Its members research, evaluate, diagnose, and treat psychiatric disorders. The academy distributes information to promote an understanding of mental illnesses, advance efforts in prevention of mental illnesses, and ensure proper treatment and access to services for children and adolescents.

American Academy of Family Physicians

www.aafp.org

The American Academy of Family Physicians is a medical specialty society that represents more than 100,300 family physicians and medical students. Its mission is to improve the health of patients, families, and communities by serving the needs of its members with professionalism and creativity. The website has access to journals and news publications and other information on policy and advocacy.

American Psychiatric Association

www.psych.org & www.healthyminds.org

The American Psychiatric Association is a national medical specialty society whose physician members specialize in diagnosis, treatment, and prevention of and research on mental illnesses, including substance use disorders. HealthyMinds.org is the association's online resource for anyone seeking mental health information, including information on many common mental health concerns, including warning signs of mental disorders, treatment options, and preventive measures.

American Psychological Association

www.apa.org

The American Psychological Association is a scientific and professional organization that represents psychology in the United States. With more than 154,000 members, it is the largest association of psychologists worldwide. The association's website has a variety of resources, brochures, and other information on psychological knowledge to benefit society and improve people's lives.

Child Welfare Information Gateway

www.childwelfare.gov

The Child Welfare Information Gateway provides information services to child welfare professionals and the public as the clearinghouse for the Children's Bureau, compiling, synthesizing, and disseminating resources on the safety, permanency, and well-being of children and families. Child welfare and related professionals can rely on the information gateway for quick access to publications, websites, and online databases covering a range of topics, including child welfare, child abuse and neglect, foster care, adoption, and the content areas for which Training & Technical Assistance Network members provide technical assistance.

Georgetown University Center for Child and Human Development (GUCCHD)

http://gucchd.georgetown.edu

The Georgetown University Center for Child and Human Development (GUCCHD) was established more than four decades ago to improve the quality of life for all children and youth, especially those with, or at risk for, special needs, and their families. The center directly serves both vulnerable children and their families, as well as influences local, state, national, and international programs and policy.

Mental Health America

www.mentalhealthamerica.net

Mental Health America (formerly known as the National Mental Health Association) is the country's leading nonprofit dedicated to helping all people live mentally healthier lives. With more than 320 affiliates nationwide, Mental Health America represents a growing movement of Americans who promote mental wellness for the health and well-being of the nation.

National Alliance on Mental Illness

www.nami.org

The National Alliance on Mental Illness is the nation's largest grassroots organization dedicated to improving the lives of individuals and families affected by mental illness. It is a national organization and has state organizations and local affiliates in more than 1,100 communities across the country.

National Association of School Psychologists

www.nasponline.org

The National Association of School Psychologists offers a wide variety of free or low-cost online resources for parents, teachers, and others working with children and youth through their website and its Center for Children and Families.

National Association of Social Workers

www.naswdc.org

The National Association of Social Workers (NASW) is the largest membership organization of professional social workers in the world with chapters in all 50 states. Social workers work in many different types of settings to ensure personal well-being, address crises, and provide counseling. The NASW website has a Help Starts Here link that provides online directories to locate professional social workers who provide individual psychotherapy and other forms of mental health assistance, including group therapy and support groups. The website also provides information on different diagnoses, such as schizophrenia, and effective forms of treatment.

National Association of State Mental Health Program Directors

www.nasmhpd.org

The National Association of State Mental Health Program Directors serves as the national representative and advocate for state mental health agencies and their directors and supports effective stewardship of state mental health systems. The association informs its members on current and emerging public policy issues, educates on research findings and best practices, provides consultation and technical assistance, collaborates with key stakeholders, and facilitates state-to-state sharing. Its website includes links to a mental health glossary; federal websites; state mental health agencies; Center for Mental Health Services; other federal agency research, training, and technical assistance centers; and other mental health and related websites.

National Center for Cultural Competence

nccc.georgetown.edu

The National Center for Cultural Competence provides national leadership and contributes to the body of knowledge on cultural and linguistic competency within systems and organizations. The center is a component of the GUCCHD and provides training, technical assistance, and consultation; contributes to knowledge through publications and research; creates tools and resources to support health and mental health care providers and systems; supports leaders to promote and sustain cultural and linguistic competency; and collaborates with an extensive

network of private and public entities to advance the implementation of these concepts.

National Council for Community Behavioral Healthcare

www.TheNationalCouncil.org

The National Council for Community Behavioral Healthcare is a member organization for America's behavioral health organizations. The National Council advocates for public policies in mental and behavioral health that ensure that people who are ill can access comprehensive health care services and offers state-of-the-science education and practice improvement resources so that services are efficient and effective. To locate mental health and addictions treatment facilities in your community, use the Find a Provider feature on the National Council's website.

National Directory of Family-Run and Youth-Guided Organizations for Children's Mental Health

www.familyorgdirectory.fmhi.usf.edu

The directory lists family run and youth-guided organizations and support groups throughout the United States, U.S. territories, and tribal nations working to support families who have children with emotional, behavioral, and mental health challenges and to improve mental health services and supports.

National Federation of Families for Children's Mental Health

www.ffcmh.org

The National Federation of Families for Children's Mental Health is a national parent-run organization supporting family run programs to meet the needs of children and youth with emotional, behavioral, or mental disorders. The federation has 125 chapters in states and communities across the country.

National Institute of Mental Health

www.nimh.nih.gov

This government site provides a wealth of excellent, up-to-date information on mental health problems and research. The site has downloadable booklets, brochures, and fact sheets about specific mental health challenges and disorders.

National Technical Assistance Center for Children's Mental Health

http://gucchdtacenter.georgetown.edu

The National Technical Assistance Center for Children's Mental Health is located within GUCCHD and is dedicated to working in partnership with families and other leaders across the country to transform systems and services for children, adolescents, and young adults who have, or are at risk for, mental health problems and their families. Using a multifaceted approach, the center provides information, technical assistance, and training in system and service strategies for achieving positive outcomes for children and youth with mental health needs and their families.

National Child Traumatic Stress Network

www.nctsn.org

The mission of the National Traumatic Stress Network is to raise the standard of care and improve access to services for traumatized children, their families, and communities throughout the United States.

Youth M.O.V.E.

www.youthmovenational.org

Youth M.O.V.E. National (Motivating Others through Voices of Experience) is a youth led national organization devoted to improving services and systems that support positive growth and development by uniting the voices of individuals who have lived experience in various systems including mental health, juvenile justice, education, and child welfare.

HELPLINES

American Psychiatric Association
Answer Center
1-888-35-PSYCH (77924) or 1-888-357-7924
Live operators available 8:30 a.m. to 6:00 p.m., eastern time, refer you to local board certified psychiatrists.

American Psychological Association
Public Education Line
1-800-964-2000
Follow the automated instructions. An operator then refers you to local board certified psychologists.

National Suicide Prevention Lifeline
1-800-273-TALK (8255)
This is a crisis hotline that can help with many issues, not just suicide. For example, anyone who feels sad, hopeless, or suicidal; family and friends who are concerned about a loved one; or anyone interested in mental health treatment referrals can call the Lifeline. Callers are connected with a professional nearby who will talk with them about what they are feeling or concerns for other family and friends. If you or someone you know is in suicidal crisis, call the hotline (toll free, 24 hours/day, 7 days/week).

SUPPORT GROUPS

National Alliance on Mental Illness
www.nami.org
The National Alliance on Mental Illness is a nonprofit, grassroots, self-help support and advocacy organization of individuals with mental disorders and their families. This website provides many resources on mental disorders, including depression, that are helpful for people who have experienced a mental illness and their families, including support groups, education, and training. Click on "Find Support" on the home page.

SECTION 2: Mental Health First Aid® for Developing Challenges and Disorders in Youth

Before being able to give Mental Health First Aid to a young person, first aiders need some basic knowledge about mental health challenges and mental disorders so that they are able to recognize that an illness may be developing. *Section 2 of the Youth Mental Health First Aid® USA* manual provides education on the signs and symptoms of a variety of mental health challenges and disorders in young people. Chapters in this section introduce depression, anxiety, attention deficit disorders, trauma, eating disorders, and substance use. Although each topic is addressed separately, it is important to note that some youth have multiple mental health disorders.

This section provides the first aider with knowledge about many types of mental health challenges and disorders, but it is important to remember that young people are still developing and often have multiple issues needing multiple resources to meet their needs. Many of these resources have been studied during the past decade and have demonstrated their helpfulness among youth, young adults, and their families.

Depression in Young People

What Is Depression?

The word *depression* is used in many different ways. People feel sad or blue when bad things happen. However, everyday blues or sadness is not a depressive disorder. People with the blues may have a short-term depressed mood, but they can manage to cope and soon recover without treatment.

The type of depression that is the focus of this chapter is *major depressive disorder*—a type of mood disorder and the most severe and most disabling form of depression. Major depressive disorder lasts for at least two weeks, affects people's ability to carry out their work and daily activities, and keeps people from having satisfying personal relationships. According to the National Survey on Drug Use and Health, in 2014, 11.4 percent of youth ages 12–17 (an estimated 2.8 million) experienced at least one major depressive episode in the past year. Among these youth, fewer than half (41.2 percent) received treatment for depression during that time.[27] Depression is a serious mental health issue that can affect even very young children.

Depression is often recurrent: a person recovers but may develop another episode later on. If a young person has an episode of depression, they are more likely to have another episode during their lifetime.[86] Young people may also experience depression as a side effect of certain medications or when discontinuing use of a medication.[87] Depression often can occur with attention deficit disorder, attention deficit/hyperactivity disorder (ADHD), other disruptive behavior disorders, anxiety disorders, and substance use disorders.[88]

FIGURE 1. PREVALENCE OF DEPRESSION AMONG U.S. YOUTH BY GENDER AND AGE[27]

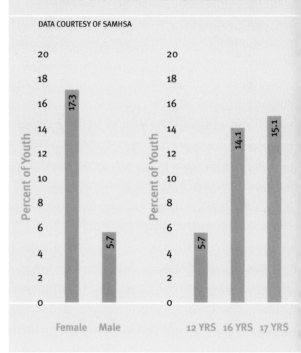

DATA COURTESY OF SAMHSA

What might a first aider notice if a young person is depressed?

When people think of depression, they typically imagine someone who appears sad and withdrawn. This is certainly true of some people with depression. However, there are other signs, particularly among young people, that may mean depression is a problem.

Not every person who is depressed has all the major symptoms. People differ in the number of symptoms they have and how severe the symptoms are. Even if a young person does not have enough symptoms to be diagnosed with a depressive disorder, some symptoms can still have a significant impact on their life.

Signs and Symptoms of Major Depressive Disorders[90]

If a young person is clinically depressed, they would have five or more of these symptoms (including at least one of the first two) nearly every day for at least two weeks:[91]

- An unusually sad mood

- Loss of enjoyment and interest in activities that were previously enjoyable

- Lack of energy and tiredness

- Feeling worthless or guilty when they are not really at fault

- Thinking about death or wishing to be dead

- Difficulty concentrating or making decisions

- Moving more slowly or sometimes becoming agitated and unable to settle

- Having sleeping difficulties or sleeping too much

- Loss of interest in food or sometimes eating too much

- Changes in eating habits, which may lead to either weight loss or weight gain

At home, young people may

- Complain of tiredness, even if they are sleeping more than usual.

- Have difficulty doing household chores, either forgetting to do them or not doing them thoroughly.

- Withdraw from family, spending a great amount of time in their bedroom.

- Snap at family members, behave irritably, or pick fights with parents or siblings.

- Avoid discussing important future events, such as decisions about further education or work opportunities.

In school, young people may

- Show a decline in school grades because they do not complete work, do not do as good a job as they used to do, or miss school.

- Fail to engage in classroom discussions or struggle to understand and communicate.

- Snap at or start fights with other students or engage in vandalism.

- Struggle to work effectively in the morning, but do better in late afternoon classes.

These symptoms can all have an impact on school achievement. Some may result in disciplinary responses. Teachers may also notice that a student chooses topics such as depression, suicide, or self-injury to write about in health or social science classes or as the subject for creative writing or art.

In a social setting, young people may

- Avoid spending time with friends altogether.

- Spend more time with friends who appear to be depressed as well.

- Become ostracized from their usual social group, either because they continually refuse invitations or friends find the individual difficult to spend time with.

- Use alcohol or other drugs to deal with emotional symptoms.

Many of the major symptoms of depression in youth and adults are also symptoms of depression in very young children. Children younger than age 12 with depression may show aggressive behaviors, be more fearful of new people and challenges, or show delays or regression in important developmental milestones.[92]

41

Bipolar Disorder

A young person who is depressed may actually have a mood disorder called *bipolar disorder* (previously known as *manic–depressive disorder*).[93] Research estimates that up to three percent of adolescents experience Bipolar Disorder.[85] People with bipolar disorder have episodes of depression, episodes of mania, and periods of normal mood in between. The time between these different episodes can vary greatly from person to person. The depression experienced by a young person with bipolar disorder includes some or all of the symptoms of depression listed earlier. Mania appears to be the opposite of depression. A person experiencing mania will have an elevated mood, be overconfident, and be full of energy. The person might be very talkative, full of ideas, have less need for sleep, and take risks they normally would not.

Bipolar disorder may have its onset in adolescence or young adulthood. However, a person cannot be diagnosed with bipolar disorder until they have experienced both an episode of mania and an episode of depression. Therefore, it may take many years before a young person is diagnosed correctly and receives the most appropriate treatment. Males and females are equally affected.

A person experiencing mania will have some or all of the following symptoms:

>> INCREASED ENERGY AND OVERACTIVITY

>> ELEVATED MOOD

The person will feel high, happy, full of energy, on the top of the world, and/or invincible.

>> NEED LESS SLEEP THAN USUAL

The person can go for days with very little sleep.

>> IRRITABILITY

The person may become irritable if others disagree with a manic person's unrealistic plans or ideas.

>> RAPID THINKING AND SPEECH

The person may talk too much, too fast, and keep changing topics.

>> LACK OF INHIBITIONS

The person may disregard risk, spend money extravagantly, or be carelessly sexually active.

>> GRANDIOSE DELUSIONS

These delusions involve very inflated self-esteem, such as a belief that the person is superhuman, especially talented, or an important religious figure.

>> LACK OF INSIGHT

The person is so convinced that manic delusions are real that they do not realize they are ill.

Young people with bipolar disorder may have symptoms that are different from those seen in adults, including more mixed episodes (feeling manic and depressed at the same time), rapid mood fluctuations, irritability, aggression, and high emotional reactivity. Fewer adolescents than adults with bipolar disorder experience the euphoria typically associated with mania.[94] In adolescents, episodes may be less distinct than in adults, may last longer, and they may have a high level of symptoms between episodes. Adolescents with bipolar disorder report they are less likely to experience sleep disturbances than adults with bipolar disorder. Bipolar disorder has a high level of co-occurrence with ADHD, substance use disorders, and anxiety disorders.[95]

Risk Factors for Depression

Depression has no single cause and often involves the interaction of many diverse biological, psychological, and social factors.[96, 97] The following factors increase a person's risk of developing depression:

- A history of depression in close family members

- Being a more sensitive, emotional, and anxious person

- Adverse experiences in childhood, such as lack of care or abuse

- Family poverty and social disadvantage

- Learning and other school difficulties

- Recent adverse events in the person's life, such as being a victim of crime, death, or serious illness in the family; having an accident; or being bullied or victimized

- Parental separation or divorce

- Lack of a close, confiding relationship with someone

- Long-term or serious physical illness

- Having another mental illness, such as an anxiety disorder, psychotic disorder, or substance use disorder

- Premenstrual changes in hormone levels

- Caring full-time for a person with a long-term disability[98]

Bullying is a common experience for many youth, and it may be a contributing factor to developing depression. Surveys have indicated that as many as half of all youth are bullied at some time during their school years and at least 10 percent are bullied on a regular basis. Youth often do not tell others that they are being bullied. Bullying behavior can be physical or verbal and can occur in-person, online, through email, and on social networking sites. Youth who are bullied experience real suffering that can interfere with their social and emotional development as well as their school performance. Some victims of bullying, many with untreated depression, have even attempted suicide rather than continue to endure such harassment and punishment.[99] The person doing the bullying probably also needs help from an adult. *Bullying* is an aggressive behavior that is intentional and involves an imbalance of power and strength. A youth who bullies may need counseling, along with supervision, clear expectations, and consistent consequences.[100]

Depression can also result from the use of medications and other substances.

- The direct effects of some medical conditions, for example, vitamin B12 deficiency, hypothyroidism, hepatitis, glandular fever, HIV, and some cancers[101]

- The side effects of certain medications or drugs (including some used to control acne)

- Intoxication from alcohol or other drugs

The symptoms of depression are thought to be due to changes in natural brain chemicals called *neurotransmitters*. These chemicals send messages from one nerve cell to another in the brain. When a person becomes depressed, the brain can have less of certain of these chemical messengers. One of these chemicals is *serotonin*, a chemical in the brain that helps to regulate a person's mood. Many antidepressant medications work by changing the activity of serotonin in the brain.

Gender Differences in Adolescent Depression[102, 103, 104, 105]

Although depression is more common in women than men, this pattern is not seen across the whole lifespan. In childhood, depression is not common, however boys tend to have slightly higher rates than girls. In adolescence, depression increases, and girls begin to have two to three times the rate seen in boys.[27]

There are several reasons why the gender difference in depression emerges in adolescence. One of these is hormonal. The rise in depression in adolescent girls is associated with the onset of puberty, with girls who reach puberty earlier having more depressive symptoms. However, other factors are involved as well. For example, adolescent girls often invest more in relationships with friends than boys do and are more likely to become depressed when there are problems in relationships. Girls are also more likely to assume caretaking roles (e.g., with parents or siblings), which can increase their risk for depression.

Risk Factors for Bipolar Disorder

The causes of bipolar disorder are not fully understood. Having a close relative with bipolar disorder, such as a parent or sibling, increases an individual's risk by about nine percent. Of course, it is important to remember that more than 90 percent of people who have a relative with bipolar disorder will not develop the illness.

No other risk factors for bipolar disorder are firmly established; however, some research has demonstrated that the following issues may lead to biochemical changes in the brain that can lead to mania and depression:[106]

>> **PREGNANCY AND OBSTETRIC COMPLICATIONS**
Such complications may affect the developing brain of the fetus or infant.

>> **BIRTH IN WINTER OR SPRING**
This issue may reflect risk to the fetus from infections or other events that vary by season.

>> **RECENT STRESSFUL LIFE EVENTS**
Stressful events are more common in the six months before onset of an episode.

>> **RECENT CHILDBIRTH**
Women appear to be at increased risk in the months after childbirth.

>> **BRAIN INJURIES**
Brain injury before age 10 may increase risk.

>> **MULTIPLE SCLEROSIS**
People with multiple sclerosis may have increased risk.

>> **SOCIAL SITUATION**
People who develop bipolar disorder are more likely to have lower income, to be unemployed and single, and to live in urban areas. However, these factors may be consequences of the very early changes produced by bipolar disorder rather than the causes.

Importance of Early Intervention

Early intervention is particularly important for youth, because depression can have negative effects on a young person's development.[107] Depression in youth is associated with delays in social, emotional, and cognitive development. Youth who have had depression are more likely to have a range of problems in adulthood, including low educational attainment, difficulties at work, unemployment, problems in personal relationships, early pregnancy, and problems with the law.

Mental Health First Aid Action Plan® for Depression[108, 109]

YOUTH MENTAL HEALTH FIRST AID® ACTION PLAN	
ACTION A	Assess for risk of suicide or harm
ACTION L	Listen nonjudgmentally
ACTION G	Give reassurance and information
ACTION E	Encourage appropriate professional help
ACTION E	Encourage self-help and other support strategies

Action A: Assess for Risk of Suicide or Harm

If you think that a young person you care about may be depressed and need help, approach the person about your concerns. It is important to choose a suitable time when both of you are available to talk as well as a space where you both feel comfortable. Let the young person know that you are available to talk when ready; do not put pressure on them to talk right away. It can be helpful to let the young person choose the moment to open up. However, if the young person does not initiate a conversation with you about how they are feeling, you should say something to them.

As you talk with the young person, be on the lookout for any indications that they may be in crisis.

CRISES ASSOCIATED WITH DEPRESSION

Two main crises that may be associated with depression are when

- The young person has **suicidal thoughts or behaviors**

- The young person is engaging in **nonsuicidal self-injury**

SUICIDAL THOUGHTS AND BEHAVIORS

Not every young person who is depressed is at risk for suicide, yet depression is a major risk factor for suicide. People who die by suicide are frequently suffering from undiagnosed, undertreated, or untreated depression.[110] A young person may feel so overwhelmed and helpless that the future appears hopeless. They may think suicide is the only way out. Sometimes a young person becomes suicidal very rapidly, perhaps in response to a trigger (such as a relationship breakup or failure at school), and acts on their thoughts quickly and impulsively. The risk is increased if the young person has also been using alcohol.

If you have concerns that the young person may be having suicidal thoughts, see *First Aid for Suicidal Thoughts and Behaviors*.

NONSUICIDAL SELF-INJURY

Self-injury (such as cutting, scratching, pinching, or burning) that is not intended to result in death is relatively common in young people. Depression is a major risk factor for nonsuicidal self-injury.[111] Young people who engage in nonsuicidal self-injury also report more emotional distress, anger problems, lower self-esteem, more risky health behaviors, and more antisocial behaviors. Youth who have emotional difficulties are more likely to engage in nonsuicidal self-injury if they have close friends or peers who have engaged in similar behaviors.[112]

If you have concerns that the young person may be engaging in nonsuicidal self-injury, see *First Aid for Nonsuicidal Self-Injury*.

If you have no concerns that the young person is in crisis, you can move on to another action.

Action L: Listen Nonjudgmentally

If you believe that the young person is not in a crisis but needs immediate attention, you can engage the person in conversation by asking how the young person is feeling and how long they have been feeling this way. Listening nonjudgmentally is important at this stage, because it can help the young person feel heard and understood while not being judged in any way. This can make it easier for the person to feel comfortable to talk freely about the problems and to ask for help.

TIPS FOR NONJUDGMENTAL LISTENING

It is very difficult to be entirely nonjudgmental all of the time. People may automatically make judgments from the minute they first see or meet others, based on their appearance, behavior, and what they say. **There is more to nonjudgmental listening than simply trying not to make those judgments—it is about ensuring that you do not express your negative judgments, because this can get in the way of helping.** If you have decided to approach a young person with your concerns about them, it is a good idea to first spend some time reflecting on your own state of mind and ensure that you are in the right frame of mind to express your concerns without being judgmental.

Although the focus of your conversation with the person you are helping is on their feelings, thoughts, and experiences, you need to be aware of your own as well. Helping someone who is in distress may evoke an unexpected emotional response in you; you may find yourself feeling fearful, overwhelmed, sad, or even irritated or frustrated.

In spite of any emotional response you have, you need to continue listening respectfully and avoid expressing a negative reaction to what the person says. This is sometimes difficult and may be made more complex by your relationship with the person or your personal beliefs about their situation. **You need to set aside these beliefs and reactions to focus on the needs of the person you are helping—the person needs to be heard, understood, and helped.**

Remember that you are providing the young person with a safe space to express themselves, and a negative reaction from you can prevent them from feeling that sense of safety.

Effective Communication Skills for Nonjudgmental Listening[113]

You can be an effective, nonjudgmental listener by paying special attention to two main areas:

- Your attitudes and how they are conveyed

- Effective communication skills, both verbal and nonverbal

ATTITUDES

The key attitudes involved in nonjudgmental listening are acceptance, genuineness, and empathy.

>> Adopting an attitude of *acceptance* means respecting the young person's feelings, culture, personal values, and experiences as valid, even if they are different from your own or you disagree with them. You should not judge, criticize, or trivialize what the young person says because of your own

beliefs or attitudes. Sometimes this may mean withholding any and all judgments that you have made about the young person and their other circumstances. For example, listen to the person without judging; these problems are not the result of weakness or laziness—the person is trying to cope.

›› *Genuineness* means that what you say and do shows the young person that they are accepted. This means not holding one set of attitudes while expressing another. Your body language and verbal cues should show your acceptance of the person. Young people are especially good at recognizing when an adult is not being genuine. Being genuine also means not trying to mimic the young person's language, slang, and mannerisms if these are not natural for you.

›› *Empathy* means being able to imagine yourself in the other person's place, showing the person that they are truly heard and understood by you. This does not mean saying something glib such as, "I understand exactly how you are feeling;" it is more appropriate to say that you can appreciate the difficulty the person may be going through. Remember that empathy is different from sympathy, which means feeling sorry for or pitying the person.

VERBAL SKILLS

Using the following simple verbal skills will show that you are listening:

■ Ask questions that show you genuinely care and want to understand.

■ Check your understanding by restating what the young person has said and summarizing facts and feelings.

■ Listen not only to what the person says, but also how they say it; tone of voice and nonverbal cues will give extra clues about how the person is feeling.

■ Respect the youth's culture by asking about and exhibiting verbal behaviors that convey this respect.

■ Use minimal prompts, such as "I see" and "Ah," when necessary to keep the conversation going.

■ Be patient if the young person is struggling to communicate.

■ Do not be critical or express frustration at the young person or their symptoms.

■ Avoid giving unhelpful advice such as "pull yourself up by your bootstraps," "get a grip," or "cheer up." If this were possible, the young person would have done it.

■ Do not interrupt the young person when they are speaking, especially to share your opinions or experiences.

■ Avoid confrontation unless necessary to prevent harmful or dangerous acts.

Remember that pauses and silences are okay. Silence can be uncomfortable for many people, but the young person may need time to think about what has been said or may be struggling to find the words they need. Interrupting the silence may make it difficult for the young person to get back on track and may damage the rapport you have been building. Consider whether the silence is awkward or just awkward for you.

With all mental health issues, it is important to understand the impact of culture on person's perceptions of depression, help-seeking behaviors, and treatment response. Many youth learn to identify their feelings through their parents and caregivers, who may perceive mental health challenges in different ways. For example, in ethnically and culturally diverse, low-income communities, women used different terms to describe depression (*blues, sadness, homesickness*), even though the physical symptoms and severity of depression were commonly reported across the different ethnic groups.[114]

NONVERBAL SKILLS

Nonverbal communications and body language express a great deal. Good nonverbal skills show that you are listening and can strengthen the rapport between you and the young person you are assisting.

Keep the following nonverbal cues in mind to reinforce your nonjudgmental listening:

- Pay close attention to what the young person says.

- Respect the youth's culture by asking about and exhibiting physical behaviors (e.g., eye contact, physical space and distance) that convey this respect.

- Maintain comfortable eye contact. Do not avoid eye contact, but do avoid staring; you can do this by maintaining the level of eye contact that the young person seems most comfortable with.

- Maintain an open body position. Do not cross your arms over your body, doing so may appear defensive.

- If it is safe to do so, sit down, even if the young person is standing; this may seem less threatening.

- It may be best to sit alongside the person, angled toward them, rather than directly opposite them.

- Do not fidget.

More information about communicating effectively with a young person is available in *Mental Health First Aid for Youth and Young Adults*.

Action G: Give Reassurance and Information

TREAT THE YOUNG PERSON WITH RESPECT AND DIGNITY

Every young person's situation and needs are unique, and it is important to respect the person's autonomy and culture while considering the extent to which they are able to make decisions for themselves.

DO NOT BLAME THE YOUNG PERSON FOR THE ILLNESS

Depression is a real health problem, and the young person cannot help being affected by depression. It is important to remind the young person that they have a health problem and that they are not to blame for feeling down.

HAVE REALISTIC EXPECTATIONS FOR THE YOUNG PERSON

You should accept the young person as they are and have realistic expectations of them. Everyday activities such as homework and household chores may seem overwhelming to the young person. You should let the young person know that they are not weak or a failure because they have depression and that you do not think less of the young person. You should acknowledge that the person is not faking, lazy, weak, or selfish.

OFFER CONSISTENT EMOTIONAL SUPPORT AND UNDERSTANDING

It is more important for you to be genuinely caring than for you to say all the right things. The young person genuinely needs additional care and understanding to help them through the illness, so you should be empathetic, compassionate, and patient. Young people with depression are often overwhelmed by irrational fears; you need to be gently understanding of someone in this state. It is important to be patient, persistent, and encouraging when supporting someone with depression. You should also offer the young person kindness and attention, even if it is not reciprocated. Let the person know that they will not be abandoned. You should be consistent and predictable in your interactions with the young person.

GIVE THE YOUNG PERSON HOPE FOR RECOVERY

You need to encourage the young person to maintain hope by saying that, with time and treatment, they will feel better. Offer emotional support and hope of a more positive future in whatever form the young person will accept.

PROVIDE PRACTICAL HELP

Ask the young person whether they would like any practical assistance with tasks, for example, "Do you need a ride or some money to get home?" Be careful not to take over or encourage dependency. You can offer and provide help in many ways, but you cannot make the changes or engage in treatment for the young person.

PROVIDE INFORMATION

Give the young person information about depression (see *Helpful Resources* at the end of this section). It is important that the resources you give are accurate and appropriate to the young person's age and situation. At the same time, do not assume that the young person knows nothing about depression because they, or someone else close to them, may have experienced depression. You may want to ask whether they are already getting help for their depression.

WHAT IS NOT SUPPORTIVE

- Do not tell the young person with depression "to snap out of it or get over it."

- Do not be hostile or sarcastic when the young person's responses are not what you would usually expect. Rather, accept the young person's responses as the best they have to offer at that time.

- Do not adopt an over involved or overprotective attitude toward a young person who is depressed.

- Do not nag the young person to try to get them to do what they normally would.

- Do not trivialize the young person's experiences by pressuring them to "put a smile on your face," "get your act together," or "lighten up."

- Do not belittle or dismiss the young person's feelings by attempting to say something positive, such as "You don't seem that bad to me."

- Do not speak with a patronizing tone of voice or use overly compassionate looks of concern.

- Do not try to cure the young person's depression or to come up with answers to their problems.

Action E: Encourage Appropriate Professional Help

Everybody feels down or sad at times, but it is important to be able to recognize that professional help is warranted when depression lasts for weeks and affects a young person's functioning in daily life.

PROFESSIONALS WHO CAN HELP

A variety of health disciplines can provide help to a young person with depression. Ideally, the health professional should have expertise in providing mental health services to youth and young adults. The first aider should seek individual professionals who have child, youth, and young adult expertise among these various professionals:

- **Primary care physicians**

- **Pediatricians**

- **Nurse practitioners**

- **Allied health professionals, such as occupational therapists, youth workers, and mental health nurses**

- **Psychiatrists and child and adolescent psychiatrists**

- **Psychologists and child and adolescent psychologists**

- **Mental health care providers**

- **Social workers**

More information about these professionals can be found in *Mental Health Challenges and Mental Disorders in Youth and Young Adults in the United States*.

TREATMENTS AVAILABLE FOR DEPRESSIVE DISORDERS

Most people recover from depression and lead satisfying and productive lives. However, only approximately two of every five youth who experience a major depressive episode receive treatment for depression.[115] A young person may not access treatment services for many reasons. Young people may not know they have a mental health problem; they may feel they will be misunderstood or stigmatized by their peers or family; or they or their family may not know how and where to seek mental or behavioral health care.

Only in the most severe cases of depression, or when there is an immediate danger that a person might harm themselves, is a person admitted to a hospital. Most people with depression can be effectively treated within the community. For some young people, it may be necessary to treat the depression with medication. These decisions should be made in consultation with the family, youth, and medical or mental health professional. The treatment of depression is very individualized and should take into account the youth's family, culture, and past treatment experience.

A range of treatments are available for both depression and bipolar disorder. There is some evidence that the following treatments are effective for depression in young people.

Psychological therapies include:

- *Cognitive behavioral therapy (CBT)*, which is based on the idea that how a person thinks affects the way the person feels. When people get depressed, they think negatively about most things. They may have thoughts about how hopeless the situation is and how helpless the person feels, with a negative view of themselves, the world, and the future. Cognitive-behavioral therapy helps the person recognize such unhelpful thoughts and change them to more realistic ones. It also helps people to change depressive behaviors by scheduling regular activities and fond past-times. CBT can include components such as stress management, relaxation techniques, and sleep management.[116]

- *Trauma-focused cognitive behavioral therapy (CBT)* incorporates elements of cognitive-behavioral and family therapy for traumatized children.

- *Interpersonal psychotherapy* helps people to resolve conflicts with other people, deal with grief or changes in their relationships, and develop better relationships.[117]

- *Wraparound care* is a team approach that involves all individuals who are relevant to the well-being of the young person (such as family members, teachers, and social service providers) in setting goals with the young person and developing an individualized set of services and supports. Wraparound services and supports are usually provided in the young person's home or community.

- *Family support and therapy* tries to help all family members change their patterns of communication and behaviors so that their relationships are more supportive and less conflict occurs.[118]

- *Problem-solving therapy* involves meeting with a therapist to clearly identify problems, think of different solutions for each problem, choose the best solution, develop and carry out a plan, and then see whether this solves the problem.[119]

MEDICATION

Research has shown that, as with adults, depression in youth and young adults is treatable. However, knowledge of antidepressant medications for youth, although growing substantially, is limited compared with what is known about using medication to treat adults with depression. In 2004, the Food and Drug Administration issued a public warning about an increased risk of suicidal thoughts and behaviors in children and adolescents treated with a group of antidepressant medications known as *selective serotonin reuptake inhibitors*. This warning was followed in 2006 with a statement that extended the warning to include young adults up to age 25. More recently, some research has suggested that the benefits of antidepressant medications likely outweigh their risks to children and adolescents with major depression and anxiety disorders.[120, 121] It is important that young people who are on medication be carefully monitored and supported by a medical professional.

BIPOLAR DISORDER TREATMENTS

There is some evidence that the following treatments help adolescents with bipolar disorder:[122]

- **Medications.** Mood stabilizers, antipsychotics, and antidepressants can be helpful for some people with bipolar disorder.[123]

- **Psychoeducation** involves providing information to the person and their family about bipolar disorder, its treatment (including the importance of continuing to use medication), and managing its effect on life.[124] Stress reduction, good sleep habits, and a stable social environment can help adolescents with bipolar disorder to stay well.

- **Psychological therapies.** *Cognitive behavioral therapy* is an approach that has proven to be helpful.[125] Cognitive behavioral therapy helps people to monitor mood swings, overcome thinking patterns that affect mood, and function better. *Interpersonal and social rhythm therapies* cover potential problem areas in the person's life (grief, changes in roles, disputes, and interpersonal challenges) and help them regulate social and sleep rhythms.[126]

- **Family therapy and support** educates family members on how they can support the person with bipolar disorder and avoid negative interactions that can trigger relapses.[127] The focus of family therapy includes family psychoeducation and developing better family communication.

Young people with depressive disorders may be more likely to seek help if a parent or another adult close to them suggests it. Encourage the young person to talk with their parent or caregiver about what they are experiencing.

DISCUSS OPTIONS FOR SEEKING PROFESSIONAL HELP

If the young person feels they do need help, discuss the options for seeking help and encourage the young person to use these options. If the young person does not know where to get assistance, help them seek assistance. It is important to encourage the young person to get appropriate professional help and effective treatment as early as possible. Ideally, the health professional should have expertise in providing mental health services to young people as well as trauma-informed treatment. Sometimes it is difficult to connect with a mental health program. You may need to provide support in navigating the system for the young person and their family.

For a younger adolescent, you may need to help them make and attend an appointment with a health professional. Older youth may not need the same level of assistance, but this depends on their maturity and the severity of the problem. It may take some time to get a diagnosis and find a health care provider with whom the person is able to establish a good relationship. You should encourage the young person not to give up seeking appropriate professional help.

WHAT IF THE PERSON DOES NOT WANT HELP?

The young person may not want to seek professional help. Find out whether there are specific reasons why this is the case. For example, the youth may be concerned that a parent cannot afford treatment, may not have a doctor the young person likes, or may be worried about being sent to a hospital. These reasons may be based on mistaken beliefs, and you may be able to help the young person overcome worrying about seeking help. If the young person still does not want help, let the young person know that if they change their mind in the future, they can speak to you. If you think the young person lacks the maturity to understand what is happening and refuses help, you need to contact the youth's parents or a health professional.

Action E: Encourage Self-Help and Other Support Strategies

Certain factors can moderate depression and help youth and young adults be successful despite mental health challenges they may encounter in their lives. Some of these factors include[128]

- Having a good social support system

- Perceiving oneself as competent and likable; having high self-esteem

- Having good problem-solving skills

- Having a healthy diet and good health practices

- Believing that they control their own life

- Parental and familial support

OTHER PEOPLE WHO CAN HELP

Encourage the young person to consider other available supports, such as family, friends, and support groups. Some young people who experience depression find it helpful to meet with others who have had similar experiences. Family and friends can be an important source of support for a young person who is depressed. Recovery from symptoms is quicker for people who feel supported by those around them.[129]

SELF-HELP STRATEGIES

Many health professionals believe self-help strategies are helpful for youth with depression. Young people who are depressed may benefit from using self-help strategies, such as

- Exercise

- Relaxation training

- Avoiding alcohol, tobacco, and other drugs[130]

- Proper nutrition and sleep[131]

A young person's ability and desire to use self-help strategies will depend on their interest and severity of depression. You should not be too forceful when encouraging the young person to use self-help strategies. Self-help strategies may be useful in conjunction with other treatments and may be suitable for people with less severe depression. It is important that severe or long-lasting depression be assessed by a health professional. It is a good idea to discuss the appropriateness of self-help strategies with a mental health professional.

LIFESTYLE AND COMPLEMENTARY THERAPIES

Very little research has been carried out on the use of alternative strategies for youth with depression. The only therapies that have some supporting evidence for their effectiveness are massage and light therapy.

- *Massage.* It is not known how massage might work to help depression, but it may be that it reduces the level of stress hormones or tension in the body.[132]

- *Light therapy* involves exposure to bright light, often in the morning. Light therapy is most useful for *seasonal affective disorder* (depression that occurs during the darker winter months) when used under the guidance of a health professional.[133]

Helpful Resources
FOR DEPRESSION AND BIPOLAR DISORDERS

WEBSITES

The Balanced Mind Foundation
www.bpkids.org

The Balanced Mind Foundation is a parent-led, not-for-profit, web-based membership organization of families raising children diagnosed with, or at risk for, pediatric bipolar disorder. The foundation educates families, professionals, and the public about early-onset bipolar disorders. This site provides information to support families with children suffering from this disorder, including fact sheets, newsletters, chat rooms, physician locators, and a support group directory for each state.

Brain & Behavior Research Foundation
www.bbrfoundation.org

This site provides information and downloadable fact sheets on depressive disorders.

Center for the Study and Prevention of Violence (CSPV)
www.colorado.edu/cspv

The center serves as an information clearinghouse with literature and resources on the causes and prevention of violence and provides direct information services to the public by offering online searchable customized databases; offers technical assistance for the evaluation and development of violence prevention programs; and maintains a basic research component through data analysis and other projects on the causes of violence and the effectiveness of prevention and intervention programs.

Depression and Bipolar Support Alliance
www.dbsalliance.org

The Depression and Bipolar Support Alliance, founded in 1985, is a patient directed national organization focusing on the most prevalent mental illnesses. The alliance fosters an environment of understanding about the impact and management of these life-threatening illnesses by providing up-to-date, scientifically based tools and information written in language the general public can understand. The alliance supports research to promote more timely diagnosis, develop more effective and tolerable treatments, and discover a cure. The organization works to ensure that people living with mood disorders are treated equitably.

Families for Depression Awareness
www.familyaware.org

Families for Depression Awareness is an organization dedicated to informing and supporting the family members of people experiencing depressive disorders to help them support their loved ones. The organization's website provides resources about depression; profiles of families who have experienced a depressive disorder; a newsletter and podcast series; and other tools and links.

National Council for Community Behavioral Healthcare

www.TheNationalCouncil.org

To locate mental health and addictions treatment facilities in your community, use the Find a Provider feature on the National Council's website.

National Institute of Mental Health

www.nimh.nih.gov

This government site provides a wealth of excellent, up-to-date information on mental health problems and research. The site has downloadable booklets, brochures, and fact sheets about specific mental health challenges and disorders.

Pendulum

http://pendulum.org

Pendulum is a nonprofit organization providing information on bipolar disorder. The website includes book reviews, discussion forums, articles, and links to other resources.

Stop Bullying Now Campaign

www.stopbullying.gov

This website from the U.S. Department of Health and Human Services features a range of tools, such as a guide to using the materials; a section on cyberbullying; and various sections from different perspectives, such as mental health, law enforcement, and education. It also has a separate section specifically for children, featuring animation and child-specific frequently asked questions.

BOOKS

These two self-help books based on CBT for depression have been found effective in trials:

Burns, D. D. (1999). *Feeling Good: The New Mood Therapy* (rev. ed.). New York, NY: Quill.

Lewinsohn, P. M., Munoz, R. A., Youngren, M. A., & Zeiss, A. M. (1992). *Control Your Depression* (Rev. ed.). New York, NY: Simon & Schuster.

OTHER BOOKS THAT MAY BE USEFUL ARE:

Bauer, M. S., Kilbourne, A. M., Greenwald, D. E., & Ludman, E. (2009). *Overcoming Bipolar Disorder*. Oakland, CA: New Harbinger.
A self-help guide for people in treatment for bipolar disorder. Includes strategies for preventing relapse, safe and effective goal setting, and medication

Bieling, P. J., & Antony, M. M. (2003). *Ending the Depression Cycle*. Oakland, CA: New Harbinger.
A depression relapse prevention workbook based on CBT principles.

Ellis, T. E. (1996). *Choosing to Live: How to defeat Suicide through Cognitive Therapy*. Oakland, CA: New Harbinger,.
This CBT-based self-help book focuses on learning thinking strategies to overcome suicidal thoughts.

Evans, D. L., & Andrews, L. W. (2005). *If Your Adolescent Has Depression or Bipolar Disorder: An Essential Resource for Parents*. New York, NY: Oxford University Press.
This guide is written for the parents and other caregivers of adolescents with a diagnosis of bipolar disorder or depression. It contains information about treatment and management, addresses myths, and includes personal stories of people who are recovering.

Greenburger, D., & Padesky, C. (1995). *Mind Over Mood: Change How You Feel by Changing How You Think*. New York, NY: Guilford Press.
This is a CBT-based self-help book for depression.

Knaus, W. J. (2006). *The Cognitive Behavioral Workbook for Depression*. Oakland, CA: New Harbinger.
This CBT manual can be used alone or in conjunction with therapy. It can also be purchased as an eBook directly from the publisher (www.newharbinger.com).

Mondimore, F. M. (2006). *Bipolar disorder: A Guide for Patients and Families* (Rev. ed.). Baltimore, MD: Johns Hopkins University Press.
This book has won awards for contributing to the public's awareness and better understanding of mental illness.

Shapiro, L. E. (2008). *Stopping the Pain: A Workbook for Teens Who Cut and Self-Injure*. Oakland, CA: Instant Help
This book is a helpful resource for those who self-injure.

HELPLINES

American Psychiatric Association
Answer Center
1-888-35-PSYCH (77924)
Live operators, available 8:30 a.m. to 6:00 p.m., EST, refer you to local board-certified psychiatrists.

American Psychological Association
Public Education Line
1-800-964-2000
Follow the automated instructions. An operator then refers you to local board-certified psychologists.

National Suicide Prevention Lifeline
1-800-273-TALK (8255)
This is a crisis hotline that can help with many issues, not just suicide. For example, anyone who feels sad, hopeless, or suicidal; family and friends who are concerned about a loved one; or anyone interested in mental health treatment referrals can call the Lifeline. Callers are connected with a professional nearby who will talk with them about what they are feeling or concerns for other family and friends. If you or someone you know is in suicidal crisis, call the hotline (toll free, 24 hours/day, 7 days/week).

SUPPORT GROUPS

Depression and Bipolar Support Alliance
www.dbsalliance.org
On the home page of this website, click on "Find Support." You will be able to find out whether a support group is meeting in your area. These support groups are peer led.

National Alliance on Mental Illness
www.nami.org
The National Alliance on Mental Illness is a nonprofit, grassroots, self-help support and advocacy organization of individuals with mental disorders and their families. This website provides many resources on mental disorders, including depression, that are helpful for people who have experienced a mental illness and their families, including support groups, education, and training. Click "Find Support" on the home page.

Anxiety in Young People

What Is an Anxiety Disorder?

Everybody experiences anxiety at some time. When people describe their anxiety, they may use terms such as *anxious, stressed, wound up, nervous, on edge, worried, tense,* or *hassled.* Although anxiety is an unpleasant state, it can be quite useful in helping a person avoid dangerous situations and motivate them to solve everyday problems. Anxiety can vary in severity from mild uneasiness to a terrifying panic attack. Anxiety can also vary in how long it lasts—from a few moments to many years.

An anxiety disorder differs from normal anxiety in the following ways:

- It is more severe.

- It is long lasting.

- It interferes with the person's studies, other activities, and family and social relationships.

Anxiety disorders affect one in eight youth ages 13 to 18 years.[29] Anxiety disorders are more prevalent than virtually all other mental disorders of childhood and adolescence.[29] The median age of onset is 11 years, which means half the people have their first episode by this age.[135] Approximately 18.1 percent of American adults ages 18 and older, in a given year, have an anxiety disorder.[136, 137]

Signs and Symptoms of Anxiety

Physical:

>> Pounding heart, chest pain, rapid heartbeat, and blushing

>> Rapid, shallow breathing, and shortness of breath

>> Dizziness, headache, sweating, tingling, and numbness

>> Choking, dry mouth, stomach pains, nausea, vomiting, and diarrhea

>> Muscle aches and pains (especially neck, shoulders, and back), restlessness, tremors, and shaking

Psychological:

>> Unrealistic or excessive fear and worry (about past and future events)

>> Racing thoughts or mind going blank

>> Decreased concentration and memory

>> Indecisiveness

>> Irritability

>> Impatience

>> Anger

>> Confusion

>> Feeling on edge

>> Nervousness

>> Sleep disturbance

>> Vivid dreams

Behavioral:

>> Avoidance of situations

>> Obsessive or compulsive behavior

>> Distress in social situations

>> Phobic behavior

>> Increased use of alcohol or other drugs.

The symptoms are similar in both adults and youth. Some anxiety symptoms are particularly common in youth. These symptoms include worry in general, but particularly worry about what others think of them, fear in social situations, and anxiety about past imperfections.[139]

What might a first aider notice if a young person has an anxiety disorder?

When people think of anxiety disorders, they typically imagine someone who is very introverted and perhaps not very communicative. This is true for some people with anxiety disorders. However, there are other signs, particularly in young people, that might indicate that anxiety is a problem.

At home, young people may

>> Complain of headaches and other physical problems to avoid going to school

>> Be tearful in the morning, saying they do not want to go to school

>> Spend more time doing homework or express unnecessary concerns that the work is not good enough

>> Demand constant reassurance from parents

>> Be touchy and irritable in interactions with family

>> Spend a long time getting ready for social occasions, worrying about their appearance or what they might do, or decide at the last minute not to attend social occasions

At school, young people may

>> Be extremely well behaved and quiet, fearful of asking questions

>> Demand extra time from teachers, asking questions constantly and needing a great deal of reassurance

>> Not hand in assignments on time because the work is seen as less than perfect

>> Complain of sudden, unexplained physical illness, such as a stomachache or headache, when exams or presentations have been scheduled

These signs can have an impact on school achievement. A specific phobia of school may result in absenteeism as well. Some of these behaviors may result in disciplinary responses.

In a social setting, young people may

>> Avoid meeting new people or socializing with groups, spending time with only a few safe friends.

>> Use alcohol or other drugs at parties to make it easier to talk to people.

>> Leave social events early.

>> Avoid speaking up for fear of embarrassment.

Types of Anxiety Disorders

There are many different types of anxiety disorders.[139] The main ones are *generalized anxiety disorder*, *panic disorder*, and *agoraphobia*. *Phobic disorders* including *social anxiety disorder, separation anxiety disorder, post-traumatic stress disorder (PTSD)*; and *obsessive-compulsive disorder (OCD)*. It is not unusual for a person to have more than one of these anxiety disorders.

Generalized Anxiety Disorder

Some young people experience long-term anxiety across a whole range of situations, and this anxiety, called *generalized anxiety disorder*, interferes with their lives. Young people with this disorder will have overwhelming, unfounded worry (about things that may go wrong or their inability to cope) and multiple physical and psychological symptoms of anxiety or tension occurring more days than not, for at least six months.[140] Young people with generalized anxiety disorder worry excessively about health, money, appearance, schoolwork, sports, and other regular activities, even when there are no signs of trouble. Young people with the disorder may have poor problem-solving skills, an intolerance of uncertainty, and the belief that worry is a helpful way to deal with problems.

Panic Disorder

It is important to distinguish between a *panic attack* and *panic disorder*. Some people have short periods of extreme anxiety called panic attacks. A panic attack is a sudden onset of intense apprehension, fear, or terror. These attacks can begin suddenly and develop rapidly. This intense fear is inappropriate for the circumstances in which it is occurring. Around one-quarter of the population has a panic attack at some stage in their life,[141] but having a panic attack does not necessarily mean that a person will develop panic disorder.[142]

A person with panic disorder experiences recurring panic attacks and, for at least one month, is persistently worried about possible future panic attacks and their possible consequences, such as a fear of losing control or having a heart attack. The person may avoid exercise or other activities that may produce physical sensations similar to those of a panic attack. They may avoid places where attacks have occurred. Some people may develop a panic disorder after only a few panic attacks, and others may experience many panic attacks without developing a panic disorder.

Phobic Disorders[143]

A person with a *phobic disorder* avoids or restricts activities because of fear. This fear appears persistent, excessive, and unreasonable. They may have an unreasonably strong fear of specific places, events, or objects and often avoid them completely.

- *Agoraphobia* involves avoiding situations in which the person fears they may have a panic attack. The focus of the anxiety is that it will be difficult or embarrassing to get away from the place if a panic attack occurs or that there will be no one present who can help. This leads them to avoid certain situations for fear of a panic attack occurring. Some may avoid only a few situations, such as parties or being in a car, or certain places, such as shopping malls. Others may avoid leaving home altogether. The younger a person is when they have their first panic attack, the more likely they are to develop agoraphobia.[144] Agoraphobia is thought by many to mean a fear of open spaces or a fear of leaving the house. Although these symptoms may occur with agoraphobia, the person cannot be said to have agoraphobia unless they have a fear of panic attacks.

- *Social anxiety disorder* is the fear of any situation in which public scrutiny may occur, usually with the fear of behaving in a way that is embarrassing or humiliating. The key fear is that others will think badly of the person. Social anxiety disorder often develops in shy children as they move into adolescence. Common fears include speaking or eating in public, dating, and social events. The anxiety occurs with peers as well as with adults.

- *Specific phobias* are intense fears of specific objects or situations. The most common fears are of spiders, insects, mice, snakes, and heights. Other feared objects or situations include an animal, blood, injections, storms, enclosed places, or traveling in buses, trains, or planes. Because they involve only specific situations or objects, these phobias are usually less disabling than agoraphobia and social phobia.

Separation Anxiety Disorder

A young person with *separation anxiety disorder* shows excessive fear or worry about being away from home or apart from a parent or caregiver. The person will worry about losing the loved one or about harm coming to them. Young people with separation anxiety may be reluctant to leave home without the loved one or to be left alone, and they may refuse to go to school because of fear of separation. Separation anxiety is most common in young children, but it can occur during adolescence as well, often as a result of having lost a parent or other close family member.

Post-traumatic Stress Disorder

Post-traumatic stress disorder (PTSD) can occur after a person experiences what they perceive to be a traumatic event. What is perceived as traumatic will vary from person to person. Common examples of events that many people find traumatic include involvement in war, accidents, assault (including physical or sexual assault, mugging or robbery, or family violence) and witnessing something terrible happen. Mass traumatic events include terrorist attacks, mass shootings, war, and severe weather events (e.g., hurricanes, tornadoes, fires, and floods).

It is common for people to feel greatly distressed immediately after a traumatic event. This distress is called *acute stress disorder*, and the distress usually lessens within a month. If the distress lasts longer than a month, they may have PTSD. Only some people who experience acute stress disorder will go on to develop a mental illness such as PTSD or depression. People are more likely to develop PTSD if their response to the event involves intense fear, helplessness, or horror.

A major symptom of PTSD is re-experiencing the trauma. This may be in the form of recurrent dreams of the event, flashbacks, intrusive memories, or unrest in situations that bring back memories of the original trauma. A young person with PTSD may avoid things associated with the event or show reduced interest in others and the outside world. The young person may show increased emotional distress in the form of irritability, jumpiness, outbursts of rage, and insomnia.[145]

Obsessive–Compulsive Disorder

Obsessive thoughts and compulsive behaviors accompany feelings of anxiety. *Obsessive thoughts* are recurrent thoughts, impulses, and images that are experienced as intrusive, unwanted, and inappropriate and cause marked anxiety. Most obsessive thoughts are about fear of contamination, symmetry and exactness, safety, sexual impulses, aggressive impulses, and religious preoccupation. *Compulsive behaviors* are repetitive behaviors or mental acts that the person feels driven to perform in response to an obsession to reduce anxiety. Common compulsions include washing, checking, repeating, ordering, counting, hoarding, or touching things over and over.[146] This type of anxiety disorder is one of the least common, but it can be a very disabling condition. OCD can begin in childhood as well as adolescence and may be a lifelong illness.

Mixed Anxiety, Depression, and Substance Abuse

It is common for young people to have some features of several anxiety disorders. A high level of anxiety over a long time will often lead to depression; so many young people have a mixture of both anxiety and depression.

Substance abuse sometimes occurs with anxiety disorders as a form of self-medication to help cope. Also, heavy use of alcohol and other drugs can lead to increased anxiety.[147, 148]

Risk Factors for Anxiety Disorders

Anxiety is mostly caused by perceived threats, but some people are more likely than others to react with anxiety when they are threatened. People most at risk are those who[149, 150]

- Have a more sensitive emotional nature and who tend to see the world as threatening

- Have a history of anxiety in childhood, including marked shyness

- Are female

- Experience a traumatic event

Some family factors increase risk for anxiety disorders:

- A difficult childhood (e.g., experiencing physical, emotional, or sexual abuse; neglect; or overstrictness)

- A family background that involves poverty or a lack of job skills

- A family history of anxiety disorders

- Parental alcohol problems

- Parental separation and divorce

Anxiety symptoms can also result from

- Some medical conditions, such as hyperthyroidism, arrhythmias, and vitamin B12 deficiency[151]

- Side effects of certain medications, including those used to treat ADHD

- Intoxication with alcohol, amphetamines, caffeine, cannabis, cocaine, hallucinogens, and inhalants

Historical trauma—the cumulative emotional and psychological wounding, during the lifespan and across generations, originating from massive group trauma experiences—has also been linked to anxiety disorders.[152] Historical trauma poses an added burden for groups that have experienced persecution, for example, American Indian/Alaska Native families, African American families, and refugee families.

Importance of Early Intervention for Anxiety Disorders

With treatment and support, youth and young adults can learn how to manage the symptoms of an anxiety disorder and function well.[153] According to the 2015 Child Mind Institute Children's Mental Health Report, while anxiety is treatable, approximately 80 percent of kids with a diagnosable anxiety disorder are not getting treatment.[31] Research has shown that children and youth with untreated anxiety disorders are at higher risk of performing poorly in school, missing out on important social experiences, experiencing early parenthood, and engaging in substance abuse. Anxiety disorders also often co-occur with other disorders such as depression. In addition, anxiety disorders can make it difficult for some young people to be assertive or make their own decisions. Some young people develop ways of reducing their anxiety that cause further problems. For example, people with phobias may avoid anxiety provoking situations. This avoidance behavior reduces their anxiety in the short term but can limit their lives in significant ways. Similarly, people with compulsions reduce their anxiety by repetitive acts such as washing hands. The compulsions then become problems in themselves. Because of these long-term consequences, it is very important that anxiety disorders are recognized early and young people get appropriate professional help.

Mental Health First Aid® Action Plan for Anxiety

YOUTH MENTAL HEALTH FIRST AID® ACTION PLAN	
ACTION A	Assess for risk of suicide or harm
ACTION L	Listen nonjudgmentally
ACTION G	Give reassurance and information
ACTION E	Encourage appropriate professional help
ACTION E	Encourage self-help and other support strategies

Action A: Assess for Risk of Suicide or Harm

Crises that may be associated with anxiety are

- The person is at an extreme level of anxiety such as a **panic attack.**

- The person has experienced a **traumatic event.**

- The person has **suicidal thoughts or behaviors.**

- The person is engaging in **nonsuicidal self-injury.**

PANIC ATTACK

A *panic attack* is a sudden onset of intense apprehension, fear, or terror. These attacks can begin suddenly and develop rapidly. This intense fear is inappropriate for the circumstances in which it is occurring. Other symptoms, many of which can appear similar to those of a heart attack, can include racing heart, sweating, shortness of breath, chest pain, dizziness, feeling detached from oneself, and fears of losing control. Although anyone can have a panic attack, people with anxiety disorders are more prone to have one.

REACTION TO A TRAUMATIC EVENT

A *traumatic event* is any incident experienced by a person that is perceived to be dangerous and threatens serious injury or death. Common examples of traumas that affect individuals include accidents, assault (including physical or sexual assault, mugging or robbery, or family violence), and witnessing something terrible. Mass traumatic events include terrorist attacks, mass shootings, warfare, and military activity, and severe weather events (hurricanes, tsunami, and wildfires). Most people who experience a traumatic event do not develop a mental illness. However, other people who experience symptoms of severe stress may go on to develop acute stress disorder, PTSD, another anxiety disorder, or depression. People at most risk of developing mental illness after a traumatic event are those who were prone to depression or anxiety before the event and those who feel horror or powerlessness during the event.

SUICIDAL THOUGHTS AND BEHAVIORS

The risk of suicide in people with anxiety disorders is not as high as for some other mental illnesses.[154] However, the risk increases if the young person also has a depressive or substance use disorder. When interacting with a young person with an anxiety disorder, the first aider should be alert to any warning signs of suicide.

NONSUICIDAL SELF-INJURY

Anxiety disorders greatly increase the risk for nonsuicidal self-injury.[155] Nonsuicidal self-injury may be a coping mechanism for feelings of unbearable anxiety.

If you have concerns that the young person may be having a panic attack, see *First Aid for Panic Attacks*.

If the young person has experienced a traumatic event, see *First Aid for Children and Youth Affected by Traumatic Events* and *First Aid for Young Adults and Adults Affected by Traumatic Events*.

If you have concerns that the young person may be having suicidal thoughts, see *First Aid for Suicidal Thoughts and Behaviors*.

If you have concerns that the young person may be engaging in nonsuicidal self-injury, see *First Aid for Nonsuicidal Self-Injury*.

If you have no concerns that the young person is in crisis, you can move on to another ALGEE action.

Action L: Listen Nonjudgmentally

See Action L in *Depression in Young People* for more tips on nonjudgmental listening. Some main points to remember are

- **Talk with the young person about how they feel and listen carefully to what they say.**

- **Do not express any negative judgments** about the young person's character or situation.

- **Be aware of your body language,** including posture, eye contact, and physical position in relation to the young person, and adjust it to respect the youth's culture.

- To ensure you understand, **reflect back what you hear and ask clarifying questions.**

- **Allow silences, be patient, do not interrupt** the young person, and use only minimal prompts such as "I see" and "Ah."

- **Do not give flippant or unhelpful advice,** such as "pull yourself together."

- **Avoid confrontation** unless necessary to prevent harmful acts.

Action G: Give Reassurance and Information

The support and information that is helpful to someone with an anxiety problem is very similar to that given to someone experiencing depression. You can support the young person in the following ways:

- Treat the young person with respect and dignity.

- Do not blame the young person for the illness.

- Have realistic expectations of the young person.

- Offer consistent emotional support and understanding.

- Give the young person hope for recovery.

- Provide practical help.

- Offer information.

WHAT IS NOT SUPPORTIVE

It is important to know that recovery from anxiety disorders may require the youth to face anxiety-provoking situations. However, this must be done with caution and without purposely putting a youth in a situation that might cause a severe reaction. Sometimes, family and friends think they are being supportive by helping a young person avoid anxiety-provoking situations, but this can slow down the recovery process and make anxiety worse. Other actions that are not supportive include dismissing the young person's fears as trivial (e.g., by saying "This is nothing to be afraid of," "Toughen up" or "Don't be so weak"), and speaking in a patronizing tone of voice. It is important to help the youth access a mental health professional who specializes in working with adolescents, because some youth report that working with professionals can be anxiety provoking.

Action E: Encourage Appropriate Professional Help

Treatments are available that can help many people with anxiety disorders to have a better life.

A variety of professionals can provide help to a young person with an anxiety disorder. Ideally, the professional should have expertise in providing mental health services to children, youth, and young adults.

- **Primary care physicians**

- **Pediatricians**

- **Nurse practitioners**

- **Allied health professionals, such as occupational therapists, youth workers, and mental health nurses**

- **Psychiatrists and child and adolescent psychiatrists**

- **Psychologists and child and adolescent psychologists**

- **Mental health care providers**

- **Social workers**

A wide range of treatments can help with anxiety disorders. These include the following:

THERAPY

Various types of therapy are used for anxiety disorders, but the following have shown to be the most effective.[156, 157]

- *Cognitive behavior therapy* is the most effective treatment for anxiety disorders. It is based on the idea that how people think (cognition) influences how they act (behavior). Individuals learn how to recognize unhelpful thoughts and actions and how to use helpful coping strategies.

- *Behavior therapy* (also known as *exposure therapy*) is often a part of CBT. It involves gradually exposing the person to the things that make them anxious. This helps individuals learn to reduce their fears without avoiding them and that their fears about the situation often do not come true or are not as bad as they thought.

TRAUMA INFORMED TREATMENT AND OTHER INTERVENTIONS[158]

No one treatment intervention is appropriate for all youth and young adults who have experienced trauma. However, these types of treatments should include some, or all, of the following principles:

- Include the child, the family, and the community.

- Be sensitive to the family's cultural background.

- Recognize the impact of culture on how illness is described and treated.

- Use interpreters carefully, when necessary.

- Recognize differences in emotional expression among different cultures.

- Create a trauma narrative using culturally appropriate methods.

- Highlight the ways in which culture may be a source of resiliency and strength.

MEDICATION

For some young people, an anxiety disorder may be treated with medication. *Antidepressant medications*[159] can be helpful in treating severe anxiety disorders, such as obsessive-compulsive disorder. The decision to use medication to treat anxiety should be made in consultation with the youth, family, and medical or mental health professional.

DISCUSS OPTIONS FOR SEEKING PROFESSIONAL HELP

Ask the person if they need help to manage how they are feeling. If the young person feels they do need help, then discuss the options for seeking help and encourage the young person to use these options. If the young person does not know where to get assistance, help them seek assistance. It is important to encourage the young person to get appropriate professional help and effective treatment as early as possible. Accessing help may sometimes be difficult, so you may also need to encourage the young person not to give up seeking appropriate professional help.

WHAT IF THE YOUNG PERSON DOES NOT WANT HELP?

The young person may not want to seek professional help. You should find out whether there are specific reasons why this is the case. For example, the young person might be embarrassed or shy or be concerned that the doctor will judge them negatively.[160] You may be able to help the young person overcome their worry about seeking help. If the young person still does not want help after you have explored the reasons, let the young person know that if they change their mind about seeking help in the future, you are available.

If the young person is uncertain about what to do, encourage them to consult a medical doctor first, because the doctor can check whether an underlying physical health problem is causing their anxiety.

Action E: Encourage Self-Help and Other Support Strategies

Certain factors reduce the risk of developing or worsening anxiety. Some of these factors include[161]

- Consistent home or family routine
- Experiencing less stress
- High self-esteem
- Feelings of self-worth
- Feeling in control of one's life
- Consistent physical activity
- Sufficient social skills
- Secure attachment style
- Economic security

OTHER PEOPLE WHO CAN HELP

Encourage the young person to consider other supports available to them, such as family, friends, and any services available through the school. Young people identify family and friends as their primary sources of support.[162] Encourage the young person to talk with a parent or caregiver.

SELF-HELP STRATEGIES

Self-help strategies can be helpful for adolescents with anxiety disorders. These include meditation, exercise, relaxation training, and avoiding alcohol, marijuana, and tobacco.[163] The young person's ability to use self-help strategies will depend on their interests and severity of symptoms. Therefore, you should not be too forceful when trying to encourage the young person to use self-help strategies. If a young person wishes to use self-help strategies, this issue should be discussed with a professional.

LIFESTYLE AND COMPLEMENTARY THERAPIES

Relaxation training has been shown to be effective for young people with anxiety disorders.[164] Relaxation training involves learning to relax by tensing or relaxing specific groups of muscles or by thinking of relaxing scenes or places. Recorded instructions are available for free on the Internet, or recordings can be purchased (see the *Helpful Resources* at the end of this section). Relaxation training is most useful when learned under the guidance of a health professional.[165]

The following complementary and alternative practices are currently used to treat anxiety and anxiety disorders:[166]

>> ACUPUNCTURE

Evidence for the use of acupuncture (the Chinese practice of inserting needles into the body at specific points to manipulate the body's flow of energy) to treat anxiety disorders is becoming stronger.

>> YOGA

Combining physical postures, breathing exercises, meditation, and a distinct philosophy, yoga is a common practice for individuals managing anxiety.

Helpful Resources
FOR ANXIETY AND TRAUMA

ANXIETY RESOURCES

In addition to the resources described at the end of Section 1, the following may also be useful resources:

WEBSITES

Anxiety & Depression Disorders Association of America
www.adaa.org/living-with-anxiety/children
This website includes an anxiety self-test for teens to fill out and take to a health professional. Click on "Teens! Take an Anxiety Disorders Self-Test."

Benson-Henry Institute for Mind Body Medicine
www.bensonhenryinstitute.org
The Benson-Henry Institute for Mind Body Medicine at Massachusetts General Hospital has an online store providing CDs, DVDs, and books on relaxation techniques.

Mental Health America
www.mentalhealthamerica.net
Visit Mental Health America's site for information on mental health, getting help, and taking action.

National Council for Community Behavioral Healthcare
www.TheNationalCouncil.org
To locate mental health and addictions treatment facilities in your community, use the Find a Provider feature on the National Council's website.

National Institute of Mental Health
www.nimh.nih.gov/health/publications/anxiety-disorders/index.shtml
This website has a wealth of information and research on anxiety disorders.

International OCD Foundation

www.ocfoundation.org

The International Obsessive-Compulsive Foundation website includes information about OCD, effective treatments, how to find a health professional who has experience treating the disorder, and links to other websites.

The site includes an online web magazine written by young people with OCD, as well as OCD experts.

BOOKS

BOOKS FOR PARENTS AND CAREGIVERS

Foa, E. B., & Andrews, L. W. (2006). *If Your Adolescent Has an Anxiety Disorder: An Essential Resource for Parents*. New York, NY: Oxford University Press.

This book incorporates clinical expertise with the experiences of parents of anxious adolescents. It includes information on anxiety disorders in adolescents, treatment options, and juggling treatment with school and social activities.

BOOKS FOR ADOLESCENTS AND YOUNG PEOPLE

Schab, L. M. (2004). *The Anxiety Workbook for Teens: Activities to Help You Deal With Anxiety and Worry*. Oakland, CA: New Harbinger.

This self-help book for adolescents teaches relaxation and coping skills and can help a young person to develop a more positive self-image. Adolescents who are motivated to follow a program of self-help may benefit from using this book, particularly with the assistance of a clinician or parent.

Phillips, N. (2005). *The Panic Book*. Concord West, New South Wales, Australia: Shrink-Rap Press

Wever, C., & Phillips, N. (2006). *The Secret Problem*. Concord West, New South Wales, Australia: Shrink-Rap Press.

These books are suitable for people of all ages and were written and illustrated by two psychiatrists. They are easy to read and incorporate important information about anxiety disorders, how to cope with them, and how to think more realistically about fears and anxiety. *The Panic Book* is about panic attacks, panic disorder and agoraphobia, and *The Secret Problem* is about OCD.

Wilson, R. R. (2003). *Facing Panic: Self-Help for People With Panic Attacks*. Silver Spring, MD: Anxiety Disorders Association of America.

Teaches seven steps to break the cycle of panic and regain control of your life.

HELPLINES

American Psychiatric Association Answer Center
1-888-35-PSYCH (77924)

Live operators, available from 8:30 a.m. to 6:00 p.m., eastern time, refer you to local board-certified psychiatrists.

American Psychological Association Public Education Line
1-800-964-2000

Follow the automated instructions. An operator then refers you to local board-certified psychologists.

National Suicide Prevention Lifeline
1-800-273-TALK (8255)

This is a crisis hotline that can help with many issues, not just suicide. For example, anyone who feels sad, hopeless, or suicidal; family and friends who are concerned about a loved one; or anyone interested in mental health treatment referrals can call the Lifeline. Callers are connected with a professional nearby who will talk with them about what they are feeling or concerns for other family and friends. Call the hotline (toll free, 24 hours/ day, 7 days/week).

TRAUMA RESOURCES

Use the resources listed in *Mental Health First Aid for Youth and Young Adults* to help create a support network for the young person, their family, and yourself.

WEBSITES

Additional resources, information, and support can be found at the following websites:

The National Child Traumatic Stress Network
www.nctsnet.org/resources/audiences/parents-caregivers
The mission of The National Child Traumatic Stress Network is to "raise the standard of care and improve access to services for traumatized children, their families and, communities throughout the United States." The network's website has resources for parents and caregivers, professionals, military children and families, educators, and the media and information in Spanish.

National Institute of Mental Health—Posttraumatic Stress Disorder
www.nimh.nih.gov/health/publications/post-traumatic-stress-disorder-easy-to-read/index.shtml
This site provides information on PTSD, including an easy to read booklet on PTSD that explains what it is, when it starts, how long it lasts, and how to get help.

WRITTEN MATERIALS

American Academy of Child & Adolescent Psychiatry
www.aacap.org
The American Academy of Child & Adolescent Psychiatry is a membership based organization, composed of more than 7,500 child and adolescent psychiatrists and other interested physicians. Its website has information on trauma, including *Your Child—Childhood Trauma and Its Effects*: www.aacap.org/cs/root/publication_store/your_child_childhood_trauma_and_its_effects

American Psychological Association (APA)
The APA offers multiple resources on trauma.
Children and trauma:
www.apa.org/pi/families/resources/children-trauma-update.aspx
APA Disaster Response Network:
www.apa.org/practice/programs/drn/fact.aspx

Psychological First Aid for First Responders
http://store.samhsa.gov/product/SMA11-DISASTER
This site provides disaster recovery workers with a tool kit on mental health awareness including materials for responding effectively to the general public during and after a disaster and for dealing with workplace stress. This site also includes materials for the general public.

Eating Disorders in Young People

What Are Eating Disorders?

Eating disorders are not just about food, weight, appearance, or willpower; they are serious and potentially life-threatening illnesses.[167] Young people with eating disorders see their self-worth largely in terms of their body shape and weight and their ability to control them. Most people with eating disorders are very distressed about their appearance, body shape, and weight, and this distress causes significant disruption to their life. A young person with an eating disorder can be underweight or overweight or fall within the healthy weight range.

Eating disorders affect approximately 2.7 percent of adolescents, ages 13 through 18, during their youth.[29] It was once a widely held belief that the only people who had eating disorders were young, White, middle- to upper-class women. During the past few years, however, there has been an increase in the number of African American, Hispanic, Asian, and Native American youth and young adults with eating disorders.[168, 169,170] Although eating disorders are more common in girls (four percent) than in boys (fewer than two percent), the number of boys and young men coming forward to say they have an eating disorder is increasing. Eating disorders typically develop at ages 18–20, but half of people with eating disorders have their first episode before this age, and a third develop an eating disorder between ages 11 and 15.[171] Many people with eating disorders may also have another mental disorder, particularly anxiety, depression, and substance use disorders.[172] Eating disorders are associated with a higher lifetime risk for suicide.

Signs and Symptoms of Eating Disorders

It is important to know the signs that indicate that a young person has or is developing an eating disorder. The following behavioral, physical, and psychological signs can indicate an eating disorder:

Behavioral:[173, 174]

>> Dieting behaviors (e.g., fasting, counting calories, and avoidance of food groups or types)

>> Evidence of binge eating (e.g., disappearance or hoarding of food)

>> Evidence of deliberate vomiting or laxative use (e.g., taking trips to the bathroom during or immediately after meals)

>> Excessive, obsessive, or ritualistic exercise patterns (e.g., exercising when injured or in bad weather, feeling compelled to perform a certain number of repetitions of exercises, or experiencing distress if unable to exercise)

>> Changes in food preferences (e.g., refusing to eat certain fatty or unhealthy foods, cutting out whole food groups such as meat or dairy, claiming to dislike foods previously enjoyed, a sudden concern with healthy eating, or replacing meals with fluids)

>> Development of rigid patterns around food selection, preparation, and eating (e.g., cutting food into small pieces and eating very slowly)

>> Avoidance of eating meals, especially when in a social setting (e.g., skipping meals by claiming to have already eaten or have an intolerance or allergy to particular foods)

- Lying about the amount or type of food consumed or evading questions about eating and weight

- Behaviors focused on food (e.g., planning, buying, preparing, and cooking meals for others but not consuming meals themselves; interest in cookbooks, recipes, and nutrition)

- Behaviors focused on body shape and weight (e.g., interest in weight-loss websites, books, and magazines or images of thin people)

- Development of repetitive or obsessive behaviors relating to body shape and weight (e.g., body checking such as pinching waist or wrists, repeated weighing of self, and excessive time spent looking in mirrors)

- Social withdrawal or avoidance of previously enjoyed activities

Physical:

- Weight loss or weight fluctuations

- Sensitivity to the cold

- Changes in or loss of periods

- Swelling around the cheeks or jaw, calluses on knuckles, or dental discoloration from vomiting

- Fainting

Psychological:

- Preoccupation with food, body shape, and weight

- Extreme body dissatisfaction

- Distorted body image (e.g., complaining of being, feeling, or looking fat when at a healthy weight or underweight)

- Sensitivity to comments or criticism about exercise, food, body shape, or weight

- Heightened anxiety around meal times

- Depression, anxiety, or irritability

- Low self-esteem (e.g., negative opinions of self; feelings of shame, guilt, or self-loathing)

- Rigid thinking (e.g., labeling of food as either good or bad)

Some Warning Signs May be Difficult to Detect.

This is because young people with an eating disorder

- May feel shame, guilt, and distress about their eating or exercising behaviors, therefore these will often occur in secret

- May use deceit to hide their eating and exercising behaviors

- Will usually deny having a problem

- May find it difficult to ask for help from family and friends

How a Young Person With an Eating Disorder May Appear[175]

Often first aiders will focus on the young person's weight and appearance, but there are other signs that may be more useful, particularly if the weight change is not very dramatic. Below are some descriptions of a young person's appearance and behavior that might indicate that an eating disorder is a problem.

At home, the young person may

- Avoid eating with the family by claiming to have already eaten with friends, to have eaten too much earlier in the day, or to not be hungry

- Be increasingly preoccupied with exercise

- Obsessively count calories or examine food labels for nutritional information

- Complain that the food is disgusting, fatty, or unhealthy

- Eat more than usual between meals or at mealtimes

- Become angry or defensive when anyone mentions weight changes

- Take large amounts of food, particularly snack foods such as chips and sweets

At school, the young person may

- Avoid eating with friends, discard lunches, or spend lunchtime exercising

- Eat lunch away from school grounds to avoid eating in front of peers

- Appear lethargic or struggle to maintain focus on schoolwork

- Not want to be involved in physical education or health classes or change in front of people in locker rooms or, alternatively, may focus intently on physical education and health classes to the point of obsession

In a social setting, the young person may:

- Avoid socializing in places where food is a focus, such as cafés and restaurants

- Talk about fat; focus on specific body parts; pinch perceived areas of fat on the body; and check their reflection in mirrors, windows, and other reflective surfaces

- Change their clothing style to conceal weight changes

- Spend a great deal of time on the Internet talking to other people with eating disorders rather than spending time with real world friends who may be concerned about or critical of their behavior

Types of Eating Disorders

Health professionals recognize a number of different types of eating disorders, including *anorexia nervosa, bulimia nervosa,* and *eating disorders not otherwise specified (EDNOS).* Binge-eating disorder is one form of EDNOS.

Anorexia Nervosa

If the young person is underweight and using extreme weight-loss strategies, they may have *anorexia nervosa.* Extreme weight-loss strategies are an attempt to control body weight and can include dieting; fasting; over exercising; using diet pills, diuretics, or laxatives; and vomiting.[176]

The main characteristics of anorexia nervosa are

- Focusing on body shape and weight as the main measure of self-worth

- Maintaining a very low body weight (weighs at least 15 percent below what is considered healthy for their height and age)

- Having an intense fear of gaining weight or becoming fat

- Alterations in the pattern of menstrual periods in girls who have reached puberty

Eating disorders, including anorexia, bulimia, and binge eating, affect up to 30 million people in the U.S.[177] Anorexia mainly affects young people. For adolescents between the ages of 13 and 18, the lifetime prevalence of eating disorders ranged from less than 1.5 percent for males to 3.8 percent for females.[29] The median age of onset during adolescence is approximately 12 years for all types of eating disorders.[89] Of those with an eating disorder, 86% report onset by age 20.[178] It often starts in adolescence with dieting that becomes out of control. For some people, the disorder is brief, but in others it becomes a long-term problem, and there is a risk of death. People who get help early on tend to have a better outcome.

Bulimia Nervosa[179]

A young person may have *bulimia nervosa* if they have regular episodes of eating unusually large amounts of food followed by any behavior that compensates for the binge, such as purging, fasting, or excessive exercising.[180] Bulimia usually starts in the same way as anorexia, but episodes of binge eating prevent the severe weight loss seen in anorexia. A person with bulimia can be slightly underweight or overweight or fall within the healthy weight range.

The main characteristics of bulimia nervosa are[181]

- Focusing on body shape and weight as the main measure of self-worth

- Repeated episodes of uncontrolled overeating (binge eating) for at least twice a week for three months or more

- Extreme weight control behavior, for example, extreme dieting, frequent use of vomiting or laxatives to control weight, diuretic and enema abuse, or excessive use of exercise

- Not meeting the characteristics of anorexia

Bulimia is more common than anorexia, and it often starts in adolescence or early adulthood. A national survey of youth found that approximately one percent (0.9) had experienced bulimia at some time in their adolescence.[89] Girls are more likely than boys to develop bulimia. There is often a delay of many years before people with bulimia seek professional help. Among adolescents with bulimia, 41.3% report purging in their adolescence.[89] Unfortunately 3.9% of all individuals with Bulimia will die from complications related to the disorder.[178]

Eating Disorders not Otherwise Specified

EDNOS describes people who have some but not all the symptoms of anorexia or bulimia nervosa. If someone does not fit the description of anorexia or bulimia, but their attitude toward food, weight, or body shape is seriously interfering with their life, they may still have a serious eating disorder. For example, a young person may have most of the symptoms of anorexia but occasionally engage in binge eating, which prevents their weight loss from reaching the point at which they would get a diagnosis of anorexia. Alternatively, the young person may have most of the symptoms of bulimia, but bingeing and purging is less frequent. Patterns of eating and weight control behavior can change over time. EDNOS should not be considered less severe than other eating disorders. EDNOS can cause significant health problems and can place the person's life at risk.

Binge-Eating Disorder

Binge-eating disorder occurs when a person has regular episodes of eating an unusually large amount of food in a short period of time and continues to eat beyond the point of feeling comfortably full.[183] These binges occur at least twice per week during a period of six months or more. The person has a sense of loss of control over their eating but does not use extreme weight-loss strategies to compensate. The young person's body weight may vary from normal to overweight to obese. People with binge-eating disorder often feel disgusted, distressed, ashamed, or guilty about their actions. A national study reported that 1.6 percent of youth, ages 13 to 18, experience binge-eating disorder during their adolescence.[89] Girls are more likely to develop binge-eating disorders.[184]

Risks Associated With Eating Disorders[185]

A young person with an eating disorder can experience a wide range of physical and emotional health problems. Serious health consequences associated with eating disorders include severe malnutrition, brain dysfunction, and heart or kidney failure. The most common complications that lead to death are cardiac arrest and electrolyte and fluid imbalances. Suicide can also result.[186] Bulimia is less frequently a cause of death than anorexia; however, heart failure and death from other causes can occur in either disorder.

Severe weight loss can cause hair and nails to grow brittle, skin to dry out and become yellow, and a covering of soft hair to develop. It can also cause the slowing of growth and delay of puberty. There can be muscle loss, loss of bone density that may lead to osteoporosis and fractures, irregular or slow heartbeat, anemia, swollen joints, light-headedness, and fainting.

Repeated vomiting can cause tooth decay (because of the acid in vomit), a chronically inflamed and sore throat, severe dehydration, stomach and intestinal ulcers, and inflammation of the esophagus.

Being overweight and obesity are associated with illness and premature death. Childhood and adolescent overweight and obesity can, in the long term, increase risk of kidney failure, cardiovascular disease, Type 2 diabetes, arthritis, and other chronic illnesses.

Risk Factors for Eating Disorders

As with other mental illnesses, there is no single cause. A range of biological, psychological, and social factors may contribute to the development of an eating disorder.[187]

BIOLOGICAL:

- Obesity (increases risk for bulimia)

- Childhood obesity (increases risk for anorexia and bulimia)

- Early start of periods in girls (age 12 or younger increases risk for anorexia and bulimia)

- Family members with an eating disorder

- Family members with other mental illnesses, such as depression, anxiety, or substance use disorders

PSYCHOLOGICAL:

- Dieting

- Low self-esteem

- Perfectionism

- Anxiety

SOCIAL:

- Conflict in the home; low contact or high expectations

- Abuse (physical, psychological, and sexual) or neglect

- Family history of dieting

- Parental obesity

- Critical comments from others about eating, weight, or body shape

- Pressure to be slim because of occupation or hobby (e.g., model, dancer, and wrestler)

- Adapting to a new culture with new ideals of body types[188]

- Environmental stress (such as racism or poverty)[189]

Dieting in Adolescents[190, 191, 192]

Dieting in adolescent girls is common, often unnecessary, and sometimes dangerous. For girls, dieting is the single most important risk factor for the development of an eating disorder. This may also be true for boys, but less research is available. Girls who diet at a moderate level are five times more likely to develop an eating disorder than those who do not diet, and girls who diet at a severe level are 18 times more likely. This risk is even higher if they also have a mental illness such as anxiety or depression.

In 2013, 14 percent of students reported fasting for 24 or more hours to lose or keep from gaining weight.[193] Additionally, 4.4 percent of students reported vomiting or taking laxatives to lose or keep from gaining weight.

Dieting should not be considered normal adolescent behavior. If there is concern that a young person is overweight, a professional opinion should be sought. If a medical professional feels that weight loss is needed, the focus should be on the young person's health rather than their weight or appearance.

Importance of Early Intervention for Eating Disorders

Anorexia and bulimia often start in adolescence. For most people, the earlier help is sought for disordered eating and exercising behaviors, the easier it will be to overcome the problem.[194] A delay in seeking treatment can lead to serious long-term consequences for physical and mental health. Early detection and treatment help prevent eating disorder behaviors from becoming more entrenched and increase the chance of full recovery. Research has shown that the sooner treatment is started, the more likely the person is to recover.[195] If a young person reaches adulthood without treatment, recovery becomes more difficult. With anorexia, there is also a high risk of death.

Eating disorders frequently co-occur with depression, anxiety, and substance use disorders.[196] Most adolescents with eating disorders recover as adults but continue to have a high level of depression and anxiety.[197]

Mental Health First Aid® Action Plan for Eating Disorders[198]

YOUTH MENTAL HEALTH FIRST AID® ACTION PLAN	
ACTION A	Assess for risk of suicide or harm
ACTION L	Listen nonjudgmentally
ACTION G	Give reassurance and information
ACTION E	Encourage appropriate professional help
ACTION E	Encourage self-help and other support strategies

Action A: Assess for Risk of Suicide or Harm

The three main crises that may be associated with eating disorders are

- The young person is experiencing a **medical emergency.**

- The young person has **suicidal thoughts or behaviors.**

- The young person is engaging in **nonsuicidal self-injury.**

MEDICAL EMERGENCIES

If a young person is significantly underweight or their health is otherwise compromised by an eating disorder, any accidental or intentional self-injury may be complicated by slower healing and increased risk of infection. For this reason, even injuries that do not appear to be serious should be checked by a doctor. (*See box at right*).

Symptoms That Indicate a Medical Emergency

Emergency help should be sought if the person has any of the following symptoms:

- Disordered thinking or not making any reasonable sense (may experience delusions or hallucinations)

- Disorientation; not knowing what day it is, where they are, or who they are

- Throwing up several times a day

- Fainting

- Collapsing or too weak to walk

- Painful muscle spasms

- Chest pain or difficulty breathing

- Blood in bowel movements, urine, or vomit

- A body mass index of less than 16

- An irregular or very low heartbeat (less than 50 beats per minute)

- Cold or clammy skin, indicating a low body temperature, or a body temperature of less than 95° Fahrenheit

SUICIDAL THOUGHTS AND BEHAVIORS

Young people with eating disorders have increased risk of suicide and suicide attempts.[199, 200]

NONSUICIDAL SELF-INJURY

Young people with eating disorders have increased risk of nonsuicidal self-injury.[201] People with eating disorders experience overwhelming feelings that may be relieved by bingeing, purging, overexercising, or engaging in other forms of nonsuicidal self-injury.

If you have concerns that the young person is experiencing a medical emergency, call 911 or seek medical care immediately.

If you have concerns that the young person may be having suicidal thoughts, see *First Aid for Suicidal Thoughts and Behaviors*.

If you have concerns that the young person may be engaging in nonsuicidal self-injury, see *First Aid for Nonsuicidal Self-Injury*.

If you have no concerns that the young person is in crisis, you can ask them how they are feeling and how long they have been feeling that way and move on to another action.

Action L: Listen Nonjudgmentally

When talking with the young person, remember to be nonjudgmental, respectful, and kind. Discuss your concerns with the young person in an open and honest way. Try to use "I" statements that are not accusing, such as "I am worried about you," rather than "you" statements, such as "You are worrying me." Try not to just focus on weight or food. Rather, focus on the eating behaviors that are concerning you. Focus on conveying empathy and not on changing the young person or their perspective. Do not comment positively or negatively on the young person's weight or appearance. Respect the youth's culture by asking about and showing behaviors (e.g., eye contact, physical space, and distance) that convey this respect.

LISTEN TO THE YOUNG PERSON'S CONCERNS
The young person may have issues in their life that need to be identified. Depression and anxiety may also be present. Allow the person to discuss other concerns that are not about food, weight, or exercise. Make sure you give the person plenty of time to discuss their feelings, and reassure the young person that it is safe to be open and honest about how they feel.

TRY TO SEE THE YOUNG PERSON'S BEHAVIOR AS ILLNESS-RELATED RATHER THAN WILLFUL OR SELF-INDULGENT
Be aware that you may find it difficult to listen to what the person has to say, especially if you do not agree with what they are saying. Do not get drawn into a discussion about the young person's appearance or weight by disagreeing with the young person's beliefs about them. It is important that you try to stay calm.

WHAT IF I DO NOT FEEL COMFORTABLE TALKING TO THE YOUNG PERSON?
It is common to feel nervous when talking to a young person about their eating and exercising behaviors. Do not avoid talking to the young person because you fear it might make them angry or upset or make the problem worse. Speaking to the young person may give them a sense of relief at having someone acknowledge their problems, or the young person may find it helpful to know that someone cares about them and has noticed that they are not coping.

See Action L in *Depression in Young People* for more tips on nonjudgmental listening.

Action G: Give Reassurance and Information

Be there for the young person by letting them know you care and are committed to supporting them. Let the young person know you want them to be healthy and happy. To help the young person feel safe, reassure them that you are not going to take control over their life. Your aim is to provide support for the young person so that they feel safe and secure enough to seek treatment and to find other supports they can trust to talk to openly about their difficulties, such as a family member, friend, or teacher.

Pick a place to talk that is private, quiet, and comfortable. Avoid approaching them in situations that may lead the young person to become sensitive or defensive, such as when either you or the young person are feeling angry, emotional, tired, or frustrated, and you are drinking, having a meal, or in a place surrounded by food. It is better to approach the young person alone, because having the whole family or a number of people confront the person at the same time could be overwhelming.

Before you approach the young person, learn as much as you can about eating disorders. Do this by reading books, articles, and brochures or gathering information from a reliable source, such as an eating disorder support organization or a health professional experienced in treating people with eating disorders (see *Helpful Resources* at the end of this section). Also, obtain accurate information about the youth's culture that may have an impact on their eating disorder. Be careful not to overwhelm the young person with too much information and advice. Remember that you do not have to know all the answers, and avoid trying to solve the young person's problems for them. Avoid speculating about the cause of the eating disorder.

If you become aware that the person is visiting "pro-ana" or "pro-mia" websites (i.e., pro-anorexia and pro-bulimia websites that promote eating-disordered behavior), you should discourage further visits. These websites can encourage further destructive behavior. If the young person is not already aware of these sites, it is important not to mention them.

Avoid making promises that you cannot keep. Explain that even if there are limits to what you can do, you are still going to try and help, and you will be there to listen if the young person wants to talk.

GIVE THE YOUNG PERSON HOPE FOR RECOVERY

Reassure the young person that people with eating disorders can get better and that past unsuccessful attempts do not mean that they cannot get better in the future. Encourage the young person to be proud of any positive steps they have taken. For example, encourage the young person to take pride when they have acknowledged the problems or agreed to professional help.

SUPPORTING A YOUNG PERSON WHO REACTS NEGATIVELY

Understand that the young person may react negatively. A young person may react negatively for many reasons, including that they

- Are not ready to make a change

- Do not know how to change without losing their coping strategies

- Have difficulty trusting others

- Think you are being pushy, nosy, coercive, or bullying

- Do not see their eating habits as a problem

If this happens, it is important not to take the negative reaction personally. Instead, be willing to repeat your concerns and remind the young person that, even if they do not agree, your support is still offered, and the young person can come and talk with you again in the future.

WHAT IS NOT SUPPORTIVE

- Do not argue, be confrontational, respond angrily, or speak harshly.

- Do not criticize, blame, or express disappointment or shock, for example, saying that what the person is doing is disgusting, stupid, or self-destructive.

- Do not make the person feel ashamed, guilty, or make generalizations, such as "You're always moody" or "You never do anything but exercise."

- Do not focus on body shape or food, in either a positive or a negative way, because this can reinforce the idea that physical appearance is important to happiness or success.

- Do not give advice about weight loss, exercise, or appearance.

- Do not give simple solutions, such as saying "All you have to do is eat."

Action E: Encourage Appropriate Professional Help

It is best to encourage the person to seek help from a professional with specific training in eating disorders. The professional should ideally have expertise in providing services to young people as well as trauma-informed treatment. Treatment can be provided by the various professionals listed below:

- **Primary care physicians** can diagnose an eating disorder, provide a physical check-up, give information on the physical health consequences of the disorder, refer to specialists, and link to community supports. Sometimes it is difficult for a primary care physician to assess or assist someone who is developing or experiencing an eating disorder. Not all doctors are formally trained in detecting and treating eating disorders.

- **Child and adolescent psychiatrists, specialty-trained nurse practitioners, and other mental health professionals** can help the person address psychological and behavioral components of the illness.[202]

- **Nutritional counselors** can provide education about nutritional needs, meal planning, and monitoring eating choices.[203]

Successful treatment involves both physical and mental aspects; therefore, eating disorders are best treated by *multidisciplinary teams* on which different kinds of professionals treat the person at the same time. Generally, a multidisciplinary team will consist of a primary care physician, a mental health professional, and a dietitian or nutritionist. Sometimes allied health professionals who have specific training in managing eating disorders may also be involved. It is best for the person if the professionals can work together and coordinate their treatment plans. Ideally, the professionals should have expertise in providing services to children and adolescents and have some training and experience in managing eating disorders.

TREATMENTS AVAILABLE FOR EATING DISORDERS

Treatment is often long term and intensive, depending on the severity of the eating disorder. As with any intervention, cultural competency is important. There is evidence that the following treatments work for eating disorders:[204]

- *Cognitive behavior therapy* aims to change eating habits and weight control behaviors as well as the person's preoccupation with body shape and weight. CBT is the best treatment for both bulimia and binge-eating disorder.[205, 206]

- *Interpersonal psychotherapy* helps the young person to identify and change problems that are contributing to the eating disorder.[207]

- *Family therapy* involves parents or caregivers in preventing severe dieting, purging, and over exercise.[208] Young people with anorexia may particularly benefit from family therapy.

- *Physical intervention.* If the young person has severe weight loss or a physical health crisis, the first goal is to ensure the person's physical health, which with anorexia in particular involves restoring the person to a healthy weight. If weight loss is severe or there are health complications, it is sometimes necessary to admit the person to a hospital to stabilize their physical health.

■ *Medication (antidepressants)* can also help with bulimia and binge-eating disorder but are not known to be as effective as CBT. There are no medications that are proven to work with anorexia.

DISCUSS OPTIONS FOR SEEKING PROFESSIONAL HELP

Explain to the young person that you think their behaviors may indicate a problem that needs professional attention. Offer to assist the young person in getting the help they need. If, however, the person is very underweight, they may not be able to take responsibility for getting professional help, because an eating disorder can affect the person's ability to think clearly. When helping a young person with an eating disorder, you should find out whether the youth is already connected to a mental health service or provider.

WHAT IF THE YOUNG PERSON DOES NOT WANT HELP?

People with an eating disorder may refuse professional help. The resistance may be related to a number of different factors. The young person may

■ Feel ashamed of their behavior

■ Fear gaining weight or losing control over their weight

■ Be afraid of acknowledging that they are unwell

■ Not think that they are ill

■ Believe that there are benefits to the behaviors, for example, controlling their weight may give them a sense of accomplishment

Do not expect the young person to immediately follow your advice, even if they ask for it. You cannot force the young person to change their attitudes or behaviors. Be sensitive to the young person's fears about seeking help. You may find it helpful to get advice from an organization that specializes in eating disorders on how to get a resistant young person to professional help.

Eating disorders are long-term problems that are not easily overcome. Although you may feel frustrated by the young person's behavior, do not threaten to end or alter your relationship with them. Do not give up on the young person. Instead, continue to be supportive, positive, and encouraging while waiting for them to accept the need to change. Be encouraging of the young person's strengths and interests that are unrelated to food or physical appearance. **Acknowledge the person's positive attributes, successes, and accomplishments, and try to view the person as an individual rather than just as someone who has an eating disorder.**

Action E: Encourage Self-Help and Other Support Strategies

Certain factors can protect against the development of eating disorders or may help to lessen the severity of an eating disorder in youth and young adults. These include[209]

■ Having a supportive, connected family

■ Having a good social support system

■ Positive self-talk

■ Having good, problem-focused coping skills

■ High self-esteem

■ School achievement

■ Emotional well-being, which may include receiving effective treatment for another mental illness or emotional problems

OTHER PEOPLE WHO CAN HELP

You can suggest that the young person surround themselves with people who are supportive, such as close family members, friends, and any school or recreational supports. There are organizations that provide information and support for people with eating disorders (see *Helpful Resources* at the end of this section).

LIFESTYLE, COMPLEMENTARY STRATEGIES, AND SELF-HELP STRATEGIES

Self-help books based on CBT have been shown to help adults with bulimia, binge-eating disorder, and EDNOS when used under the guidance of a health practitioner.[210] Self-help books do not help reduce bingeing and purging, but they do help decrease other symptoms such as depression.[211] No specific self-help strategies have been shown to be effective for anorexia. Online therapy for eating disorders is available but has not yet been evaluated (see *Helpful Resources* at the end of this section).

Self-help strategies may assist with co-occurring problems such as depression and anxiety. Although exercise is a useful treatment for depression, care should be taken with any exercise undertaken by people with eating disorders. People who are underweight may be using exercise to lose more weight and maintain their eating disorder. People who are overweight may need to ease into an exercise program more slowly. In either case, exercise should only be done with professional advice and monitoring.

Helpful Resources
FOR EATING DISORDERS

In addition to the resources described in previous sections, the following may also be useful resources:

WEBSITES

Mental Health America
www.mentalhealthamerica.net

Visit Mental Health America's site for information on mental health, getting help, and taking action.

National Association of Anorexia Nervosa and Associated Disorders
www.anad.org

The National Association of Anorexia Nervosa and Associated Disorders website includes information about eating disorders, how to seek treatment, and support groups for people with eating disorders and their families.

National Eating Disorders Association
www.nationaleatingdisorders.org

The National Eating Disorders Association website has stories of recovery from eating disorders, information about seeking treatment, and additional resources for school professionals and caregivers.

National Institute of Mental Health
www.nimh.nih.gov

The National Institute of Mental Health website has links to information and research about eating disorders.

Something Fishy
www.something-fishy.org

This website provides useful information and links for those with an eating disorder or for friends and families. It also has online support options such as web boards and links to chat rooms.

Substance Abuse and Mental Health Services Administration

www.samhsa.gov

The Substance Abuse and Mental Health Services Administration website has links to information about eating disorders.

BOOKS AND OTHER WRITTEN RESOURCES

GurzeBooks

www.gurze.com

This website offers all types of books on eating disorders. Listed are self-help books, many based on CBT; information for people with eating disorders, their families, and therapists; and autobiographical books documenting recovery from an eating disorder.

Walsh, B. T., & Cameron, V. L. (2005). *If Your Adolescent Has an Eating Disorder: An Essential Resource for Parents.* New York, NY: Oxford University Press.

This guide is written for the parents and other caregivers of adolescents with eating disorders. It contains information about treatment and management, addresses myths, and includes personal stories from people who are recovering.

Walsh, B. T., & Arnold, C. (2007). *Next to Nothing.* New York, NY: Oxford University Press.

Carrie Arnold developed an eating disorder as an adolescent and nearly lost her life to the disease. Here she tells the story of her descent into anorexia, how and why she fell victim to this mysterious illness, and how she was able to seek help and recover after years of therapy and hard work. With input from Dr. Timothy Walsh, a leading authority on eating disorders, this book is also a practical guide to recovery that offers the scientific information and personal support needed to manage and maintain recovery on a daily basis and an appendix for caregivers of young people with eating disorders.

Kolodny, N. (2004). *A Beginner's Guide to ED Recovery.* Carlsbad, CA: Gurze Books.

A self-help guide written specifically for teen and college-age readers (and their loved ones) who are confronting an eating disorder for the first time.

HELPLINES

American Psychiatric Association Answer Center
1-888-35-PSYCH (77924)

Live operators, available from 8:30 a.m. to 6:00 p.m., eastern time, refer you to local board-certified psychiatrists.

American Psychological Association Public Education Line
1-800-964-2000

Follow the automated instructions. An operator then refers you to local board-certified psychologists.

National Suicide Prevention Lifeline
1-800-273-TALK (8255)

This is a crisis hotline that can help with many issues, not just suicide. For example, anyone who feels sad, hopeless, or suicidal; family and friends who are concerned about a loved one; or anyone interested in mental health treatment referrals can call the Lifeline. Callers are connected with a professional nearby who will talk with them about what they are feeling or concerns for other family and friends. If you or someone you know is in suicidal crisis, call the hotline (toll free, 24 hours/day, 7 days/week).

SUPPORT GROUPS

Eating Disorders Anonymous

www.eatingdisordersanonymous.org

Following the 12-step approach used by Alcoholics Anonymous, Eating Disorders Anonymous can help people struggling with eating disorders. The website lists meetings nationwide.

Overeaters Anonymous

www.oa.org

Following the 12-step approach used by Alcoholics Anonymous, Overeaters Anonymous can help people struggling with compulsive eating and binge eating. The website lists Overeaters Anonymous meetings nationwide.

Psychosis in Young People

What Is Psychosis?

Psychosis is a general term used to describe a mental health problem in which a person has lost some contact with reality, resulting in severe disruptions in thinking, emotion, and behavior.[212] Psychosis can have a severe impact on a person's life. Relationships, work, school, other usual activities, and self-care can be difficult to initiate or maintain.[213]

People usually experience psychosis in episodes. An episode can involve the following phases, which vary in length from person to person:[214]

- *At risk* (premorbid phase)—the person does not experience any symptoms but has risk factors for developing psychosis.

- *Becoming unwell* (prodromal phase)— the person has some changes in their emotions, motivation, thinking, and perception or behavior. Whether the person is developing a disorder in which psychosis can occur or another mental illness may be unclear.

- *Unwell* (acute phase)—the person has symptoms, such as delusions, hallucinations, and disorganized thinking and a decrease in the ability to maintain social relationships, work, or study.

- *Recovery*—the person's individual process to attain a level of well-being.

- *Relapse*—the person may only have one episode in their life or may go onto have other episodes.

Common Signs and Symptoms When Psychosis is Developing[215]

- Changes in emotion and motivation include: depression; anxiety; irritability; suspiciousness; blunted, flat, or inappropriate emotion; change in appetite; reduced energy and motivation; or significantly increased energy.

- Changes in thinking and perception include: difficulties with concentration or attention; sense of alteration of self, others, or outside world (e.g., feeling that self or others have changed or are acting differently in some way); odd ideas; and unusual perceptual experiences (e.g., a reduction or greater intensity of smell, sound, or color).

- Changes in behavior include: sleep disturbance, social isolation or withdrawal, and reduced ability to carry out studies or social roles.

Although these signs and symptoms may not be very dramatic on their own, together they may suggest that something is not quite right. It is important not to ignore or dismiss these warning signs, even if they appear gradually and are unclear. You should not assume that the young person is just going through a phase or that the symptoms will go away on their own.

The signs and symptoms of psychosis may vary from person to person and can change over time. People experiencing the early stages of psychosis often go undiagnosed for some time before receiving treatment. A major reason for this delay is that psychosis often begins in late adolescence or early adulthood, and the early signs and symptoms involve behaviors and emotions that may not be unusual for this age group.

What may be perceived as a mild form of mental illness in one culture may be defined as normal behavior in another, what may be described as a psychosis in one culture may not be in another culture. For example, individuals in western societies who regularly engage in animated conversations with dead relatives are likely to be viewed as experiencing a hallucination. In a culture that has an indigenous worldview, such as many Native American/Alaska Native and Asian communities, the same behavior may more likely be considered healthy and the person seen as fortunate for having direct communication with the spirit world. Therefore, it is important for the first aider to be aware of the young person's cultural background.

Many young people will have some of these symptoms without developing a psychosis. Others showing these symptoms will eventually be diagnosed as having a psychotic disorder.

Types of Disorders in Which Psychosis may be Present

Psychosis can be present in many disorders including *PTSD, schizophrenia, psychotic depression, bipolar disorder, schizoaffective disorder,* and *drug-induced psychosis.*

Schizophrenia

Psychosis is most commonly associated with schizophrenia. Contrary to common belief, schizophrenia does not mean "split personality." The term *schizophrenia* comes from the Greek for "fractured mind" and refers to changes in mental function in which thoughts and perceptions become disordered. Numerous studies have found that about one in every 100 people around the world has schizophrenia. Symptoms usually begin in late adolescence or early adulthood. However, schizophrenia with an onset before age 18 is less

common, and an onset of the disorder in childhood (before age 13) is exceedingly rare.[216]

Schizophrenia is hard to recognize in its early phases. Many of the symptoms are similar to the symptoms of depression, bipolar disorder, or other illnesses. As a result, misdiagnosis is common, especially with youth and young adults.

The behavior of youth and young adults with schizophrenia may differ from that of adults with this illness. Some early warning signs in children and youth include[217, 218, 219, 220]

- Trouble discerning dreams from reality

- Seeing things and hearing voices that are not real

- Confused thinking

- Vivid and bizarre thoughts and ideas

- Extreme moodiness

- Peculiar behavior

- Feeling that people are out to get them

- Behaving younger than chronological age

- Severe anxiety and fearfulness

- Confusing television or movies with reality

- Severe problems in making and keeping friends

The major symptoms of schizophrenia include[221]

›› DELUSIONS
These are false beliefs, for example, of persecution, guilt, having a special mission, or being under outside control. Although the delusions may seem bizarre to others, they are very real to the person experiencing them.

›› HALLUCINATIONS
These are false perceptions. Hallucinations most commonly involve hearing voices but can also

involve seeing, feeling, tasting, or smelling things. The person may hear more than one voice or experience many types of hallucinations. They are perceived as very real by the person, but are not actually there. The hallucinations can be very frightening, especially voices making negative comments about the person.

›› THINKING DIFFICULTIES

It may be challenging for the young person to concentrate, recall memories, or plan, which makes it more difficult to reason, communicate, and complete daily tasks.

›› LOSS OF DRIVE

The person lacks motivation even for self-care. It is not laziness.

›› BLUNTED OR INAPPROPRIATE EMOTIONS

The person does not react to the things around them or reacts inappropriately. Examples include speaking in a monotone voice, lack of facial expressions or gestures, lack of eye contact, or reacting with anger or laughter when these are not appropriate.

›› SOCIAL WITHDRAWAL

The person may avoid contact with other people, even family and close friends. This withdrawal may be due to the difficulty of interacting with others because of the other signs listed above.

Psychotic Depression

Sometimes depression can be so intense it causes psychotic symptoms. For example, people may experience delusions involving feeling very guilty about something that is not their fault, believing that they are severely physically ill, or that they are being mistreated or observed. Some people may also experience hallucinations, most commonly hearing voices.

Schizoaffective Disorder

Sometimes it is difficult to tell the difference between schizophrenia and bipolar disorder because the person has symptoms of both illnesses. A person with *schizoaffective disorder* has symptoms of psychosis and elevated or depressed mood or both but does not meet criteria for bipolar disorder.

Substance-Induced Psychosis

This psychosis is brought on by intoxication with or withdrawal from alcohol or drugs. The psychosis usually appears quickly and lasts a short time (from a few hours to a few days) until the effects of the drugs wear off. The most common symptoms are visual hallucinations, disorientation, and memory problems. Hallucinations and delusions will occur shortly after consuming a drug, or they may also occur during or after the withdrawal period. Both legal and illegal drugs can contribute to an episode of psychosis, including marijuana, cocaine, amphetamine (e.g., speed or meth), hallucinogens, inhalants, opioids (e.g., morphine, codeine, and oxycodone), sedatives, hypnotics, and minor tranquilizers (also known as anxiolytics).[222]

What might a first aider notice if a young person is developing a psychotic disorder?

In thinking of disorders in which psychosis can occur, a first aider might imagine someone who is very out of touch with reality, perhaps talking to themselves or expressing concerns about being watched. This is certainly an accurate description of some people with these disorders, but a first aider may see the following signs that might indicate that psychosis may be a problem.[223]

At home, the young person may

- Become increasingly secretive or avoid answering questions

- Spend more time alone in their bedroom

- Begin expressing strange ideas

- Have sudden outbursts or explosive, highly emotional reactions

- Appear changed in a way that you cannot quite describe. It is important not to dismiss a gut feeling that something is not quite right

- Experience auditory hallucinations and sometimes try to drown them out. For example, a young person may listen to music on headphones and refuse to take them off when talking to family members or eating a family meal or turn the television up to a loud volume and react angrily when asked to turn it down

At school, the young person may

- Appear unmotivated

- Distance themselves from peers

- Show a decline in completing work, not do as good a job as they used to, or miss school

- Have inappropriate or no reactions to others

- Do things to drown out auditory hallucinations (e.g., listening to music on headphones in class)

These behaviors can all have an impact on school achievement, and some may result in disciplinary responses.

In a social setting, the young person may

- Withdraw from friends

- Use alcohol or other drugs to dull unfamiliar feelings and upsetting emotions

- Appear not to react or react inappropriately to friends

- Appear suspicious or accuse friends of acting against them (e.g., talking about the person behind their back or plotting against them)

Risk Factors for Disorders in Which Psychosis can Occur

Psychosis is caused by a combination of factors including genetics, biochemistry, and stress.[224] Biological factors could be genetic vulnerability, changes in the brain, or dysfunction in the neurotransmitters in the brain. Stress or drug use may trigger symptoms in people with these risk factors.

Psychosis can be drug induced or drug assisted. Commonly known as substance-induced psychosis, the most common substances involved are, in order, marijuana, alcohol, cocaine, crack, and hallucinogens.[225] Methamphetamines are also known to trigger the onset of psychosis and have a high incidence of abuse among adolescents and adults with disorders in which psychosis can occur.[226] Substance use during adolescence increases risk, particularly in people who have other risk factors.

Other risk factors are far less significant, increasing risk by only a very small amount:[227]

>> **EVENTS DURING THE MOTHER'S PREGNANCY**
Infections in the mother in the first and second trimesters of pregnancy have been linked with higher incidence. A possible explanation is that the mother's immune response interferes with the brain development of the fetus. Severe nutritional deficiency and very stressful life events during pregnancy might also increase risk.

>> BIRTH COMPLICATIONS

A range of complications are associated with approximately double the risk, perhaps because of a lack of oxygen (hypoxia) to the infant's brain.

>> BIRTH IN WINTER OR SPRING

Birth during the late winter or early spring is associated with five–10 percent greater risk that may be related to infection, malnutrition, or risk of genetic mutation.

>> OLDER AGE OF FATHER

Older age at the time of conception roughly doubles the risk. The explanation is not known but may be related to impaired sperm and genetic mutation.

Importance of Early Intervention for Psychosis

Early intervention for people with psychosis is important. Young people who get proper treatment can lead productive and fulfilling lives into adulthood. Earlier treatment may reduce the decline in functioning and long-term impairments commonly associated with schizophrenia. Therefore, accurate and early intervention and diagnosis are critical. Research has shown that the longer the delay between the onset of psychosis and the start of treatment the less likely the person is to recover.[228]

Other consequences of delayed treatment include[229]

- Poorer long-term functioning

- Increased risk of depression and suicide

- Slower psychological maturation and slower uptake of adult responsibilities

- Strain on relationships with friends and family and subsequent loss of social supports

- Disruption of study

- Increased use of alcohol and other drugs

- Loss of self-esteem and confidence

- Greater chance of problems with the law

Mental Health First Aid® Action Plan for Psychosis

YOUTH MENTAL HEALTH FIRST AID® ACTION PLAN	
ACTION A	Assess for risk of suicide or harm
ACTION L	Listen nonjudgmentally
ACTION G	Give reassurance and information
ACTION E	Encourage appropriate professional help
ACTION E	Encourage self-help and other support strategies

Action A: Assess for Risk of Suicide or Harm

Crises that may be associated with psychosis are

- The person is in a **severe psychotic state**.

- The person has **suicidal thoughts or behaviors**.

- The person is showing **aggressive behavior**.

ACUTE PSYCHOSIS

People with disorders in which psychosis can occur can have periods when they become very unwell. They can have overwhelming delusions and hallucinations, disorganized thinking, and bizarre and disruptive behavior. They may appear very distressed or their behavior will be disturbing to others. When a person is in this state, they are at increased risk for accidents and are vulnerable to becoming a victim of crime or other unintentional harm.

SUICIDAL THOUGHTS AND BEHAVIORS

Disorders in which psychosis can occur involve a high risk of suicide. Approximately five percent of people with schizophrenia complete suicide.[230] About 10–20 percent of individuals with bipolar disorder take their own life.[231] Having a concurrent depression or a substance use disorder further increases the risk.

The main factors to be taken into account when assessing risk of suicide in people experiencing psychosis are[232, 233]

- Depression

- Suicidal thoughts, threats, or behavior

- Previous suicide attempt

- Poor adherence to treatment

- Fears of the impact of the illness

- Alcohol and other drug misuse

AGGRESSIVE BEHAVIOR

A very small percentage of people experiencing psychosis may threaten violence.[234] The vast majority of people with mental health challenges and disorders are not dangerous to others. Only a small proportion (as much as 10 percent) of violence in society is carried out by people with mental health disorders.[235, 236] The use of alcohol or other drugs has a stronger association with violence than do mental health disorders. The risk of violence is greater when the person with psychosis is not being adequately treated or is using alcohol or other drugs.

As you talk with the person, be on the lookout for any indications that the person may be in crisis.

If you have concerns that the young person is in a severe psychotic state, see *First Aid for Acute Psychosis*.

If you have concerns that the person may be having suicidal thoughts, see *First Aid for Suicidal Thoughts and Behaviors*.

If you have concerns that the person is showing aggressive behavior, see *First Aid for Aggressive Behaviors*.

If you have no concerns that the person is in crisis, you can ask them about how they are feeling and how long they have been feeling that way and move on to another action.

Action L: Listen Nonjudgmentally

If you are concerned about a young person, approach them in a caring and nonjudgmental manner to discuss your concerns. If possible, you should approach the young person privately about their experiences in a place that is free of distractions. Let the young person know that you are concerned about them and want to help. It is important to allow the young person to talk about their experiences and beliefs if they want to. However, if the young person is unwilling to talk with you about their experiences, do not try to force them. People experiencing symptoms of psychosis or developing a disorder associated with psychosis will often not reach out for help. Someone who is experiencing profound and frightening changes such as psychotic symptoms will often try to keep them a secret. If the young person is unwilling to talk with you, let them know that you will be available if they would like to talk in the future.

As much as possible, let the young person set the pace and style of the interaction. You should recognize that the young person may be frightened by their thoughts and feelings. Respect the youth's culture by exhibiting verbal and nonverbal behaviors that demonstrate this respect.

Try to

- Understand the symptoms for what they are.

- State the specific behaviors you are concerned about.

- Empathize with how the person feels about their beliefs and experiences.

- Adjust your verbal and nonverbal communication to the young person's concerns (e.g., if they are suspicious and avoiding eye contact, be sensitive to this and give them the space needed).

Do not

- Challenge the person or their beliefs.

- Criticize or blame them.

- Take delusional comments personally.

- Use sarcasm.

- Use patronizing statements.

- State any judgments about the content of an individual's beliefs and experiences.

- Touch the young person without their permission.

- Speculate about a diagnosis.

DEALING WITH DELUSIONS AND HALLUCINATIONS

Delusions and hallucinations are very real to the person experiencing them, so it is common for people with these experiences to be unaware that they are ill. It is important to recognize that the delusions and hallucinations are very real to the young person.

Do not

- Dismiss, minimize, or argue with the person about the delusions or hallucinations.

- Act alarmed, horrified, or embarrassed by the person's delusions or hallucinations.

- Laugh at the person's symptoms of psychosis.

- Encourage or inflame the person's paranoia, if the person exhibits paranoid behavior.

You can respond to the young person's delusions without agreeing with them by saying something, such as "I can see that you are upset."

DEALING WITH COMMUNICATION DIFFICULTIES

The young person may be behaving and talking differently because of symptoms of acute psychosis. The young person may be unable to think or communicate clearly. They may also find it difficult to tell what is real from what is not. The person you are trying to help might not trust you or might be afraid of being perceived as different and may not be open with you.

Ways to deal with communication difficulties include

- Responding to disorganized speech by speaking clearly.

- Repeating things if necessary.

- Being patient and allowing plenty of time for the person to process the information and respond to what you have said.

- Being aware that even if the person is showing a limited range of feelings, it does not mean that they are not feeling anything.

- Not assuming the person cannot understand what you are saying, even if their response is limited.

Action G: Give Reassurance and Information

Reassure the young person that you are there to help and be supportive and that you want to keep them safe. When a person is in a severe psychotic state, it is usually difficult and inappropriate to give information about psychosis. When the person is more lucid and in touch with reality, you could ask whether they would like some information about their own wellness or, if appropriate, about psychosis. If the young person does want information from you, it is important that you give them resources that are accurate and appropriate to the situation (see *Helpful Resources* at the end of this chapter).

Convey a message of hope by assuring the young person that help is available and things can get better.

Try to find out what type of assistance the young person needs by asking what will help them to feel safe and in control. If possible, offer the person a few choices of how you can help so that the individual feels somewhat in control. Do not make any promises that you cannot keep because it can create an atmosphere of distrust and add to the young person's distress.

Treat the young person with respect and dignity. It is important that you seek a connection with the young person and are honest in your interactions. Even if the young person does not seem to be capable of making good decisions, it is important to respect their ability to be involved in making decisions related to their own care.

Action E: Encourage Appropriate Professional Help

DISCUSS OPTIONS FOR SEEKING PROFESSIONAL HELP

Find out if the youth is already connected to a mental health service or provider. Assist the young person to seek professional help, making sure that the young person (and, if needed, the family) is supported both emotionally and practically in accessing services. If the young person or the parents or caregivers lack confidence in the medical advice received, encourage them to seek a second opinion from another medical or mental health professional. People with disorders in which psychosis can occur need to be treated with hope for recovery and in a spirit of partnership.

A variety of professionals can provide help to a child, adolescent, or young adult experiencing psychosis. Ideally the health professional should have expertise in providing mental health services to young people as well as trauma-informed treatment. These professionals include

- **Primary care physicians**

- **Pediatricians**

- **Nurse practitioners**

- **Allied health professionals, such as occupational therapists, youth workers, and mental health nurses**

- **Psychiatrists and child and adolescent psychiatrists**

- **Psychologists and child and adolescent psychologists**

- **Mental health care providers**

- **Social workers**

- **Peer support providers or specialists**

TREATMENTS AVAILABLE FOR PSYCHOSIS

Professional help may be able to improve quality of life of a young person experiencing symptoms of psychosis by helping them to learn to manage their illness, facilitate good employment or education opportunities, and maintain good family and social relationships. Recovery from psychosis varies from person to person. Some people recover quickly with intervention, and others may require support over a longer time. Recovery from the first episode usually takes a number of months. If symptoms remain or return, the recovery process may be longer. Some people may take months or even years before recovery is achieved. Most people recover from psychosis and lead satisfying and productive lives.

There are a variety of options that have good evidence in the treatment of psychosis.

Schizophrenia Treatments[237, 238]

Treatment for schizophrenia includes biological, educational, and social interventions.

There is evidence that the following specific treatments help people with schizophrenia:

- *Antipsychotic medications* are effective for psychotic symptoms such as delusions and hallucinations. However, they are less effective for other symptoms such as lack of motivation, poor memory, and problems with concentration.

- *Antidepressant medications* are effective for treating the symptoms of depression that may also be experienced by young people with schizophrenia.

- *Physical health checks* with a general practitioner can ensure that any side effects from medications (e.g., weight gain) do not cause significant problems in the future.

- *Psychoeducation* teaches the young person and the family about the illness and how best to manage it, which helps to reduce family tension and relapses.

- *Cognitive behavior therapy* can help reduce psychotic symptoms by helping the young person to think about ways to reduce the impact of the illness on their life and by encouraging the person to take medication.

- *Social skills training* is used to improve social and life skills.

- *Assertive community treatment* is an approach for people experiencing more severe mental illness. The person's care is managed by a team of health professionals, such as a psychiatrist, nurse, psychologist, and social worker. Care is available 24 hours a day and is tailored to the person's individual needs. Support is provided to family members as well. Assertive community treatment has been found to reduce relapses and the need for hospitalization.

- *Wraparound care* is a team approach that involves all individuals who are relevant to the well-being of the young person (such as family members, teachers, and social service providers) in setting goals with the young person, and developing an individualized set of services and supports. Wraparound services and supports are usually provided in the young person's home or community.

- *Family therapy and education* may help family members to cope with the young person's illness.

Medication can be important to the management and treatment of schizophrenia, but it should be viewed as a means to facilitate other treatment. Treatment with only medication is not as effective as when it is combined with other forms of treatment. A young person with a disorder in which psychosis is occurring will need to work closely with their family, medical professionals, and other formal and informal supports to determine the best way to manage their illness. Any treatment should consider the youth's family, culture, and any past treatment experiences.

What if the person does not want help?

The young person (or the family) may refuse to seek help even if the young person realizes they are not well. The young person's and family's confusion and fear about what is happening may lead them to deny that anything is wrong. In this case, you should encourage them to talk to someone they trust. It is also possible that a person may refuse to seek help because they lack insight that they are not well. The young person might actively resist your attempts to encourage them to seek help. How you offer help should depend on the type and severity of the young person's symptoms.

If the young person's psychosis is not severe, you may wish to seek the advice of a mental health professional with expertise in early psychosis and young people. The professional may be able to help you to develop a strategy to make sure the young person is seen by an appropriate provider. Avoid trying to persuade the young person using negative methods such as lecturing, nagging, or threatening. It is important to remain friendly and patient and maintain a good relationship so that the young person may seek help from you in the future.

If the young person's psychosis is severe, they are at risk of harming self or others, and they are unwilling to engage in treatment, then involuntary committal (i.e., placing a person in a psychiatric hospital against their will) may be necessary. A young person who is experiencing severe psychosis may benefit from a

short stay in the hospital to get back on track. States have different laws and procedures for involuntary commitment. In Florida, judges, law enforcement officials, physicians, or mental health professionals can request involuntary examination of an individual for as long as 72 hours. There must be evidence that the person has a mental illness and is a danger to self or others, or cannot take care of themselves. **However, never threaten the young person with hospitalization.** The parent, caregiver, or guardian should be contacted as soon as possible and given all relevant information.

Action E: Encourage Self-Help and Other Support Strategies

Certain factors can lessen the severity of psychosis and help youth and young adults be successful despite mental health challenges they may encounter in their lives. Some of these factors include[239]

- Having a good social support system

- Having good problem-solving skills

- Parental and familial support

- Positive self-talk

- Having spiritual or religious beliefs

- Having good physical as well as mental health, including healthy diet and exercise

OTHER PEOPLE WHO CAN HELP
Youth and young adults with psychosis need to live in a stable and secure social and family environment that includes support from family and friends and good educational and work opportunities.[240] Try to determine whether the person has a supportive social network and, if the person does, encourage them to use these supports.

Family and friends are an important source of support.[241] A young person is less likely to relapse if they and the family have supports that help them maintain a positive and supportive relationship. Family and friends can help by

- Listening to the person without judging or being critical

- Keeping the person's life as stress free as possible

- Encouraging appropriate treatment and support

- Checking whether the person is feeling suicidal and taking immediate action if the person is suicidal

- Providing the same support as they would for a physically ill person, including sending get-well cards, flowers, and other gifts, and calling, texting, or visiting the person

- Helping minimize disruptions to school and other important areas of the young person's life by supporting them to complete homework, attend events, and spend time with friends

- Having an understanding of psychosis

- Looking for support from a caregivers' support group and peer support

- Helping the person to develop a services and supports plan, relapse prevention plan, or crisis or safety plan

- Discouraging unhealthy coping strategies, such as the use of alcohol and other drugs

SCHOOLS AND COMMUNITIES[242]

Young people with psychosis may experience disruptions in education as a result of hospitalizations and poor functioning. Schools can help by working with the young person to develop a personal education plan to help meet educational goals. Parents should contact the adolescent's school to discuss options for extra help. Older adolescents may benefit from help in getting a job or attending career training.

Support groups can be helpful to a young person experiencing psychosis. Other family members can benefit from joining caregivers' support groups.[243]

LIFESTYLE, COMPLEMENTARY STRATEGIES, AND SELF-HELP STRATEGIES

People experiencing psychosis should avoid the use of alcohol, marijuana, and other drugs. People sometimes take drugs as a way of coping when psychosis is developing, but these drugs can make the symptoms worse, initiate relapse, and make the problem difficult to diagnose.[244] The use of marijuana can slow down recovery.[245]

Many people experiencing psychosis also experience depression or anxiety. Self-help strategies recommended for depression and anxiety, such as exercise, may also be appropriate for young people with psychosis.

Helpful Resources
FOR PSYCHOSIS

WEBSITES

Brain & Behavior Research Foundation
www.bbrfoundation.org

The Brain & Behavior Research Foundation awards grants that support advances and breakthroughs in scientific research to alleviate the suffering of people with mental illness. This site provides downloadable fact sheets on psychotic disorders.

Mental Health America
www.mentalhealthamerica.net

Visit Mental Health America's site for information on mental health, getting help, and taking action.

National Alliance on Mental Illness

www.nami.org

The National Alliance on Mental Illness is a nonprofit, grassroots, self-help support and advocacy organization of individuals with mental disorders and their families. This website provides many resources on psychosis. The National Alliance on Mental Illness also offers peer support groups for families and consumers.

National Council for Community Behavioral Healthcare

www.TheNationalCouncil.org

To locate mental health and addictions treatment facilities in your community, use the "Find a Provider" feature on the National Council's website.

National Institute of Mental Health

www.nimh.nih.gov

This government site gives a wealth of excellent, up-to-date information and research on psychosis in the form of downloadable booklets and fact sheets.

Schizophrenia.com

www.schizophrenia.com

This website is a member of the Internet Mental Health Initiative and is a source of information, support, and education to the family members, caregivers, and individuals whose lives have been affected by schizophrenia.

STEP (Schizophrenia Treatment and Evaluation Program)

med.unc.edu/psych

Based at the University of North Carolina (UNC) Hospitals, this program has a web page full of straightforward, practical, easy-to-digest information.

BOOKS AND OTHER WRITTEN RESOURCES

The "First Person Account" special features in the quarterly journal "Schizophrenia Bulletin", www.schizophreniabulletin.oxfordjournals.org

Smith, B. (2010). *A Family Guide to Severe Mental Illness*. Chapel Hill: University of North Carolina Schizophrenia Treatment and Evaluation Program and Mental Health Association in Orange County www.unccmh.org/clients-and-families/learn-about-mental-illness/a-family-guide/introduction

Originally published in 2003, this manual was made possible by a grant from the Carolina Center for Public Service at the University of North Carolina. It was produced by the UNC Schizophrenia Treatment and Evaluation Program and the Mental Health Association in Orange County as part of a collaborative project to provide education about mental illness to families in rural areas. This manual is the third edition. The purpose of this manual is to provide information about severe mental illness, its treatment, its impact on families, and ways to cope. The manual concentrates on two categories of disorders—mood disorders and psychotic disorders—because they encompass the most severe mental illnesses. Mood disorders include major depression and bipolar disorder (sometimes called manic depression); psychotic disorders include schizophrenia and schizoaffective disorder.

National Institute of Mental Health. (2009). *Schizophrenia*. Rockville, MD: Author. www.nimh.nih.gov/health/publications/schizophrenia/index.shtml

A detailed booklet that describes symptoms, causes, and treatments, with information on getting help and coping.

Compton, M. T., & Broussard, B. (2009). *The First Episode of Psychosis: A Guide for Patients and Their Families*. Oxford, England: Oxford University Press.

This guide is for people who have had a first psychotic episode and their families. It encourages them to take an active, informed role in their care.

Gur, R. E., & Johnson, A. B. (2006). *If Your Adolescent Has Schizophrenia: An Essential Resource for Parents*. New York, NY: Oxford University Press.

This guide is written for the parents and other caregivers of adolescents with a diagnosis of schizophrenia. It contains information about treatment and management, addresses myths, and includes personal stories from people who are recovering.

Temes, R. (2002). *Getting Your Life Back Together When You Have Schizophrenia*. Oakland, CA: New Harbinger.

This is a self-help guide for people starting a treatment program for schizophrenia. It includes information about what to expect from medication and therapy and strategies for improving overall quality of life.

SUPPORT GROUPS

National Alliance on Mental Illness
www.nami.org
Click on "Find Support" on the home page.

Recovery, Inc.
www.communityresources.net
Recovery International, a Chicago-based self-help mental health organization, sponsors weekly group peer-led meetings in many communities, as well as telephone and Internet-based meetings. Click on "Find a Meeting" on the home page to find the next Recovery, Inc. meeting in your area.

Schizophrenics Anonymous
www.sanonymous.com
Schizophrenics Anonymous is made up of self-help groups established to support the recovery of people who experience schizophrenia. The website lists the location of self-help groups.

Substance Use and Substance Use Disorders in Young People

What is Substance Use and Abuse?

Different substances (alcohol and other drugs) affect the brain in different ways. People use substances because of these effects, which include increasing feelings of pleasure or decreasing feelings of distress. Young people may experiment with substances, using only a small amount once or twice during adolescence, or they may develop a pattern of heavy use that can lead to dependence or addiction. Any substance use by an adolescent, other than that prescribed and used as directed by a doctor, should be regarded as serious. Substance use has potential harmful effects on the developing brain and the young person's mental health; a strong association with a high level of risk-taking behavior; and the potential to develop into a substance-related disorder.[246] In 2014, the National Survey on Drug Use and Health reported that approximately 8.1 percent of people age 12 years and older suffered from a substance use disorder.[27]

Substance-related disorders are divided into two groups: *substance use disorders* (which include substance abuse and substance dependence) and *substance-induced disorders*. *Substance abuse* involves repeated use of a substance or substances leading to difficulty in fulfilling responsibilities at school, home, or work; physically hazardous situations (e.g., driving); legal problems; recurrent social and interpersonal problems; or all of these.[247] *Substance dependence* is when an individual continues to use a substance despite significant substance-related problems (i.e., tolerance, withdrawal, and compulsive use). Substance use disorders include

- Use of alcohol or other drugs that leads to problems at work, school, or home or to legal problems or damage to health

- Dependence on alcohol or other drugs, that is, needing increased amounts over time to get the same effect, difficulty in controlling or reducing use, being unable to cope without using the substance, and giving up or reducing important social, occupational, or recreational activities because of substance use[248]

Co-occurring Substance Use and Mental Health Disorders

Mental health problems often co-occur with substance use.[249] Nearly 43 percent of youth receiving mental health services in the United States have been diagnosed with a co-occurring substance use disorder.[250] Also, among young people receiving treatment for alcohol or drug use, 54–95 percent also have conduct disorder or oppositional defiant disorder; approximately half have a mood disorder; and 15–42 percent exhibit anxiety disorders.[251]

Alcohol

Alcohol makes people less alert and impairs concentration and coordination. In small quantities, alcohol causes people to relax and lower their inhibitions. They can feel more confident and often act more extraverted. However, alcohol use can have serious effects on physical and mental health, particularly if it starts in adolescence. In 2013 66.2% of students reporting having at least one drink of alcohol on at least one day during their life with the prevalence of having ever drunk alcohol higher among female (67.9%) than male (64.4%) students.[252] Alcohol is a factor in approximately one-quarter of all adolescent deaths from motor vehicle crashes.[253] Long-term alcohol abuse is associated with liver disease, cancer, cardiovascular disease, and neurological damage as well as psychiatric problems such as depression, anxiety, and antisocial personality disorder.[254]

Alcohol is used by more young people in the United States than tobacco or illicit drugs.[255] Although it is illegal for people under the age of 21 to consume alcohol, research has shown that many adolescents start to drink at a young age. In 2013, 18.6 percent of students had reporting drinking alcohol (other than a few sips) for the first time before the age of 13 years.[256] In the 2014 National Survey on Drug Use and Health, 11.5 percent of 12 to 17 year olds reported being current alcohol users.[257] In 2009, 24 percent of high school students reported episodic heavy or binge drinking.[258] People who reported starting to drink before the age of 15 were four times more likely to also report meeting the criteria for alcohol dependence at some point in their lives.[259] In 2010, Native Americans and Alaska Natives were at a much higher risk than other minority populations for heavy drinking, binge drinking, and alcohol dependence.[261]

Is beer or wine safer to drink than liquor?

No. One 12-ounce beer has about the same amount of alcohol as one 5-ounce glass of wine or a 1.5-ounce shot of liquor. The amount of alcohol consumed is what most affects a person, not the type of alcoholic drink.

Other Drugs

Although the use of other drugs is less common than the use of alcohol, young people misuse a wide variety of other drugs.

Marijuana (cannabis)

Marijuana is a mind-altering drug and is a mixture of dried, shredded leaves, stems, seeds, and flowers of the hemp plant. Marijuana has street names such as *pot, herb, weed, grass, boom, Mary Jane, gangster,* or

chronic. In some states, medical marijuana is legally prescribed to relieve pain.

The main active chemical in marijuana is tetrahydro-cannabinol (THC).[262] The effects of cannabis on the user vary depending on how much THC it contains, and the THC content of cannabis has been increasing since the 1970s. Use of cannabis can interfere with performance at work or at school and lead to increased risk of accidents if used while driving. Long-term heavy use of marijuana has been found to produce abnormalities in certain parts of the brain.[263]

Marijuana is by far the most commonly used illicit drug in the United States for adolescents as well as the population as a whole. The 2014 National Survey on Drug Use and Health showed that 7.4 percent of people age 12–17 used marijuana in the past month along with 2.7 percent of adolescents meeting criteria for a marijuana use disorder.[264]

Marijuana use is associated with mental health problems. People who use marijuana are more likely to have a range of mental health problems, including anxiety and depression, but it is unclear which comes first—the substance use or the mental health problem. Also, marijuana use by adolescents and young adults has been found to increase the risk of developing schizophrenia, particularly in people who are vulnerable because of a personal or family history of the illness.[265]

Opioid Drugs

Opioid drugs include *heroin, morphine, opium, codeine,* and *oxycodone.* Opioids are processed from morphine, which is a naturally occurring substance taken from the poppy plant. Some opioids are prescribed for pain relief, but they may also be illegally used or abused without a prescription. Heroin is not a widely used drug in the United States. In 2014, only 0.1 percent of adolescents aged 12 to 17 reported using heroin in the past year.[266] However, it is a highly addictive drug, and most people who use it become dependent. Heroin produces a short-term feeling of euphoria, well-being, and relief of pain. Most people who are dependent on heroin also have associated problems such as depression, alcohol dependence, and criminal behavior. People who use heroin are at higher risk for suicide.

Pharmaceutical Drugs Used for Nonmedical Purposes

A number of prescription and over-the-counter drugs, such as those used to treat anxiety and sleep problems, are used by some people for nonmedical purposes. Although illicit drug use has declined among youth, rates of non-medical use of prescription and over-the-counter medication remain high with 17.8 percent of students reporting in 2013 that they took a prescription drug without a doctor's prescription.[267] Prescription medications most commonly abused by youth include *pain relievers, tranquilizers, stimulants,* and *depressants.*[268] Adolescents also misuse over-the-counter cough and cold medications containing the cough suppressant dextromethorphan to get high. Prescription and over-the-counter medications are widely available, free or inexpensive, and are falsely believed to be safer than illicit drugs. Misuse of prescription and over-the-counter medications can cause serious health effects, addiction, and death.[269]

Cocaine

Cocaine is a highly addictive stimulant drug. Cocaine is generally sold on the street in the form of a white powder known as *coke, C, snowflake,* or *blow.* Although sometimes thought of as a modern drug problem, cocaine has been abused for more than a century, and the coca leaves from which it is made have been used for thousands of years. Cocaine gives very strong euphoric effects, and people can develop dependence after using it for a short time. With long-term use, people can develop mental health problems, such as paranoia, aggression, anxiety, and depression. Cocaine can also bring on an episode of drug-induced psychosis. In 2014, the National Survey on Drug Use and Health reported that 0.2 percent of adolescents aged 12 to 17 were current users of cocaine.[270]

Amphetamines (Including Methamphetamine)

Amphetamines are stimulant drugs that temporarily increase energy and apparent mental alertness. However, as the effect wears off, a person may experience a range of problems including depression, irritability, agitation, increased appetite, and sleepiness. Amphetamines come in many shapes and forms and are taken in many ways. They can be in the form of powder, tablets, capsules, crystals, or liquid.

High doses of amphetamine can lead to aggression, intense anxiety, paranoia, and psychotic symptoms. Withdrawal symptoms can include temporary depression. A particular mental health risk is *speed psychosis*, which involves symptoms similar to schizophrenia, including hallucinations, delusions, or both. The person will recover as the drug wears off but is vulnerable to further episodes of drug-induced psychosis if the drug is used again.

Some types of amphetamine have legitimate medical uses. They are used under prescription to treat attention deficit disorders and some other medical conditions. Care should be taken to minimize the chances of these medications being sold or passed on to peers for nonmedical use.

Methamphetamine has a chemical structure similar to that of amphetamine, but it has stronger effects on the brain. The effects of methamphetamine can last six–eight hours. After the initial rush, there can be a state of agitation, which can sometimes lead to violent behavior. Methamphetamine (also called crystal meth) is a white, odorless, bitter-tasting crystalline powder that easily dissolves in water or alcohol and is taken orally, by snorting the powder through the nose, by needle injection, or by smoking.[271]

The 2014 National Survey on Drug Use and Health reported that about 45,000 adolescents (0.2 percent) aged 12 to 17 reported being current methamphetamine users.[260]

Although methamphetamine use has decreased for most of the U.S. population, methamphetamine has become a major concern to many Native American communities during the past decade. Tribal leaders and reservation police departments consider the epidemic to be the largest threat to public safety and attribute higher rates of domestic violence, assault, burglaries, uncontrolled violent behavior, and child abuse and neglect on the reservation to the drug.[272, 273]

Hallucinogens

Hallucinogens are drugs that affect a person's perceptions of reality. Some hallucinogens also produce rapid, intense emotional changes. A particular problem associated with hallucinogens is flashbacks, during which users re-experience some of the perceptual effects of the drug when they have not recently been using it. In 2013, 7.1 percent of students reported using hallucinogenic drugs one or more times during their life.[274]

Ecstasy

Ecstasy (3,4-Methylenedioxymethamphetamine, or MDMA, also known as E) is a stimulant drug that has hallucinogenic properties. While intoxicated, ecstasy users report that they feel emotionally close to others. Some young people use it at dance parties. Users can develop an adverse reaction that in extreme cases can lead to death. To reduce this risk, users need to maintain a steady fluid intake and take rest breaks from vigorous activity. When coming off the drug, they often experience depressed mood. The long-term

effects of using ecstasy are of particular concern. The evidence that ecstasy damages nerve cells in the brain that use the chemical messenger serotonin is considerable.[275] Research among people who have used ecstasy has regularly shown that they have reduced sexual interest and a range of mental health problems.[276] It is important to note that although ecstasy refers to the drug MDMA, people buying ecstasy may be buying pills that contain other substances, which means that ecstasy users are risking the use of other drugs and poisonous substances. Lifetime use of ecstasy among high school students decreased from 11 percent in 2001 to 6.6 percent in 2013.[277]

Inhalants

Inhalants are breathable chemical vapors that produce mind-altering effects. Inhalants may be solvents (e.g., paint thinners, gasoline, and glue), gases (e.g., aerosols or butane lighters), nitrites, and other substances. Common slang for inhalants includes laughing gas, snappers, poppers, whippets, bold, and rush.

Inhalants are usually used in one of these ways:

- Sniffing or snorting fumes from containers

- Spraying aerosols directly into the nose or mouth

- Sniffing or inhaling fumes from substances sprayed or placed into a plastic or paper bag ("bagging")

- "Huffing" from an inhalant-soaked rag stuffed in the mouth

- Inhaling from balloons filled with nitrous oxide

The effects of inhalants range from an alcohol-like intoxication and euphoria to hallucinations, depending on the substance and the dosage. Use of inhalants starves the brain of oxygen, causing a brief rush. Because the intoxication lasts only a few minutes, abusers often try to make the feeling last longer by inhaling repeatedly during the course of several hours. Depending on the type of inhalant abused, the harmful health effects will differ. The table below lists a few examples.[278]

Examples and Effects by Type of Inhalant		
INHALANT	**EXAMPLES**	**EFFECTS**
Toluene	• Spray paint • Glue • Dewaxer • Fingernail polish	• Hearing loss • Spinal cord or brain damage • Liver and kidney damage
Trichloroethylene	• Cleaning fluid • Correction fluid	• Hearing loss • Liver and kidney damage
Hexane	• Glue • Gasoline	• Limb spasms • Blackouts
Nitrous oxide	• Whipped cream dispensers • Gas cylinders	• Limb spasms • Blackouts
Benzene	• Gasoline	• Bone marrow damage

Many people do not think of inhalants as drugs because most of them are commonly found at home or work. Young people are the most likely to abuse inhalants, partly because inhalants are readily available and inexpensive.

Inhalants are often among the first drugs that young adolescents use. In fact, they are one of the few classes of substances that are abused more by younger adolescents than older ones. In 2013, 8.9% of students had sniffed glue, breathed the contents of aerosol spray cans, or inhaled any paints or sprays to get high one or more times during their life.[277] Inhalant abuse can become chronic and continue into adulthood. Female students reported a higher prevalence of ever using inhalants (10 percent) than male students (7.9 percent). The prevalence in high school was highest in 9th grade (10.1 percent). During approximately the last twenty years, there has been a significant decrease in the overall prevalence of students ever having used inhalants from 20.3 percent (1995) to 8.9 percent (2013).[279]

Tobacco

Although the number of younger Americans who smoke has been going down since the late 1990s, the rates of cigarette smoking among students in 2013 was at 15.7% reporting smoking cigarettes once in the past month.[279] Nearly all first use of tobacco takes place before high school graduation. In fact, almost 90 percent of adults who are regular smokers started at or before age 19. Of adolescents aged 12 to 17 that report to be current smokers, 24.1 percent report to smoke cigarettes every day.[280] The younger a person is when they begin to smoke the more likely they are to be an adult smoker. In addition, about one in seven high school boys use some form of spit or other type of smokeless tobacco. More than two percent of high school girls use spit or smokeless tobacco. Those who drop out of school have higher rates of smoking and tobacco use.[281]

Cigarette smoking causes serious health problems among young people, including

- Coughing

- Shortness of breath

- Frequent headaches

- Increased phlegm (mucus)

- Respiratory illnesses

- Worse cold and flu symptoms

- Reduced physical fitness

- Lung problems

- Addiction to nicotine

As they get older, adolescents who continue to smoke can expect problems, such as

- Early heart disease and stroke

- Gum disease and tooth loss

- Chronic lung diseases, such as emphysema and bronchitis

- Hearing loss

- Vision problems, such as macular degeneration

People who smoke are also more likely to get into fights, carry weapons, attempt suicide, have mental health problems such as depression, and engage in high-risk sexual behaviors. Adolescent tobacco users are more likely to use alcohol and illegal drugs than are nonusers.

People who use tobacco have a high rate of mental health problems. Smokers are about twice as likely to have a mental illness as people who have never smoked.[282] Smoking is particularly high in people with schizophrenia (approximately 62 percent).[283] Tobacco is used by some people with mental illness as a type of self-medication.

What might a first aider notice if a young person is abusing alcohol or other drugs?

If a young person is using substances only occasionally, use may be difficult to recognize. If substance use becomes more frequent, the signs may become more noticeable over time.

At home, the young person may

- Become increasingly secretive or avoid answering parents' questions, particularly when it comes to where they go and what they do with friends

- Take alcohol from liquor cabinets or other sources in the home

- Appear to suffer from a hangover some mornings

- Eat a large amount of snack foods, as a result of increased appetite from cannabis use

- Spend money more quickly than they used to or be unable to explain what they are spending their money on

At school, the young person may

- Show a decline in school grades as a result of not completing work, not doing as good a job as they used to, or missing school

- Have difficulty maintaining focus and concentration

- Decrease the time spent in healthy extracurricular activities, such as sports

These behaviors can all have an impact on school achievement, and some may result in disciplinary responses.

In a social setting, the young person may

- Spend increased amounts of time with friends who use substances rather than those who do not

- Use more substances than what is considered usual in the social group or start to suggest bringing substances to parties or other social events

- Use substances to become intoxicated rather than to experiment

- Seem to have a different personality when using substances compared with their usual self or experience distress, as a result of behavior, when intoxicated

Risk Factors for Substance Use and Abuse

Most of the knowledge about the risk factors for substance use relates to alcohol, but the risk factors for other drug abuse or use are likely to be similar. It is important to remember that a risk factor for one youth may not be a risk factor for another.

Many factors may influence an adolescent's decision to drink:[284]

- Adolescents may associate alcohol use with becoming an adult.

- Drinking may be considered normal in the adolescent's peer or cultural group.

- Portrayal and marketing of alcohol in the media may encourage drinking.

- Parents' use of and attitudes about alcohol also influence drinking.

A number of factors increase the risk of an adolescent drinking heavily:

- Experiencing emotional or psychological problems

- Not feeling connected to family, school, or community

- Behavior problems

- Family history of alcohol problems

Some adolescents who drink heavily will go on to develop an *alcohol use disorder*. People with alcohol use disorders drink to excess, endangering themselves and others.[285] Factors that increase the risk include[286]

- Early use of alcohol

- Availability and tolerance of alcohol in society

- Alcohol use in the family

- Social disadvantage and negative life events

- Biological factors such as genetic predisposition and alcohol sensitivity

- Enjoyment from drinking

- Other mental health problems

Importance of Early Intervention

Substance use problems typically begin in adolescence and early adulthood, so this time is critical for early intervention.[287] The brains of adolescents and young adults are still developing and are more sensitive to the effects of alcohol and other drugs than the brains of older adults.[288] Because the brains of adolescents are still developing, alcohol and other drugs have a more serious effect in this age group.[289] For example, alcohol abuse in adolescents affects the development of areas of the brain that control decision making and memory,[290] and marijuana use in adolescence is associated with lower IQ and poorer memory.[291]

Early and frequent use of alcohol and other drugs increases the risk of developing substance use disorders including substance dependence or addiction, and other mental disorders such as depressive, anxiety, and psychotic disorders.[292] In addition, any use of alcohol and other drugs by a young person may indicate an underlying mental health problem or emotional distress. Young people may self-medicate these problems by using substances, but, in the long term, this is likely to make the problems worse.

Many people with alcohol and drug problems do not receive treatment. A failure to seek help can cause problems with family and education; damage physical health; and increase the risk of developing other mental illnesses, such as depression and anxiety disorders. Early intervention will also prevent many of the long-term ill effects on a person's physical health, social relationships, educational progress, financial status, and job prospects. It will also reduce the possibility of serious problems with the law. While under the influence of substances, a young person is more likely to engage in risk-taking behavior or get into dangerous situations.[293, 294]

These include

- **Physical injuries** resulting from risk-taking behavior, such as imitating dangerous stunts seen on television or the Internet, driving while intoxicated, or getting into a car with an intoxicated driver

- **Aggression and antisocial behavior,** such as getting into fights or engaging in criminal activity including vandalism or theft

- **Sexual risk taking.** Young people are more likely to engage in unsafe sex practices or sex with multiple partners while affected by substances. Young people may consent to sexual activity that they would not agree to while sober or be more susceptible to nonconsensual sex, such as date rape. Sexual risk taking may result in unwanted pregnancy or sexually transmitted infections.

- **Becoming a victim of crime.** While affected by alcohol and other drugs, young people are also at increased risk of becoming victims of violent crime, including physical or sexual assault.

- **Suicide and self-injury.** When people are intoxicated, they are more likely to act on suicidal thoughts or to injure themselves. Alcohol increases feelings of anxiety, depression, and anger; reduces inhibitions; and inhibits the use of more effective coping strategies.

Ongoing substance misuse can interfere with normal functioning in a number of ways.

These include

- **Educational problems** including a decline in school performance, increased absenteeism, and failure to complete education

- **Legal problems** associated with violence, property damage, theft, vandalism, or traffic offenses

- **Social and family problems,** such as increased conflict or withdrawal. Long-term substance use and substance use disorders can lead to physical illnesses and other serious problems. Although these problems typically do not occur until later in life, substance misuse that starts during adolescence increases the long-term risk.

Mental Health First Aid® Action Plan for a Substance Use Disorder

YOUTH MENTAL HEALTH FIRST AID® ACTION PLAN	
ACTION A	Assess for risk of suicide or harm
ACTION L	Listen nonjudgmentally
ACTION G	Give reassurance and information
ACTION E	Encourage appropriate professional help
ACTION E	Encourage self-help and other support strategies

Action A: Assess for Risk of Suicide or Harm

The main crises that may be associated with substance use are

- The person has **acute effects from alcohol abuse**.

- The person has **acute effects from drug abuse**.

- The person is showing **aggressive behaviors**.

- The person has **suicidal thoughts or behaviors**.

ACUTE EFFECTS OF ALCOHOL USE

If the person is using alcohol heavily, it is possible they will experience acute effects from *alcohol intoxication, alcohol poisoning,* or *alcohol withdrawal*.

- *Alcohol intoxication* substantially impairs thinking and behavior. When intoxicated, the person may engage in a wide range of risky activities, such as having unprotected sex, getting into arguments or fights, or driving a car. The person may also be at higher risk of attempting suicide.

- *Alcohol poisoning* is a dangerous level of intoxication that can lead to death. The amount of alcohol that causes alcohol poisoning is different for every person.

- *Alcohol withdrawal* refers to the unpleasant symptoms a person experiences when they stop drinking or drink substantially less than usual. It is not simply a hangover. Untreated alcohol withdrawal may lead to seizures.

ACUTE EFFECTS OF DRUG USE

If the person is using drugs, it is possible they will experience acute effects from *drug intoxication, drug overdose, overheating* or *dehydration*.

- *Drug intoxication* can lead to impairment or distress, poor judgment, and engagement in risky behaviors or aggressive behavior. The effects vary depending on the type and amount of the drug and also vary from person to person. Illicit drugs can have unpredictable effects because they are not manufactured in a controlled way.

- *Overdose* occurs when the intoxication level leads to risk of death.

- *Overheating or dehydration* can occur while on some drugs (e.g., ecstasy) when in a hot environment or without adequate water intake.

- *Sudden sniffing death* can occur when a person who has been using inhalants gets a fright or tries to run. This sometimes occurs when a young person is caught using inhalants by an adult who gets angry or shouts at them. The heart and lungs can fail suddenly, and death can occur very quickly.

AGGRESSIVE BEHAVIORS

People abusing substances or who have substance use disorders have an increased risk of aggression toward others.[295] Many crimes are committed by people who are intoxicated with alcohol or other drugs.

SUICIDAL THOUGHTS AND BEHAVIORS

People are more likely to act on suicidal thoughts when they are intoxicated. Of all people who complete suicide, 26 percent have a substance use disorder.[296]

As you talk with the person, be on the lookout for any indications that the person may be in crisis.

If you have concerns that the young person has acute effects of alcohol use (intoxication, alcohol poisoning, or severe withdrawal), see *First Aid for a Medical Emergency Resulting from Alcohol Abuse*.

If you have concerns that the young person has acute effects of drug use (drug intoxication, overdose, overheating, dehydration), see *First Aid for Acute Effects of Alcohol and Drug Abuse or Misuse*.

If you have concerns that the young person is showing aggressive behavior, see *First Aid for Aggressive Behaviors*.

If you have concerns that the young person may be having suicidal thoughts, see *First Aid for Suicidal Thoughts and Behaviors*.

If you have no concerns that the person is in crisis, you can ask them about how they are feeling and how long they have been feeling that way and move on to another action.

Action L: Listen Nonjudgmentally

If the young person is not in crisis, take the time to plan how and when to speak with them. Before speaking with the young person, reflect on the situation, organize your thoughts, and decide what you want to say. Arrange a time to talk with the young person in a quiet, private environment at a time when there will be no interruptions and you are in a calm frame of mind. Do not talk to the young person when they have been using substances; wait until the effects have worn off to start the conversation. It can be hard for an adult to listen nonjudgmentally to a young person who is using substances. These substances are often illegal and because of the high risk of injury or other harms, adults can be fearful of consequences of their use.

Some of the main things to keep in mind to listen nonjudgmentally are to

- Express your concerns openly and honestly.

- Interact with the person in a supportive way rather than threatening, confronting, or lecturing.

- Avoid expressing moral judgments about the substance use.

- Be assertive, but do not blame or be aggressive.

- Do not criticize the young person's substance use. You are more likely to be able to help in the long term if you maintain a noncritical but concerned approach.

- Do not label the young person, for example, by calling them a "pothead" or a "drunk."

- Try not to express your frustration about the young person's substance misuse.

- When the young person finishes talking, repeat back what you have heard and allow the young person to clarify any misunderstandings.

■ Respect the youth's culture by exhibiting verbal and nonverbal behaviors that demonstrate this respect.

Consider the following when making your approach:

>> THE YOUNG PERSON'S OWN PERCEPTION OF USING DRUGS AND ALCOHOL

Ask the person about their substance use (e.g., about how much the young person is using) and whether they believe their substance use is a problem.

>> THE PERSON'S READINESS TO TALK

Ask about areas of the person's life that the substance use may be affecting, for example, the youth's mood, performance in school, and relationships. The person may deny that they are using at all or might not recognize that they have a substance use problem, and trying to force the person to admit to substance misuse may cause conflict.

>> USE "I" STATEMENTS

Express your point of view by using "I" statements, for example, "I am concerned about how much you've been drinking lately," rather than "you" statements such as "You have been drinking too much lately."

>> RATE THE ACT, NOT THE YOUNG PERSON

Identify and discuss the person's behavior rather than criticizing their character, for example, "Your drug use seems to be getting in the way of your friendships" rather than "You're a pathetic druggie." Remember, your role is to intervene, not to enforce the law.

>> THE PERSON'S RECALL OF EVENTS

When discussing the person's substance use, bear in mind that the young person may recall events that occurred while they were using differently from how they actually happened or may not recall events at all.

>> STICK TO THE POINT

Focus on the person's substance use and do not get drawn into arguments or discussion about other issues.

Action G: Give Reassurance and Information

Give the young person information about substance use, substance use disorders, and associated risks. Try to find out whether the young person feels they need help to change the substance use and discuss what you are willing and able to do. Have a helpline phone number or the address of a reputable website with you to give to the young person (see *Helpful Resources* at the end of this section).

SUPPORTING THE YOUNG PERSON WHO WANTS TO CHANGE

Tell the person what you are willing and able to do to help. This help may range from simply being a good listener to organizing professional help. If you are assisting an adolescent and you are not the parent, caregiver, or guardian, encourage them to talk to their parent, caregiver, or guardian about what is going on. Discuss with parents or caregivers what a good response might be; rather than parents or caregivers getting angry and the young person being disciplined, encourage them to find more useful ways of talking through the problem.

Have realistic expectations for the person (relapse is a common part of the recovery process). Do not expect a change in the person's thinking or behavior right away. Bear in mind that

■ Changing substance use habits is not easy.

■ Willpower and self-resolve are not always enough to help the person stop misusing substances.

- Giving advice alone may not stop the young person from abusing substances.

- A person may try to change or stop substance use more than once before they are successful.

- If the young person finds it difficult to give up the substance use altogether, cutting down is still worthwhile.

HELPING THE YOUNG PERSON WHO DOES NOT WANT TO CHANGE

If a young person wants to continue using substances, you may need to take extra steps to help them change. However, it is important that you maintain a good relationship. Let the person know how important it is for health reasons that they stop using alcohol and other drugs during adolescence. Provide the young person with information about substance abuse (e.g., reputable websites or pamphlets). Encourage the young person to question any assumptions they may have that most adolescents use substances and help the young person realize that many of their peers are not using and can be supportive.

You can speak with a health professional who specializes in substance use to determine how best to help the young person, or you could consult with others who have dealt with such problems about effective ways to help.

While working to encourage the young person to change the substance use, you should set boundaries around what behaviors you are willing and not willing to accept from them. If you are the young person's parent, it can be helpful to set rules such as being home by a particular time, informing you about where they are and who they are with when unsupervised, and having a plan to get home safely. If you are in a school environment, you need to know the school's policies and procedures for managing students who use substances at school. Most schools have very specific policies and procedures in place for managing these situations.

If the young person continues to use substances, do not

- Use negative approaches (e.g., lecturing or making the person feel guilty) because they are unlikely to promote change.

- Try to control them by bribing, nagging, threatening, or crying.

- Make excuses for them or cover up the young person's substance use or related behaviors.

- Make the young person move out of the family home (if you are in a position to make this determination).

Action E: Encourage Appropriate Professional Help

Assist the young person to access professional help and obtain a good assessment. Seek information about local services, particularly provided by those who specialize in substance abuse. Help the young person or their parents to access these services. Ensure that the young person is supported to make and keep appointments. It may not always be easy to find or access local services, especially in more rural communities. However, "e-counseling" (counseling by email or live Internet chat) and telephone counseling may be an option, if other professional help is unavailable or difficult to access.

PROFESSIONALS WHO CAN HELP

A variety of health professionals can provide help to a young person who is misusing substances. Ideally, the health professional should have expertise in providing mental health services to young people as well as trauma-informed treatment. If the young person is uncertain about what to do, encourage them or a parent to consult a primary care physician first. The doctor may be able to provide treatment or might refer the young person to a drug or alcohol specialized service or to a mental health professional if there are other mental health problems. Ideally, the health professional should have knowledge about mental health and substance use services for children and adolescents.

TREATMENTS AVAILABLE FOR ALCOHOL AND OTHER DRUG ABUSE

The treatments for substance abuse disorders depend on the severity of the problem and what other physical and mental health problems the young person also has. If a young person is substance dependent, *detoxification* and *withdrawal management* may be needed, which can involve a stay in a treatment facility, medication, and ongoing therapy. For young people who are not substance dependent, the following types of care may help:[297, 298]

- *Cognitive behavior therapy* helps a person to understand the link between their thoughts and behaviors and to learn coping skills to prevent relapse.

- *Motivational enhancement therapy* uses a directive approach to providing feedback that focuses on strengthening the young person's commitment to change and recovery.

- The *Adolescent Community Reinforcement Approach* seeks to replace factors that have supported alcohol or drug use with activities and behaviors that support recovery. Treatment includes individual therapy with the youth, the caregivers, and family therapy. Treatment also includes community partners to ensure appropriate screening, referral, planning, and connections to other community resources and activities. Community partners may include schools, police, referral agencies, and others.

TREATMENT FOR CO-OCCURRING SUBSTANCE USE AND MENTAL HEALTH CHALLENGES

Young people who abuse substances often do so to try to cope with a mental health problem or illness. It is thus important that any other mental illness be treated as well, preferably at the same time, through an integrated treatment approach. A number of specialized programs are designed to provide more integrated mental health and substance use services targeted to youth with co-occurring disorders. *Integrated Co-occurring Treatment*[299] uses an integrated treatment approach, embedded in an intensive home-based method of service delivery, to provide a set of core services to youth with co-occurring substance use and serious emotional disability and their families.[300]

The parent, caregiver, or guardian should be contacted as soon as possible and given all relevant information.

WHAT IF THE PERSON DOES NOT WANT PROFESSIONAL HELP?

Be prepared for a negative response when suggesting professional help. The young person may not want such help when it is first suggested and may find it difficult to accept. Continue to suggest professional help to the person. However, do not pressure the person or use negative approaches because they may be counterproductive. Discuss with the young person their reasons for not wanting help. These reasons may be based on mistaken beliefs about treatment, which you may be able to correct. Reassure the person that professional help is confidential.

Remember that the person cannot be forced to get professional help except under certain circumstances, for example, if a violent incident results in the police being called or after a medical emergency. If the young person is substance dependent or otherwise severely impaired by the use, a doctor or a young person's parent or guardian may seek involuntary treatment for them. However, involuntary treatment is very rare in this age group.

WHAT CAN YOU DO IF YOU OR SOMEONE YOU KNOW ABUSES ALCOHOL?

Consult your personal health care provider if you feel you or someone you know has an alcohol problem. Other resources include the **National Drug and Alcohol Treatment Referral Routing Service available at 1-800-662-HELP (4357)**. This service can provide you with information about treatment programs in your local community and allow you to speak with someone about alcohol problems.

Action E: Encourage Self-Help and Other Support Strategies

Certain factors can protect against the development of substance use and abuse. These include[301, 302]

- Having a supportive, connected family, including an extended family network

- Having a good social support system

- Positive self-talk

- Having good, problem-focused coping skills

- High self-esteem

- Emotional well-being, which may include receiving effective treatment for another mental illness or emotional problems

- Community bonding

- Community-sponsored substance abuse prevention efforts and programs

- Availability of constructive recreation

- High monitoring of youth's activities

- Reinforcement for positive social involvement

- No tobacco and other substance use or abuse in their family

- Regular school attendance and academic achievement

During adolescence, fitting in with friends becomes very important. Young people may use substances as a way to obtain acceptance from peers. Young people may find themselves in situations in which they experience peer pressure to use substances. Tell the young person that the decision as to whether to use alcohol or other drugs is theirs, not their friends'. Help the young person to prepare for this by talking about specific situations that may occur and helping develop various refusal techniques.

A young person can handle or avoid situations involving substance misuse. Help the individual develop strategies to do this. Talk about ways you can help. If appropriate, tell the young person to call you if faced with a situation in which other people are using substances. Talk to the young person about ways to minimize any embarrassment this may cause. Peer support may be a helpful strategy. Link the young person with a mentor or recovery coach.

Peers can be a positive and a negative influence. Encourage the young person to develop friendships with peers who have healthy, positive lifestyles and good coping strategies rather than with those who abuse substances. Talk to the young person about qualities that really count in friends, such as being kind and trustworthy rather than popular and cool. Encourage the young person to turn to friends who are supportive of the decision not to use alcohol or other drugs.

People are more likely to start using substances again if there is an emotional upset or because of the biological component to substance use. Parents and others can try to reduce this possibility by offering additional support and recommending good coping strategies when negative events occur. Help the parents or caregivers access needed self-care services, such as those listed in the *Helpful Resources* below.

Helpful Resources
FOR SUBSTANCE USE AND
SUBSTANCE USE DISORDERS

WEBSITES

Alcoholics Anonymous (AA)
Narcotics Anonymous (NA)
Alateen
www.aa.org
www.na.org
www.al-anon.alateen.org

Alcoholics Anonymous is an international fellowship that declares its "primary purpose is to stay sober and help other alcoholics achieve sobriety." Narcotics Anonymous sprang from the Alcoholics Anonymous program. Books and information pamphlets are currently available in many languages. Membership is open to all people with an alcohol or drug addiction.

Centers for Disease Control and Prevention
www.smokefree.gov

Smokefree.gov, created by the Centers for Disease Control and Prevention, provides ideas about how to stop using tobacco. It includes downloadable resources and contacts for online and phone counseling.

National Clearinghouse for Alcohol and Drug Information
www.cocommunity.net/agency
www.findtreatment.samhsa.gov

SAMHSA's National Clearinghouse for Alcohol and Drug Information is a one-stop resource for information about substance abuse prevention and addiction treatment.

National Council for Community Behavioral Healthcare
www.TheNationalCouncil.org

To locate mental health and addictions treatment facilities in your community, use the "Find a Provider" feature on the National Council's website.

National Institute on Alcohol Abuse and Alcoholism
www.niaaa.nih.gov

The National Institute on Alcohol Abuse and Alcoholism is the lead agency for government research on alcohol use disorders and health.

National Institute on Drug Abuse (NIDA)
www.drugabuse.gov

The website provides links to information for parents, teens, health professionals, teachers, and others about drugs of all types.

NIDA for Teens
http://teens.drugabuse.gov/about.php

The National Institute on Drug Abuse, a component of the National Institutes of Health, created this website to educate adolescents between 11 and 15 (as well as their parents and teachers) on the science behind drug abuse. The institute enlisted the help of teens in developing the site to ensure that the content addresses appropriate questions and timely concerns. The site delivers science-based facts about how drugs affect the brain and body so that kids will be armed with better information to make healthy decisions. Elements such as animated illustrations, quizzes, and games are used throughout the site to clarify concepts, test the visitor's knowledge, and make learning fun through interaction.

The Partnership at Drug Free.org

www.drugfree.org

The Partnership at Drugfree.org is a nonprofit organization that helps parents prevent, intervene, and find treatment for drug and alcohol use by their children. The site offers resources and provides community education programs and public awareness campaigns to help parents prevent, intervene, and find treatment for drug and alcohol use by their children.

SAMHSA's Prevention of Substance Abuse and Mental Illness

www.samhsa.gov/prevention

The SAMHSA website has information about substance use disorders of all kinds. It has information for the public, including families, health professionals, schools, and individuals. It also includes a treatment finder to locate a substance use treatment provider in your area. This web page has a list of links and resources on substance use and tobacco prevention.

WRITTEN MATERIALS

STUDENTS AND YOUNG ADULTS

From the **National Institute on Drug Abuse** at www.drugabuse.gov/students-young-adults
These materials were developed specifically for students and young adults.

NIDA for Teens

http://teens.drugabuse.gov
The NIDA for Teens website includes facts on drugs, real stories, videos, downloads, and activities.

Marijuana: Facts for Teens/La Marihuana: Información Para los Adolescentes
www.drugabuse.gov/marijbroch/teens
Provides facts about marijuana and its potential harmful effects. Available in English and Spanish.

NIDA DrugFacts

www.drugabuse.gov/publications/term/160/DrugFacts

Information about drug abuse trends related to high school students and youth.

Mind Over Matter from NIDA for Teens

http://teens.drugabuse.gov/mom/index.php

Fact sheets: "The Effects of Drug Abuse on Your Body and Brain for Grades 5–9" for cocaine, hallucinogens, inhalants, marijuana, methamphetamine, opiates, prescription drug abuse, steroids (anabolic), and tobacco addiction

Heads Up (Scholastic Website)

http://headsup.scholastic.com/articles/heads-up-free-copies-of-past-issues

Current and past compilations on "Real News About Drugs and Your Body for Grades 6–10."

FOR PARENTS AND OTHER ADULTS

National Institute on Alcohol Abuse and Alcoholism

http://pubs.niaaa.nih.gov/publications/aa67/aa67.htm

Publications and resources from the National Institute on Alcohol Abuse and Alcoholism.

Additionally, the National Family Dialogue partnered with Faces and Voices of Recovery to develop teleconferences that can be listened to and followed along with a PowerPoint presentation and other handouts.

HELPLINES

When someone has a drug problem, it is not always easy to know what to do. If someone you know is using drugs, encourage them to talk to a parent, school guidance counselor, or other trusted adult. There are also anonymous resources, such as these helplines:

Alateen
1-800-352-9996

National Cocaine Hotline
1-800-COCAINE (262-2463)
The hotline provides information, crisis intervention, and referrals to local rehab centers for all types of drug dependency. It operates 24 hours a day, seven days a week.

National Suicide Prevention Lifeline
1-800-273-TALK (8255)
This is a crisis hotline that can help with many issues, not just suicide. For example, anyone who feels sad, hopeless, or suicidal; family and friends who are concerned about a loved one; or anyone interested in mental health treatment referrals can call the Lifeline. Callers are connected with a professional nearby who will talk with them about what they are feeling or concerns for other family and friends. Call the hotline (toll free, 24 hours/day, 7 days/week).

National Youth Crisis Hotline
1-800-442-HOPE (4673)
The hotline provides counseling and referrals to local drug treatment centers, shelters, and counseling services, as well as responds to youth dealing with pregnancy, molestation, suicide, and child abuse.

Treatment Referral Helpline
1-800-662-HELP
This helpline, offered by SAMHSA's Center for Substance Abuse Treatment, refers callers to treatment facilities, support groups, and other local organizations that can provide help for their specific need. You can also locate treatment centers in your state by going to www.findtreatment.samhsa.gov.

HELPLINES FOR TOBACCO CESSATION

National Cancer Institute Smoking Quitline
1-877-44U-QUIT (87848)
(English and Spanish)

Smoking Cessation Centers
1-800-QUIT-NOW (7848669)
(Number used in 17 states; English and Spanish)

SUPPORT GROUPS

Al-Anon & Alateen
www.al-anon.org
www.al-anon.alateen.org
Provides information and support for the family members and friends of people with alcohol problems, including a list of meetings in the United States and Canada.

Narcotics Anonymous & Alcoholics Anonymous
www.na.org
www.aa.org
These websites will give you information on Narcotics Anonymous and Alcoholics Anonymous and will give you the website and contacts for groups in your area.

Attention Deficit and Disruptive Behavior Disorders in Young People

What Are Disruptive Disorders?

Disruptive disorders can be described as the difficulty children and youth have following the rules that most other young people accept.[303] These behaviors cause significant difficulties with family and friends and at school or work. Disruptive behavior disorders are the most common psychiatric disorders of childhood.

Types of Disruptive Disorders

Disruptive behaviors are frequently found in young people who have *Attention Deficit Hyperactivity Disorder* (ADHD). Children, youth, and young adults who exhibit more extreme forms of these behaviors may be diagnosed with *oppositional defiant disorder (ODD)* or *conduct disorder.*

ADHD is a disorder in which inattention, overactivity, impulsivity, or a combination are common. Youth with ADHD may have the following behaviors:[304, 305]

- Difficulty paying attention to details

- Easily distracted

- Difficulty finishing schoolwork

- Putting off anything requiring sustained mental effort

- Disorganized and prone to making mistakes

- Appearing to not listen when spoken to or follow through on given tasks

A young person with ADHD will have at least some of these signs before they are seven years old and the signs will be severe enough to affect their school and relationships. ADHD affects about three–five percent of school-age children.[306]

ODD is defined as a pattern of defiance, disobedience, and hostility toward authority figures including parents, teachers, and other adults. Children and young people with ODD may repeatedly lose their temper, argue with adults, deliberately refuse to comply with requests or rules of adults, deliberately annoy or spite other people, blame others for their own mistakes, and be repeatedly angry and resentful. Being touchy or easily annoyed, stubbornness, and testing of limits are common. Before puberty, the condition is more common in boys, but after puberty the rates in both genders are equal.

Conduct disorder is characterized by aggressive behaviors, such as by fighting; bullying; intimidating; physically assaulting; sexually coercing; being cruel to people or animals; vandalism; theft; truancy; early tobacco, alcohol, and substance use and abuse; and precocious sexual activity.

When a young person's behavior is clearly disruptive in interpersonal and family relationships and/or at school, but not enough symptoms are present to warrant the diagnosis of either conduct disorder or ODD, the young person may still have a *disruptive behavior disorder not otherwise specified* (NOS).

Many symptoms of ODD, conduct disorder, and ADHD overlap. For example, academic difficulties, poor social skills, and an over representation among males are predominant features of all of these disorders. There is also a high level of comorbidity among these three behavior disorders. Disruptive disorders often co-occur with other mental health challenges, including mood disorders, substance abuse, and ADHD.

Approximately two-thirds of youth with ADHD will also have a disruptive behavior disorder.

What might a First Aider notice?

Most youth with ADHD continue to have symptoms when entering adolescence. Although hyperactivity tends to decrease as a child ages, teens who continue to be hyperactive may show the following behaviors:

- Feel restless.

- Try to do too many things at once.

- Choose tasks or activities that have a quick payoff, rather than those that take more effort but provide bigger, delayed rewards.

- Struggle with school and other activities in which they are expected to be more self-reliant.

- Have difficulty sticking with treatment.

Risks Associated with Disruptive Disorders and ADHD

Significant risk factors in the development of disruptive behavior disorders include learning difficulties, hyperactivity, prenatal complications, and violence in the home.[307] Other factors may include school failure, brain damage or dysfunction, severe head trauma, low birth weight, and maternal and familial psychiatric illness.

The cause of ADHD seems to be biological or genetic, and environmental factors and life experiences may influence the severity of the disorder.[308]

Possible causes or risk factors of ADHD include[309]

- Environmental agents (use of cigarettes and alcohol by mothers during pregnancy, maternal postnatal depression,[310] high levels of lead in young preschool children).

- Traumatic brain injury (children who have been in accidents that resulted in brain injury occasionally show some signs of behavior similar to that of ADHD, but only a small percentage of children with ADHD have been found to have suffered a traumatic brain injury).

- Food additives and sugar (some research has suggested that attention disorders are caused by, or symptoms are exacerbated by, refined sugar or food additives).

- Genetics and hereditary factors (ADHD hereditary factors appear to run in families and to have a strong genetic influence).

- Brain abnormalities (some studies have shown structural differences in the brains of ADHD patients).

The cause of conduct disorder is not fully known, but several social risk factors have been identified. The social risk factors for conduct disorder include early maternal rejection, separation from parents with no adequate alternative caregiver available, early institutionalization, family neglect, abuse or violence, mental illness of parents, parental marital discord, large family size, crowding, and poverty.[311] These factors are thought to lead to a lack of attachment to the parents or to the family and eventually to lack of regard for the rules and rewards of society.[312]

No single factor causes ODD. Possible risk factors for ODD include having a parent with a mood or substance abuse disorder; being abused or neglected; harsh or inconsistent discipline; lack of supervision; lack of positive parental involvement; severe marital discord in the home; parents with a history of ADHD, ODD, or conduct problems; family instability (e.g., parents' divorce, financial instability, multiple moves, or frequently changing schools or child care); or exposure to violence.[313]

Importance of Early Intervention

The earlier in life that youth receive appropriate help for their attention deficit or disruptive behaviors the greater their chance of leading productive and fulfilling lives. A failure to seek help can cause problems with family and education; damage physical health; and increase the risk of developing other mental illnesses, such as depression and anxiety disorders.

ADHD is a long-term, chronic condition. If not treated appropriately, ADHD may lead to drug and alcohol abuse, failure in school, problems keeping a job, and trouble with the law.[314]

Young people with ODD conduct disorder have problems at school or work, have higher injury rates, and are prone to school expulsion and problems with the law. Their relationships with peers and adults are often poor. Sexually transmitted diseases are common. If youth have been removed from home, they may have difficulty staying in an adoptive or foster family or group home placement. Girls with conduct disorder are at a higher risk of running away from home and may become involved in prostitution. Rates of depression, suicidal thoughts, suicide attempts, and suicide itself are all higher in children and youth diagnosed with a conduct disorder.[315]

Mental Health First Aid® Action Plan for Attention Deficit and Disruptive Behavior Disorders

YOUTH MENTAL HEALTH FIRST AID® ACTION PLAN	
ACTION A	Assess for risk of suicide or harm
ACTION L	Listen nonjudgmentally
ACTION G	Give reassurance and information
ACTION E	Encourage appropriate professional he
ACTION E	Encourage self-help and other support strategies

Action A: Assess for Risk of Suicide or Harm

Crises that may be associated with disruptive disorders and ADHD include

- The person goes into an extreme level of anxiety, such as a **panic attack**.

- The person **displays physical or verbal aggression**.

- The person is **engaging in alcohol or other substance use or abuse**.

- The person has **suicidal thoughts or behaviors**.

- The person is engaging in **nonsuicidal self-injury**.

As you talk with the person, be on the lookout for any indications that the person may be in crisis.

If you have concerns that the young person is showing aggressive behavior, see *First Aid for Aggressive Behaviors*.

If you have concerns that the young person has **acute effects of alcohol use** (intoxication, alcohol poisoning, or severe withdrawal), see *First Aid for a Medical Emergency Resulting from Alcohol Abuse*.

If you have concerns that the young person has **acute effects of drug use** (drug intoxication, overdose, overheating, or dehydration), see *First Aid for Acute Effects of Alcohol and Drug Abuse or Misuse*.

If you have concerns that the young person may be having suicidal thoughts, see *First Aid for Suicidal Thoughts and Behaviors*.

If you have no concerns that the youth is in crisis, you can ask the young person the following questions: How are you feeling? How long have you felt like that? Then move on to another action.

Action L: Listen Nonjudgmentally

It can be hard for an adult to listen nonjudgmentally to a young person who is misbehaving. Before speaking with the young person, reflect on the situation, organize your thoughts, and decide what you want to say. Arrange a time to talk with the person. Talk with the youth in a quiet, private environment at a time when there will be no interruptions and you are in a calm frame of mind. Talk to the person about your concerns openly and honestly. Express your concerns nonjudgmentally in a supportive, nonconfrontational way. Be assertive, but do not blame or be aggressive. Respect the youth's culture by exhibiting verbal and nonverbal behaviors that demonstrate this respect.

Some of the main things to keep in mind in order to listen nonjudgmentally are

- Listen to the young person without judging them as bad or immoral.

- Interact with the person in a supportive way rather than threatening, confronting, or lecturing.

- Avoid expressing moral judgments about the young person's behavior.

- Do not criticize the young person's behavior. You are more likely to be able to help the young person in the long term if you maintain a noncritical but concerned approach.

- Do not label the young person, for example, by calling them a "troublemaker" or a "screw-up."

- Try not to express your frustration about the young person's behavior.

- When the young person finishes talking, repeat back what you have heard and allow the young person to clarify any misunderstandings.

Consider the following when making your approach:

>> THE YOUNG PERSON'S OWN PERCEPTION OF THEIR BEHAVIOR
Ask the youth about their behavior and whether they believe the behavior is a problem.

>> THE YOUNG PERSON'S READINESS TO TALK
Ask about areas of the young person's life that the behavior may be affecting, for example, the youth's performance in school and relationships. Be aware that the person may deny that the behavior is a problem at all and that trying to force the youth to admit to this may cause conflict.

>> USE "I" STATEMENTS
Express your point of view by using "I" statements, for example, "I am concerned about your behavior lately," rather than "you" statements, such as "You have been behaving very poorly lately."

>> **RATE THE ACT, NOT THE YOUNG PERSON**

Identify and discuss the youth's behavior rather than criticizing their character, for example, "Your behavior seems to be getting in the way of your friendships" rather than "You're a troublemaker." Remember, your role is to intervene, not to enforce the law.

>> **THE YOUNG PERSON'S RECALL OF EVENTS OR BEHAVIORS**

When discussing the youth's behavior, bear in mind that the youth may recall events or behaviors that occurred differently from how they actually happened or not at all.

>> **STICK TO THE POINT**

Focus on the youth's behavior and do not get drawn into arguments or discussion about other issues.

At home, the following strategies can help young people with ADHD:[316]

- Give rules that are clear and easy to understand.

- Help the youth stay focused and organized, such as posting a chart listing household chores and responsibilities with spaces to check off completed items.

- Keep responses as calm and matter of fact as possible.

- When the youth has trouble controlling their impulsivity and tempers flare, sometimes a short time out can be calming.

See Action L in *Depression in Young People* for more tips on nonjudgmental listening.

Action G: Give Reassurance and Information

Try to find out whether the young person feels in need of help to change the behavior and discuss what you are willing and able to do. Give the young person information about attention deficit and disruptive behavioral disorders and associated risks. Have a helpline number or the address of a reputable website with you to give the young person (see *Helpful Resources* at the end of this section). Have realistic expectations for the person. Do not expect a change in the person's thinking or behavior right away.

SUPPORTING THE YOUNG PERSON WHO WANTS TO CHANGE

Tell the person what you are willing and able to do to help, which may range from simply being a good listener to organizing professional help. If you are assisting a youth and you are not the parent, caregiver, or guardian, support the youth in talking to parents, caregivers, or guardians about what is going on. Discuss with parents or caregivers what a good response might be; rather than parents or caregivers getting angry and the young person being disciplined, encourage them to find more useful ways of talking through the problem. Ensure that the youth is in treatment and receiving recovery service and supports as needed.

HELPING THE YOUNG PERSON WHO DOES NOT WANT TO CHANGE

If a young person does not want to change, you may need to take extra steps to help them see the benefit of changing and the consequences of not changing. However, it is important that you maintain a good relationship.

You can speak with a health professional who specializes in attention deficit and disruptive behavioral disorders to determine how best to help the young person or you could consult with others who have dealt with such problems about effective ways to help.

While working to encourage the young person to change the behavior, you should set boundaries around what behaviors you are willing and not willing to accept. If you are the young person's parent, it can be helpful to set rules, such as being home by a particular time, informing you about where they are and with whom when unsupervised, and having a plan to get home safely. If you are in a school environment, you need to know the school's disciplinary policies and procedures. Most schools have very specific policies and procedures in place for managing these situations. In school settings, the young person may need extra support in organizing time to accomplish tasks.

If the young person continues to engage in disruptive and destructive behaviors, do not

- Use negative approaches (e.g., lecturing or making them feel guilty) because they are unlikely to promote change.

- Try to control them by bribing, nagging, threatening, or crying.

- Make excuses for them or cover up the young person's behaviors.

- Make the young person move out of the family home (if you are in a position to make this determination).

Tips to Help Children and Young Adults With ADHD Stay Organized and Follow Directions[317]

>> SCHEDULE
If you live or work closely with the youth, keep the same routine every day, from wake-up time to bedtime. Include time for homework, outdoor play, and indoor activities. Keep the schedule on the refrigerator or on a bulletin board. Write changes on the schedule as far in advance as possible.

>> ORGANIZE EVERYDAY ITEMS
Have a place for everything. Keep everything in its place, including clothing, backpacks, books, and toys.

>> USE HOMEWORK AND NOTEBOOK ORGANIZERS
Use organizers for school material and supplies. Stress the importance of writing down assignments, bringing home the necessary books, and making lists or keeping an appointment book.

>> BE CLEAR AND CONSISTENT
Children and young adults with ADHD need consistent rules and structure they can understand and follow.

>> GIVE PRAISE OR REWARDS WHEN RULES ARE FOLLOWED
Children and young adults with ADHD often receive and expect criticism. Look for good behavior and praise it.

Action E: Encourage Appropriate Professional Help

Behavioral health specialists are helpful in supporting young people and their families with disruptive disorders and ADHD. Ideally, the health professional should have expertise in providing mental health services to young people as well as trauma-informed treatment. Seek information about local services, and help the young person or a parent to access these services. The parent, caregiver, or guardian should be contacted as soon as possible and given all relevant information. Ensure that the young person is supported to make and keep appointments. It may not always be easy to find or access local services, especially in more rural communities. The professional can decide whether "e-counseling" (counseling by email or live Internet chat) and telephone counseling are a good option, if other professional help is unavailable or difficult to access (see *Helpful Resources* at the end of this section).

ADHD is a condition that affects individuals across the lifespan. This fact is one reason treating ADHD is a partnership between the health care provider, parents or caregivers, school, and the child or youth. Among the most effective methods to date is the judicious use of medication and behavior management. Currently, available treatments focus on reducing the symptoms of ADHD and improving functioning.[318]

For many children, ODD does improve over time; however, research has also shown that many children with ODD eventually develop conduct disorder. There is no single treatment for all youth and young adults with ODD. Treatment usually will last several months or longer and may require multiple episodes either continuously or as periodic booster sessions. Individual approaches should be specific to the child's problems, behaviorally based, and geared to the child's age.

Several psychosocial interventions can effectively reduce antisocial behavior in disruptive disorders.

- *Therapy and counseling* may be particularly helpful for youth with ODD. Therapy will often include both individual therapy and family therapy.

- *Problem-solving skills training* may be helpful for youth with ODD and focuses on helping the child acquire new problem-solving skills and resisting negative peer group influences.[319]

- *Parent management training* is also helpful for youth with ODD and involves teaching parents or caregivers how to reinforce appropriate behaviors and not harshly punish negative ones.

- *Multisystemic therapy* is an intensive home and family focused treatment that includes therapy as well as training for a parent on how to deal with the youth's demands or behavior. In addition to learning appropriate reactions to behaviors, parents may be encouraged to find ways to strengthen emotional ties with their child.

- *Medication*. For many young people, ADHD medications reduce hyperactivity and impulsivity and improve their ability to focus, work, and learn. Medication may also improve physical coordination. However, a one-size-fits-all approach does not apply for all youth with ADHD. What works for one child might not work for another. One child might have side effects with a certain medication, and another child may not. Sometimes several different medications or dosages must be tried before finding one that works for a particular child. Any child taking medications must be monitored closely and carefully by caregivers and doctors.[320] Medication combined with therapy or other treatment may be the more effective than either treatment alone.[321] Treatment for ODD may also include the use of medication, although medication alone would rarely be considered an adequate or appropriate intervention for children with ODD. The research on the safety and efficacy of medications for ODD is also limited. No medications have been demonstrated to be consistently effective in treating conduct disorder.[322]

- *Academic and social counseling* involves working with the youth and their teacher or school on social interaction, and providing academic help to reduce rates of school failure can help prevent some of the negative educational consequences of ODD or conduct disorder.[323]

The most effective treatment plan will be individualized to the needs of each child and family.

WHAT IF THE YOUNG PERSON DOES NOT WANT PROFESSIONAL HELP?

Be prepared for a negative response when suggesting professional help. The young person may not want such help when it is first suggested and may find it difficult to accept. Be persistent, but do not pressure the person or use negative approaches because they may be counterproductive. Discuss with the young person their reasons for not wanting help. The reasons may be based on mistaken beliefs about treatment that you may be able to correct. Reassure the person that professional help is confidential.

Remember that the person cannot be forced to get professional help except under certain circumstances, for example, if a violent incident results in the police being called or following a medical emergency.

Action E: Encourage Self-Help and Other Support Strategies[324, 325]

Certain factors can lessen the severity of disruptive disorders and help youth and young adults be successful despite mental health challenges they may encounter in their lives. Significant protective factors for the development of disruptive disorders, including ODD and conduct disorders, include the ability to express feelings and have a good relationship with parents or caregivers. For youth with ADHD, protective factors may moderate further development of behavior problems, particularly ODD. Some of these factors include[326, 327]

- Positive social contact with peers

- Positive role models

- Adaptability

- Good social skills

- Positive involvement in community

- Meaningful activities

- Spirituality

- Attachment to caregivers or supportive adults

- Consistent consequences and well-defined expectations

Talk to the young person about available supports, and help the young person choose ones they feel will be most helpful.

Peers can be a positive and a negative influence. Encourage the young person to develop friendships with peers who have healthy, positive lifestyles and good coping strategies. Talk to the young person about qualities that really count in a friend, such as being kind and trustworthy rather than popular and cool. Encourage the young person to turn to friends who are supportive of the decision to seek and receive help.

ALTERNATIVE AND COMPLEMENTARY TREATMENTS

Having a healthy, balanced diet and exercise and physical activity are important to health development and growth. There is little systemic research on alternative or complementary treatments (e.g., dietary interventions, chiropractic, or biofeedback) that have clear conclusions about their efficacy in treating symptoms of ADHD.

Helpful Resources
FOR ATTENTION DEFICIT AND
DISRUPTIVE BEHAVIOR DISORDERS

WEBSITES

American Academy of Child & Adolescent Psychiatry Resource Centers
www.aacap.org

The American Academy of Child & Adolescent Psychiatry Resource Centers site contains consumer friendly definitions, answers to frequently asked questions, clinical resources, expert videos, abstracts from the academy's journal, scientific proceedings, and facts for families relevant to each disorder. There are resource centers for ADHD, ODD, conduct disorder, and others.

American Academy of Pediatrics
www.healthychildren.org

This site is the American Academy of Pediatrics' ADHD resource web page.

Centers for Disease Control and Prevention
www.cdc.gov/ncbddd/adhd

This site is the Centers for Disease Control and Prevention's ADHD resource web page.

Children and Adults with Attention Deficit/Hyperactivity Disorder (CHADD)
www.chadd.org

Children and Adults with Attention-Deficit/Hyperactivity Disorder is a national organization that provides education, advocacy, and support for individuals with ADHD. In addition to its website, CHADD also publishes a variety of printed materials on research advances, medications, and treatments affecting individuals with ADHD.

National Institute of Mental Health
www.nimh.nih.gov/health/topics/attention-deficit-hyperactivity-disorder-adhd/index.shtml

The site has information and research for children and youth with ADHD, ODD, and other conduct disorders.

National Resource Center on ADHD (a program of CHADD)
www.help4adhd.org

The website has the nation's clearinghouse for science-based information about all aspects of ADHD.

SAMHSA Service Locators
http://store.samhsa.gov/mhlocator

Within the federal government, SAMHSA offers a services locator for mental health and substance abuse treatment programs and resources nationwide.

HELPLINES

American Psychiatric Association Answer Center
1-888-35-PSYCH (77924)

Live operators, available 8:30 a.m. to 6:00 p.m., eastern time, refer you to local board-certified psychiatrists.

American Psychological Association Public Education Line
1-800-964-2000

Follow the automated instructions. An operator then refers you to local board-certified psychologists.

National Suicide Prevention Lifeline
1-800-273-TALK (8255)

This is a crisis hotline that can help with many issues, not just suicide. For example, anyone who feels sad, hopeless, or suicidal; family and friends who are concerned about a loved one; or anyone interested in mental health treatment referrals can call the Lifeline. Callers are connected with a professional nearby who will talk with them about what they are feeling or concerns for other family and friends. If you or someone you know is in suicidal crisis, call the hotline (toll free, 24 hours/day, 7 days/week).

SECTION 3: **Mental Health First Aid® for Youth in Crisis**

"A core aspect of giving mental health first aid is being fully present and listening." — Foreword in *Mental Health First Aid® USA* manual.

Section 3 of this manual provides guidance on how to assist a young person either at a time of crisis or in an ongoing situation with significant emotional distress. It is meant to give the first aider some tools that can be used to provide basic help during a crisis and refer to professional care. This section also gives some additional resources that may be helpful to link a young person to available professional or self-help supports.

Parents, caregivers, and family members are a vital part of any young person's life and may be an important support for the young person. This support requires that caregivers and family members be provided information and resources so that they in turn can appropriately assist the child.

Youth and young adults who are experiencing emotional stresses do not necessarily have mental health disorders. However, these individuals may still display many of the behaviors listed in the previous section and still require support of a first aider, family members, and others to help them overcome the stresses they are experiencing.

Last, to ensure that first aiders maintain their own wellness; this section outlines some self-care suggestions for the individual providing Mental Health First Aid.

CHAPTER 3.1

First Aid for Suicidal Thoughts and Behaviors

An Important Note

Self-injury can indicate a number of different things. Some people who are hurting themselves may be at risk of suicide. Others engage in a pattern of self-injury over weeks, months, or years and are not necessarily suicidal. As a first aider, the following advice is of use only if the young person you are helping is suicidal. If the young person you are assisting is self-injuring but is not suicidal, please refer to *First Aid for Nonsuicidal Self-Injury*.

Facts on Suicide

In 2014, suicide was the second leading cause of death for young people ages 10 to 24 years.[328] The percentage of Latina females attempting suicide is higher than that of most other female racial groups. Suicide is the second leading cause of death among Asian American and Pacific Island youth between the ages of 15 and 19.[329] Suicide continues to be the second leading cause of death for young American Indian/Alaska Natives and remains at that rate until their mid-30s.[330] Suicide accounts for the death of almost 20 percent of American Indian/Alaska Natives youth.[331] American Indian/Alaska Natives teenage girls die by suicide at three times the rate of their peers in different cultural populations.[332]

Lesbian, gay, bisexual, transgender, and questioning (LGBTQ) youth are also at increased risk.[333] Being LGBTQ alone does not put an adolescent at higher risk for suicide, but living in the closet, being outed by someone else, or being ridiculed are specific stressors for this population.[334, 335] African American and Latino LGBTQ youth may also be at increased risk because they are less likely than White youth to come out to family and friends.[336]

Although most people who have a mental illness do not die by suicide, having a mental illness does increase the likelihood of suicide compared with people who do not have one.

How to Tell Whether a Young Person is Suicidal

Important signs that a young person may be suicidal are[337]

- Threatening to hurt or kill themselves.

- Seeking access to pills, weapons, or other means to kill themselves.

- Talking or writing about death, dying, or suicide (including in schoolwork, creative writing, and artwork).

- Expressing hopelessness, no reason for living, or having no sense of purpose in life.

- Having rage, anger, or seeking revenge.

- Acting recklessly or engaging in risky activities, seemingly without thinking.

- Feeling trapped.

- Increasing alcohol or drug use.

- Withdrawing from friends, family, or society.

- Having a dramatic change in mood (may even be a shift from being sad and depressed to happy, with a sense of resolve; often with no clear indication of how or why the shift in mood occurred).

- Sleeping all the time or being unable to sleep.

- Being anxious or agitated.

- Giving away prized possessions.

Young people may show one or many of these signs, and some may show signs not on this list. Another factor to consider is whether the young person has had family or friends die by suicide or whether there has been a recent suicide or multiple suicides in the community.

If you see some warning signs that the young person may be feeling suicidal, talk to the youth about what you have noticed. Let the young person know that you are concerned and are willing to help. It is important to ask the young person directly about suicidal thoughts. Although it may be uncomfortable, do not avoid using the word *suicide*. It is important to ask the question without dread and without expressing any negative judgment. Appearing confident in the face of the suicide crisis can be reassuring for the young person. The question must be direct and to the point. For example, the first aider could ask,

- "Are you having thoughts of suicide?"

- "Are you thinking about killing yourself?"

Some young people may not be able to respond to these questions, but you should observe their other behaviors as well. Not everyone is going to tell you the truth about how they feel. Although some people think that asking about suicide can put the idea in a person's mind, this is not true.[338] Another myth is that someone who talks about suicide is not really serious.[339] Remember that talking about suicide may be a way for the person to indicate just how badly they are feeling.[340]

When administering Mental Health First Aid to a young person experiencing a suicidal crisis, the role of family members or other caregivers cannot be overstated. For the young person, *family* may mean the biological or legal parents, siblings, other relatives, foster parents, legal guardians, caregivers, or other individuals with primary relationships to the child whether they be blood, adoptive, legal, or social relationships. Family can include any natural, formal, or informal support people identified by the family, youth, or both. Remember, parent, caregiver, or family notification is a vital part of suicide prevention for young people. Communicate your concerns and the situation to the parent, caregiver, or family in a calm and reassuring manner.

How to Assist

When a person is suicidal, you should always seek professional help. If the person has a weapon or is behaving aggressively toward you, you must seek assistance from law enforcement for your own safety.

How should I talk with a young person who is suicidal?[342]

It is important to

- Tell the person that you are concerned and that you want to help.

- Express empathy for the young person and what they are going through.

- Respect the culture of the young person and respond in ways that demonstrate this respect. For example, consider issues such as eye contact, physical space, and language as well as the role and relationship of the first aider with the young person.

- Clearly state thoughts of suicide are common and that help is available to discuss these thoughts, because this may instill a sense of hope.

- Tell the young person that thoughts of suicide do not have to be acted on.

Encourage the young person to do most of the talking, if they are able to. Suicidal thoughts are often a plea for help and a desperate attempt to escape from problems and distressing feelings. The young person needs the opportunity to talk about their feelings and reasons for wanting to die and may feel great relief at being able to do this.[343, 344]

Listen to the youth, and talk about some of the specific problems the youth is experiencing. Discuss healthful ways to deal with problems, which may seem impossible to cope with, but do not attempt to solve the problems yourself.

How can I tell how serious or urgent the situation is?[345]

First, you need to determine whether the young person has definite intentions to take their life, or whether the young person has been having more vague suicidal thoughts, such as, "What's the point of going on?" To do this, you need to ask the young person if they have a plan for suicide.

The three questions you need to ask are

- "Have you decided how you would kill yourself?"

- "Have you decided when you would do it?"

- "Have you taken any steps to secure the things you would need to carry out your plan?"

A higher level of planning means a greater risk. However, you must remember that the lack of a plan is not enough to ensure the person's safety. **All thoughts of suicide must be taken seriously.**

Next, you need to know about the following extra risk factors:

- Has the young person been using alcohol or other drugs? The use of alcohol or other drugs can make a person more susceptible to acting on impulse.

- Has the young person made a suicide attempt in the past? A previous suicide attempt makes a person more likely to make a future suicide attempt.

How can I keep the young person safe?

Once you have established that there is a risk of suicide, you need to take action to keep the young person safe. A young person who is **actively** suicidal should not be left on their own. If you cannot stay with the young person, arrange for someone else to do so. In addition, give the person a safety contact who is available at all times (such as one of the suicide hotline numbers, a friend or family member who has agreed to help, or an informal or professional help giver).

It is important to help the young person think about people or things that have supported them in the past, and find out whether these supports are still available. These supports might include a family member or friend, teacher, coach, doctor, psychologist, or other mental health worker; or an individual from a church, community organization, or recreational club.

Do not use guilt or threats to prevent suicide. For example, do not tell the young person they will go to hell or ruin other people's lives if they complete suicide.

Suicide Hotlines

If you or someone you know is in suicidal crisis, call a suicide hotline (toll free, 24 hours/day, 7 days/week).

1-800-SUICIDE (784-2433)
1-800-273-TALK (8255)
1-800-799-4TTY (4889) for hearing & speech impaired

What About Professional Help?

During the Crisis

Help the young person and parents or caregivers to access professional help as soon as possible. This may mean taking the young person to the emergency department of a hospital, a community mental health center, or a doctor's office. If you call ahead to make an appointment, explain that you are assisting a young person who is at risk of suicide, and ask what information is needed to provide immediate services. Even a busy doctor will ensure that a young person who is suicidal gets the help they need quickly. It will be helpful to have as much information as possible, such as health insurance coverage and mental health history. The most important thing is that the young person is not left alone. People rarely act on suicidal thoughts with other people present.

If the suicidal person has a weapon or is behaving aggressively toward you, you must seek assistance from the police to protect yourself. Let the police know that you believe this is a mental health issue and that the person may be suicidal.

As a first aider, it is helpful to know the local emergency resources and that EMTs may be the primary responders. At the point at which the EMTs arrive, your job as a first aider is to provide them with the information they request to the best of your ability.

What the Emergency Department Needs to Know[346]

Inform the emergency department personnel if the young person has

- Access to a gun, medications, or other means of suicide.

- Stopped taking prescribed medicines.

- Stopped seeing a mental or behavioral health provider or physician.

- Written a suicide note.

- Given possessions away.

- Been in or is currently in an abusive relationship.

- Recently suffered a loss or other traumatic event.

- An upcoming anniversary of a loss.

- Started using alcohol or drugs.

- Recovered well from a previous suicidal crisis after a certain type of intervention.

Accessing services is not always easy, especially in rural areas. For example, for some tribal rural communities or western frontier regions, it may be hours to the nearest service.

After the Crisis Has Passed

Emergency department care is short term and crisis oriented. After the suicide crisis has passed, help ensure that the young person gets whatever ongoing psychological and medical help they need. The health professional that helped during the crisis can assist in referring the young person to appropriate mental health care. Accessing the appropriate services, supports, and treatment is not always easy and may take days or weeks, even in an apparent crisis. If you as the first aider have an ongoing role with the young person, it may be helpful to assist the young person and the family, friends, and involved professionals in developing a safety plan that includes steps and actions to keep the youth safe as well as steps and actions to take should there be another suicidal crisis.

What if the Young Person Makes Me Promise not to Tell Anyone Else?

You should never agree to keep the risk of suicide a secret. However, you should respect the young person's right to privacy and involve the young person in decisions regarding who else needs to know about their suicidal intentions. If the young person continues to refuse to involve anyone else, you will need to act against their wishes and contact a mental health professional and the young person's parents or caregivers. If you have to do this, tell the young person whom you have told, explain that you are acting to keep them safe, and tell the young person again that you care about them.

Self-Care

Do your best for the young person you are trying to help. Despite our best efforts, some people will still die by suicide. The suicide or attempted suicide of an adolescent or young adult may have considerable impact on caregivers and first aiders involved. As a first aider, it is important to pay attention to your own emotional state and physical needs (proper diet and sleep) and to make sure that you are asking for and

accepting care from your social support network. Seek and accept support from trusted colleagues, friends, and family, and allow yourself time for reflection and healing. Remember to respect the young person's right to privacy; if you talk to someone, do not share the name of the young person you helped or any personal details that might make the young person identifiable to the person you choose to share with.

Use the resources listed in *Depression in Young People* to help create a support network for the young person, their family, and you.

Self-Care

- Have I decided what I will do for self-care?

- Who can I speak with now?

- Who can I call if I feel upset or distressed later?

First Aid for Nonsuicidal Self-Injury

An Important Note

This first aid advice applies only if the young person is self-injuring for reasons other than suicide. Some people engage in nonsuicidal self-injury even when suicidal, which means that even though a person is having thoughts of suicide, self-inflicted injuries are not intended to result in death. Some people say that engaging in nonsuicidal self-injury helps them avoid acting on suicidal thoughts. If the young person you are helping is engaging in nonsuicidal self-injury and is also suicidal, you will also need to refer to *First Aid for Suicidal Thoughts and Behaviors*.

How to Tell Whether a Young Person is Engaging in Nonsuicidal Self-Injury

Do not ignore suspicious injuries you have noticed on the young person's body. If you suspect that someone you care about is deliberately injuring themselves, you need to discuss it with them.

You may observe many different types of nonsuicidal self-injury:[347, 348]

- Cutting, scratching, or pinching their skin, enough to cause bleeding or a mark that remains on the skin

- Banging or punching objects or self to the point of bruising or bleeding

- Ripping and tearing their skin

- Carving words or patterns into their skin

- Interfering with the healing of wounds

- Burning their skin with cigarettes, matches, or hot water

- Pulling out large amounts of hair compulsively

- Overdosing deliberately on medications when it is NOT meant as a suicide attempt

- Changing eating or sleeping habits

- Having frequent "accidents"

- Tattooing or body piercing excessively

Apart from seeing evidence of injuries described above, there are other signs that may indicate that the young person is engaging in self-injury. These include

- Blood on clothing

- First aid supplies being used up more quickly than expected

- Always wearing long sleeves or long pants, even when the weather is hot

You may also notice the adolescent or young adult viewing photos and websites (e.g., YouTube) about self-injury or talking about media focused on how to self-injure.

Facts on Nonsuicidal Self-Injury

Many terms are used to describe self-injury, including *self-harm* and *self-mutilation*. *Nonsuicidal self-injury* is used to refer to situations in which the self-injury is not intended to result in death. It is not always easy to tell the difference between nonsuicidal self-injury and a suicide attempt. The only way to know is to ask the person directly if they are suicidal. Do not assume that a person who says they are not suicidal is being truthful. If you see other behaviors that indicate the youth may be suicidal, refer to *First Aid for Suicidal Thoughts and Behaviors*.

Children and adolescents engage in nonsuicidal self-injury with ninth grade females most at risk, as they engage in nonsuicidal self-injury at three times the rate of their male counterparts.[349]

There may be many reasons for engaging in self harm. Some youth and young adults may self-mutilate to take risks, rebel, reject their parents' values, display their individuality, or merely be accepted by peers or others. Some youth, however, may injure themselves out of desperation or anger to seek attention, to show their hopelessness and worthlessness, or because they have suicidal thoughts. These young people may have serious mental health disorders, such as depression, psychotic disorder, PTSD, and bipolar disorder. Additionally, some children and youth who engage in self-injury may develop borderline personality disorder as adults. Some young children may engage in self-injurious acts from time to time but often grow out of it. Some young people with developmental delays (i.e., when a child's physical, cognitive, behavioral, emotional, or social development falls behind the normal age range) or developmental disabilities may show these behaviors. Youth and young adults who have been abused or abandoned may also self-injure.[350]

Other reasons for self-injury may be

- To manage painful feelings of current or past trauma

- To punish themselves

- To exert influence over others

- To end feelings of unreality or being detached from themselves

- To avoid or combat suicidal thoughts

- To feel pain or relief

- To show control of their body[351]

Self-injury is seen differently by groups and cultures within society. Understanding cultural influences is important in recognizing and responding to a young person's self-harming behaviors. Certain forms of self-harming behavior are sometimes culturally acceptable, for example, body art and piercings or religious convictions that reinforce self-harm, such as physical penance.

How to Assist

How should I talk with a young person who is deliberately injuring?

Let the young person know that you have noticed the injuries or other signs. Avoid expressing a strong negative reaction to the self-injury and discuss it calmly with the young person. When asking the person about the self-injury, it is important that you have reflected on your own state of mind and are sure you are prepared to calmly deal with their answer.

Self-injury is a coping mechanism; therefore, stopping self-injury should not be the focus of the conversation. Instead, look at alternative ways to relieve the distress. Do not trivialize the feelings or situations that have led to the self-injury. Do not punish the person, especially by threatening to withdraw care.

What should I do if I witness someone deliberately injuring?

If you have interrupted someone in the act of self-injury,

- Intervene in a supportive and nonjudgmental way.

- Remain calm and avoid expressions of shock or anger.

- Express your concern for the person's well-being.

- Ask whether you can do anything to alleviate the distress.

- Ask whether any medical attention is needed.

- Respect the culture of the young person and respond in ways that demonstrate this respect. For example, consider issues such as eye contact, physical space, and language as well as the role and relationship of the first aider with the young person.

Share your concerns and the situation with a parent, caregiver, or family member in a calm and reassuring manner.

What About Professional Help?

Medical Emergency

If the young person has harmed themselves by taking an overdose of medication or consuming poison, call 911 immediately, because the risk of death or serious harm is high. **Do not try to make the person vomit.** Do not stick your finger down the person's throat or give anything by mouth unless told to do so by the Poison Control Center (1-800-222-1222) or a doctor. Deliberate overdose is more frequently intended as a suicide attempt but is sometimes a form of self-injury. Regardless of the young person's intentions, emergency medical help must be sought for self-poisoning or overdose.

If the injury is life threatening, emergency medical help must be sought. Call 911 if the young person is confused, disoriented, or unconscious or if they have bleeding that is rapid or pulsing. When EMTs arrive, your job is to provide them with the information they request to the best of your ability.

Obtaining Mental Health Care

Help the young person and parents or caregivers to access mental health services. Services may be available through a community mental health center, a physician, a child or adolescent psychiatrist, or other mental health professional. Accessing services is not always easy, especially in rural areas. For example, for some tribal rural communities or western frontier regions, it may be hours to the nearest service. As a first aider, it is helpful to know the local emergency resources and that EMTs may be the primary responders.

It is also important to help family members access services, such as support groups and other types of peer support. Self-injury is not an illness in itself, but may be a symptom of past trauma, a mental health challenge or disorder, or serious psychological distress. Help should be sought even if you are not sure whether it seems necessary. For example, if the injuries do not appear to be severe, if there is no evidence that self-injury has become a long-term pattern, or if the young person says they were just trying it out, help should be sought anyway. A clinical assessment can determine whether there is an underlying problem, and treatment can prevent self-injury from becoming a long-term coping strategy. Ideally, the health professional should have expertise in providing mental health services to children, youth, and young adults.

Further information about helping a young person to access professional treatment can be found in *Depression in Young People.*

How can I keep the young person safe?

Encourage the young person to speak to someone they trust, such as a teacher, coach, or other supportive adult, the next time the young person feels the urge to self-injure. Ensure that first aid supplies, such as bandages and antibiotic ointments, are accessible to the young person. Offer to work with the young person, the family or caregivers, and other service providers in developing a safety plan that clearly states what the youth should do to stay safe when they feel like self-injuring. In addition to professional help, directing the young person and the family to self-help resources may also be helpful.

In an Emergency

- Call 911 for all emergency medical services.

- If you believe someone has taken poison, call the American Association of Poison Control Centers at 1-800-222-1222 or the Poison Control Center in your area.

Self-Care

Assisting a young person who is engaging in self-injury can be a very intense and draining experience. It is important to pay attention to your own emotions and needs (including proper diet and sleep). Seek and accept support from trusted colleagues, friends, and family. Allow yourself time for reflection and healing. If you talk to someone, remember to respect the young person's right to privacy; do not share their name or any personal details that might make the young person identifiable to the person you choose to share with.

Self-Care

- Have I decided what I will do for self-care?

- Who can I speak with now?

- Who can I call if I feel upset or distressed later?

First Aid for Panic Attacks

Facts on Panic Attacks

More than one in four people have a panic attack at some time in their life.[352] Few people go on to have repeated attacks, and fewer still go on to develop panic disorder or agoraphobia. Although anyone can have a panic attack, people with anxiety disorders are more prone. Panic attacks are not always indicative of a mental disorder, and as many as 10 percent of otherwise healthy people experience a panic attack per year.[353, 354] Panic disorder is about twice as common among women as men.[355] Age of onset is most common between late adolescence and middle adulthood, with onset relatively uncommon past age 50.[356]

Some panic attacks do not appear to be triggered by anything specific. Other panic attacks may be associated with a feared situation—for example, a person with social phobia may experience a panic attack in a social setting—or brought on by traumatic reactions from past events.

How to Tell Whether a Young Person is Having a Panic Attack

A *panic attack* is a distinct episode of high anxiety, with fear or discomfort that develops abruptly and has its peak within 10 minutes. During the attack, several of the following symptoms are present:[357]

- Palpitations, pounding heart, or rapid heart rate

- Sweating

- Trembling and shaking

- Shortness of breath and/or feelings of choking or smothering

- Chest pain or discomfort

- Abdominal distress or nausea

- Dizziness, light-headedness, or feeling faint or unsteady

- Feelings of unreality or being detached from oneself

- Fears of losing control or going crazy

- Fear of dying

- Numbness or tingling

- Chills or hot flashes

If a young person is experiencing the above symptoms, and you suspect that they are having a panic attack, you should first ask the young person whether they know what is happening and whether they have ever had a panic attack before. If you are helping someone you do not know, approach them calmly and introduce yourself. Young people with panic attacks and anxiety often do not have the words to describe what is happening to them. They may exhibit behavior out of the ordinary, such as tantrums, frequent stomachaches, clinginess, separation anxiety, or a refusal to go to school.[358]

How to Assist

What if I am uncertain whether the person is really having a panic attack and not something more serious such as a heart attack?

The symptoms of a panic attack sometimes resemble the symptoms of a heart attack or other medical problem. It is not possible to be totally sure that a person is having a panic attack. Only a medical or mental health professional can tell if it is something more serious. If the young person has not had a panic attack before and does not think they are having one now, you should follow physical first aid guidelines. The first step is to help the person into a supported sitting position (e.g., against a wall).

Ask the young person or check to see whether they are wearing a medical alert bracelet or necklace. If the young person is, follow the instructions on the alert or seek medical assistance. If the young person loses consciousness, apply physical first aid principles. Check for breathing and pulse, and call 911 or an ambulance. When the EMTs arrive, your job is to provide them with the information they request to the best of your ability.

What should I do if I think someone is having a panic attack?

If the young person says that they have had panic attacks before and believes that they are having one now, ask whether the individual needs any kind of help and provide it if possible. Even if the young person knows it is a panic attack, if the young person has chest pain or difficulty breathing, the youth may still want to go to an emergency room or call 911 for help. The feelings and experiences of the young person generally provoke a strong urge to escape or flee the place where the attack begins.[359]

To help calm a young person who is having a panic attack,

- Reassure the person that they are experiencing a panic attack.

- Remain calm.

- Speak to the person in a reassuring but firm manner.

- Be patient.

- Speak clearly and slowly, and use short sentences.

- Invite the person to sit down somewhere comfortable.

- Maintain a comfortable distance from the youth.

- Ask the young person directly what they think might help rather than making assumptions about what they need.

- Do not belittle the person's experience.

- Acknowledge that the terror feels very real, but reassure the person that a panic attack, although very frightening, is not life threatening or dangerous.

- Reassure the young person that they are safe and that the symptoms will pass.

What should I say and do when the panic attack has ended?

After the panic attack is over, help the young person to get information about panic attacks. Tell the young person that if the panic attacks recur and are causing them distress, they should speak to an appropriate professional. Assist the young person and their parents or caregivers to access professional help if they feel they need it.

You should be aware of the services in your community that work with young people with panic attacks. Reassure the young person that effective treatments are available for panic attacks and panic disorder. In addition, you may find it helpful to refer the youth and the family to other resources, such as those listed at the end of *Anxiety in Young People*.

Note: Breathing

It has been widely believed for many years that focusing on breathing during a panic attack can help, either by distracting the person or bringing about a state of calm. Many people still find this to be helpful, and you should not try to stop someone from focusing on breathing if this has helped them before. However, many experts now say that it is not a good idea to actively encourage a person to focus on breathing because it can become an emotional crutch, leading to difficulty with treatments later on.[360] Instead, simply support the person, and if the individual feels distressed, encourage them to seek professional help if the feelings persist.

Self-Care

Assisting a young person who is experiencing a panic attack can be an intense and draining experience. It is important to pay attention to your own emotions and needs (such as proper diet and sleep). Seek and accept support from trusted colleagues, friends, and family. Allow yourself time for reflection and healing. If you talk to someone, remember to respect the young person's privacy; do not share the young person's name or any personal details that might make them identifiable to the person you choose to share with.

Use the resources listed in *Anxiety in Young People* to help create a support network for the young person, the family, and you.

Self-Care

- Have I decided what I will do for self-care?

- Who can I speak with now?

- Who can I call if I feel upset or distressed later?

First Aid for Children and Youth Affected by Traumatic Events

Note

The next two sections address the issue of traumatic events for individuals. Separate guidelines are provided for assisting older adolescents and adults (see *First Aid for Young Adults and Adults Affected by Traumatic Events*). If you are assisting a youth or young adult, consider their age and reaction to the event when choosing which guidelines to use. For younger youth and those whose behaviors in response to an event seem to be more childlike, the child guidelines may be most appropriate. For older youth and those who are responding to the event in a somewhat mature manner, the adult guidelines may be the most appropriate. Use your best judgment and consider how the youth responds, adjusting your approach as necessary.

Facts on Trauma and Traumatic Events[361]

A *traumatic event* is any incident experienced by a person that is perceived to be dangerous and threatens serious injury or death. A traumatic event may be a large-scale disaster or may only happen to a single individual. Common examples of traumas that affect individuals include accidents, assault (including physical or sexual assault, mugging, robbery, or family violence), and witnessing something terrible happen. Mass traumatic events include terrorist attacks, mass shootings, warfare and military activity, and severe weather events (e.g., hurricanes, tornadoes, fires, and floods). Coping with the death of an important person in one's life is especially difficult for children and youth. Young children may also experience traumatic stress in response to painful medical procedures or the sudden loss of a parent or caregiver.[362]

Early childhood trauma generally refers to traumatic experiences that occur to children from birth to six. *Youth Mental Health First Aid® USA* does not focus on early childhood. However, the impact of early childhood trauma may not be apparent until adolescence. Events and reminders of the trauma may bring back fears, intense physical reactions, and posttraumatic stress reactions long after the trauma has occurred.[363] For more information on early childhood trauma, visit the National Child Traumatic Stress Network at www.nctsn.org.

Young People at Heightened Risk of Experiencing Traumatic Events

Young people who are racial and ethnic minorities, are from low-income families, are LGBTQ, or are male are all at increased risk of exposure to trauma. Significantly more boys than girls are exposed to community violence. African American and Hispanic young people have increased risks to their health and life that may result in the development of traumatic stress reactions.[364, 365, 366] In addition, serious injury disproportionately affects boys, youth living in poverty, and Native American youth.[367]

Refugee children experience trauma resulting from war and political violence, displacement and loss of home, malnutrition, separation from caregivers, detention and torture, and many other events affecting their health and well-being.[368]

Adolescents and young adults who identify as LGBTQ or who may be perceived to be LGBTQ may also be more likely to experience harassment or bullying from other youth and significant adults in their lives and may be subjected to verbal, sexual, and physical abuse as well as other forms of trauma.[369]

Historical trauma poses an added burden for American Indian/Alaska Native children and families.[370] *Historical trauma* is cumulative emotional and psychological wounding during the lifespan and across generations, originating from massive group trauma experiences.

Mental Health First Aid Response

Mental Health First Aid often does not occur immediately after the traumatic event. Sometimes, trauma is not a single incident; rather, it may be recurring abuse or bullying. The memories of a traumatic event can suddenly or unexpectedly return weeks, months, or even years afterward. Mental Health First Aid should be used when the first aider becomes aware of the problem.

It is important to know that people can differ in how they react to traumatic events:

- One person may perceive an event as deeply traumatic, but another may not.

- Particular types of trauma affect some individuals more than others.

- A history of trauma may make some people more susceptible to later traumatic events, whereas others become more resilient.

- Youth may respond differently than adults, depending on their age and psychological maturity.

How to Tell Whether a Child has Been Affected by a Traumatic Event

A child who has experienced a traumatic event may react strongly right away; others may have a delayed reaction. If you are helping a youth you know and see on a regular basis, you should be continually observing the youth for signs of distress during the next few weeks or months.

How to Assist

What are the first priorities for helping a youth after a traumatic event?

- Ensure your own safety before offering help to anyone. Before deciding to approach a child or adolescent to offer your help, check for potential dangers (e.g., from fire, weapons, or debris), including any person who may become aggressive.

- If you are helping a child or youth whom you do not know, introduce yourself and explain that you are there to help.

- Find out the youth's name and use it when talking to them.

- Remain calm.

- Do what you can to protect the youth (whether by taking them to a safer location or removing any immediate dangers).

- Reassure the youth that they won't be left alone, so far as this is possible, and ensure them that you, or another adult (such as a professional helper), are available to take care of them.

- Respect the culture of the youth by exhibiting physical and verbal behaviors that demonstrate this respect. For example, it may be more comfortable for the youth if you demonstrate that you care by placing your hand on the youth's shoulder instead of hugging them.

- If you have to leave the youth alone for a few minutes to attend to others, reassure the youth that you will be back soon. However, try not to behave toward the youth in such a way that they feel in continued danger.

- If the youth is injured, give the youth first aid for the injuries and seek medical assistance.

- Watch for signs that their physical or mental state is declining, and be prepared to seek emergency medical assistance.

- Be aware that the youth may suddenly become disoriented or may have internal injuries that reveal themselves more slowly.

- Try to determine what the youth's immediate needs are for food, water, shelter, or clothing.

- Do not take over the role of any professional helpers (police, EMTs, or others).

- Do not make any promises you may not be able to keep. For example, do not promise the youth that you will get them home soon when this may not be the case.

- If you are not the youth's parent or caregiver, and you believe it is appropriate to do so (e.g., will not further endanger the youth), ensure the youth that a parent or caregiver is informed of what has occurred. Do this in a calm and reassuring manner.

What are the priorities if I am helping after a mass traumatic event?[371]

Mass traumatic events are those that affect large numbers of people. They include severe environmental events (such as fires and floods), acts of war and terrorism, and mass shootings. In addition to the more general guidelines in the following section, there are a number of things you need to do.

- Try to keep the youth together with any loved ones and caregivers who are present. If they are not present, or have been separated from the youth in the course of the event, ensure that the youth is reconnected with them as soon as possible.

- Ask the youth what would make them feel better or safer.

- Direct the youth away from traumatic sights and sounds (including media images), people who are injured and very distressed people (e.g., anyone who is screaming, agitated, or aggressive).

- Ask bystanders and the media to stay away from the youth.

How do I talk to a youth who has experienced a traumatic event?[372]

If you know the youth, then you can use these guidelines to offer them ongoing support after a traumatic event. If you do not know the youth, then you can use these guidelines for talking to the youth at any time that you come into contact with them after the traumatic experience; at the scene of a trauma or, later on, at home, in a classroom, or elsewhere.

- It is more important to be genuinely caring than to say all the right things.

- Tell the youth that you understand and care and that you will do your best to keep them safe.

- Talk to the youth using age-appropriate language and explanations.

- Allow the youth to ask questions and answer them as truthfully as possible. Be patient if the youth asks the same question many times, and try to be consistent with answers and information. If you cannot answer a question, admit that you do not know the answer.

- If the youth knows accurate, upsetting details, do not deny them. When someone has died, it can be tempting to soften this news by telling a youth that the person has gone to sleep, but this is best avoided because it may result in the youth's becoming fearful of sleep.

- Do not force or coerce the youth to speak. Never coerce a youth to talk about feelings or memories of the trauma before they are ready to do so.

- If the youth wants to talk about their feelings, then allow them to do so. Some youth prefer to express feelings through writing, drawing, or playing with toys or video games.

- Never tell the youth how they should or should not be feeling. Do not tell the youth to be brave or not to cry, and do not make judgments about feelings.

- Do not get angry if the youth expresses strong emotions; instead, tell them it is okay to feel upset when something bad or scary happens.

- Respect the youth's culture. For example, do not bring up religious or spiritual issues unless you know the youth's specific religious or cultural background.

A youth has told me that they are being abused. What should I do?

Remain calm and reassure the youth that they have done the right thing by telling you and that what happened was not their fault. Tell the youth that you believe them. You need to know the local laws or regulations about reporting suspected child abuse and follow them. For more information, see *Appendix 1, Mandatory Reporters of Child Abuse and Neglect: Summary of State Laws.* Contact the appropriate authorities and work with them to ensure the child's safety. Do not confront the alleged abuser. If it is appropriate for you to do so, perhaps if you have a relationship with the parent or caregiver and you are certain they are not conducting the abuse, notify them. Communicate your concerns and the situation in a calm and reassuring manner. It may be more appropriate for a mental health professional to contact the parents or caregiver and help them through the crisis.

Dealing with temper tantrums and avoidance behaviors

The youth may avoid things that remind them of the trauma (e.g., specific places, driving in the car, certain people, or separation from parents or guardians). Try to figure out what triggers sudden fearfulness, regression, or aggression in the youth. If the youth has temper tantrums or becomes fearful, cries, and becomes clingy to avoid something that reminds them of the trauma, ask the youth what they are afraid of. Do not get angry or call the youth "babyish" if they start acting more immature, for example, by bedwetting, misbehaving, or thumb sucking. If the youth avoids things that remind them of the trauma but does not appear very distressed, ask what they are afraid of and assure them that they are safe.

Should the Youth Receive Professional Help?

Not all youth will need professional help to recover from a traumatic event. The following guidelines can help you to determine whether help is needed.

You should seek professional help for the youth if, for four weeks or more after the trauma,[373]

- The youth is unable to enjoy life at all.

- The youth display sudden, severe, or delayed reactions to the trauma.

- The youth is unable to escape intense, ongoing distressing feelings.

- The youth's reactions and behaviors are interfering with usual activities.

- The youth withdraws from caregivers or friends.

- The youth has temper tantrums or becomes fearful, crying, and clingy to avoid something that reminds them of what happened.

- The youth still feels very upset or fearful.

- The youth acts very differently compared to before the trauma.

- The youth feels jumpy or has nightmares because of, or about, the trauma.

- The youth cannot stop thinking about the trauma.

If at any time the youth becomes suicidal, you should seek immediate professional help.

Self-Care

It is difficult to absorb another person's sadness and trauma, and helping an individual affected by a traumatic event can cause fatigue and traumatic stress symptoms (also called *vicarious trauma* or *compassion fatigue*). It is critical that any first aider prioritize their own emotional well-being. It is important to pay attention to physical needs (proper diet and sleep), and make sure you are asking for and accepting care from your social support network.[374] Seek and accept support from trusted colleagues, friends, and family. Allow yourself time for reflection and healing. If you talk to someone, remember to respect the young person's right to privacy; do not share the person's name or any personal details that might make them identifiable to the person you choose to share with.

Use the *Helpful Resources* listed in *Anxiety in Young People* to find further information and support.

Self-Care

- Have I decided what I will do for self-care?

- Who can I speak with now?

- Who can I call if I feel upset or distressed later?

First Aid for Young Adults and Adults Affected by Traumatic Events

Note

Separate guidelines are provided for assisting children and youth (see *First Aid for Children and Youth Affected by Traumatic Events*). If you are assisting a youth, consider their age and reaction to the event when choosing which guidelines to use. For younger youth and those who seem to behave in a childlike way in response to the event, the child guidelines may be the most appropriate. For older adolescents and those who are responding to the event in a somewhat mature manner, these adult guidelines may be the most appropriate. Use your best judgment and consider how the youth responds, adjusting your approach as necessary.

How to Assist

What are the first priorities for helping someone after a traumatic event?

Ensure your own safety before offering help to anyone. Check for potential dangers, such as fire, weapons, debris, or other people who may become aggressive, before deciding to approach a person to offer help.

If you are helping someone whom you do not know, introduce yourself and explain your role.

Find out the person's name and use it when talking. Remain calm, and do what you can to create a safe environment by taking the person to a safer location or removing any immediate danger.

If the person is injured, it is important to get treatment. If you are able, offer the person first aid and seek medical assistance. If the person seems unhurt, you need to watch for changes in the person's physical or mental state and be prepared to seek emergency medical assistance. Be aware that a person may suddenly become disoriented or may have internal injuries that reveal themselves more slowly.

Determine what the person's immediate needs are for food, water, shelter, or clothing. If there are professional helpers nearby (police, ambulance, or others) who are better able to meet those needs, do not take over their role.

If the person has been a victim of assault, you need to consider the possibility that forensic evidence may need to be collected (e.g., cheek swabs or evidence on clothing or skin). Work to preserve such evidence when possible. For example, the person may want to change their clothes and shower, which may destroy forensic evidence. It may be helpful to put clothing in a bag for law enforcement to take as evidence and suggest to the person that they wait to shower until after a forensic exam. Although collecting evidence is important, you should not force the person to do anything they don't want to do. Do not make promises you may not be able to keep. For example, do not say you will get the person home soon if this is not possible or likely.

What are the priorities if I am helping after a mass traumatic event?

Mass traumatic events are those that affect large numbers of people. They include severe environmental events (such as fires and floods), acts of war and terrorism, and mass shootings. In addition to the general principles outlined above, there are a number of things you need to do:

>> **FIND OUT WHAT EMERGENCY HELP IS AVAILABLE**
   If professional helpers are at the scene, follow their directions.

>> BE RESPONSIVE TO THE COMFORT AND DIGNITY OF THE PERSON YOU ARE HELPING

Offer a blanket or coat to cover them, or ask bystanders or media to move away. Try not to appear rushed or impatient.

>> GIVE TRUTHFUL INFORMATION, BUT ALSO ADMIT WHEN YOU DO NOT KNOW SOMETHING

Tell the person about information sources offered to victims, such as information briefings, fact sheets, and special telephone information helplines, as they become available. Do not give the person any information they do not want to hear, because this can be traumatic in itself.

How do I talk to someone who has just experienced a traumatic event?

- When talking to a person who has experienced a traumatic event, it is more important to be genuinely caring than to say all the right things.

- Show the person that you understand and care, and ask them how they would like to be helped.

- Speak clearly and avoid clinical and technical language, and communicate with the person as an equal rather than as a superior or expert.

- If the person seems unable to understand what is said, you may need to repeat yourself several times.

- Providing support does not have to be complicated; it can involve small things like spending time with the person, having a cup of tea or coffee, chatting about day-to-day life.

- Respect the person's culture by exhibiting verbal and physical behaviors that demonstrate this respect. For example, do not bring up religious or spiritual issues unless you know the person's specific religious or cultural background.

Behavior, such as withdrawal, irritability, and bad temper, may be a response to the trauma, so try not to take such behavior personally. Be friendly, even if the person is being difficult. The person may not be as distressed about what has happened as you might expect, and this is fine. Do not tell the person how they should be feeling. Tell the individual that everyone deals with trauma at their own pace. Be aware that cultural differences may influence the way some people respond; for example, in some cultures, expressing vulnerability or grief around strangers is not considered appropriate.

Should we talk about what happened? How can I support someone in doing so?

It is very important you do not force the person to talk. Remember, you are not the person's therapist. Encourage the person to talk about reactions only if the individual feels ready. If the person does want to talk, do not interrupt to share your own feelings, experiences, or opinions. Be aware that the person may need to talk repetitively about the trauma, so you may need to be willing to listen on more than one occasion. Avoid saying anything that might trivialize the person's feelings, such as "Don't cry" or "Calm down" or anything that minimizes the experience, such as "You should just be glad you're alive."

The person might experience *survivor guilt*, the feeling that it is unfair that others died or were injured when the person was not.

How can I help the person to cope over the next few weeks or months?

If you are helping someone you do not know, unless you are responsible in some professional capacity, it is not expected that you will have further contact. If it is someone close to you, such as a friend or family member, your support can be very helpful.

- Encourage the person to tell others what they need or when they want something rather than assume others will know. Also, encourage the person to identify sources of support, including loved ones and friends, but remember that it is

important to respect the person's need to be alone at times.

- Encourage the person to get plenty of rest and to do things that feel good (such as take baths, read, exercise, or watch television). Encourage the person to think about coping strategies they have successfully used in the past and to spend time in places that are safe and comfortable.

- Be aware that the person may suddenly or unexpectedly remember details of the event and may or may not wish to discuss these details. If this happens, the general principles outlined above can help you to assist the person.

- Discourage the person from using negative coping strategies, such as working too hard, using alcohol or other drugs, or engaging in self-destructive behavior.

When should the person seek professional help?

Not everyone will need professional help to recover from a traumatic event. If the person wants to seek help, offer your support. Be aware of professional help that is available locally, and if the person does not like the first professional they speak to, tell them that it is okay to try a different one. If the person has not indicated a desire for professional help, the following guidelines can help you to determine whether help is needed.

If at any time the person becomes suicidal, seek professional help. *First Aid for Suicidal Thoughts and Behaviors* may be useful in helping you to do this. Also, if at any time the person abuses alcohol or other drugs to deal with the trauma, encourage professional help.

First Aid for a Medical Emergency Resulting from Alcohol Abuse and *First Aid for Acute Effects of Alcohol and Drug Abuse or Misuse* may be useful in helping you to do this.

After four weeks, some return to normal functioning is expected. Encourage professional help if, for four weeks or longer after the trauma, they

- Are still very upset or fearful

- Seem unable to escape intense, ongoing feelings of distress

- Withdraw from family or friends or important relationships are suffering

- Feel jumpy or have nightmares related to the trauma

- Cannot stop thinking about the trauma

- Are unable to enjoy life at all

- Have post trauma symptoms that are interfering with their usual activities

Self-Care

It is difficult to absorb the sadness and trauma of another person, and helping an individual affected by a traumatic event can cause fatigue and traumatic stress symptoms (also called *vicarious trauma* or *compassion fatigue*). It is critical that any first aider prioritize their own emotional well-being. It is important to pay attention to physical needs (proper diet and sleep), and make sure you are asking for and accepting care from your social support network.[375] Seek and accept support from trusted colleagues, friends, and family. Allow yourself time for reflection and healing. If you talk to someone, remember to respect the young person's right to privacy; do not share the young person's name or any personal details that might make them identifiable to the person you choose to share with.

Use the resources listed in *Mental Health First Aid for Youth and Young Adults* to help create a support network for the young person, their family, and yourself.

Use the *Helpful Resources* listed in *Anxiety in Young People* to find further information and support.

Self-Care

- Have I decided what I will do for self-care?

- Who can I speak with now?

- Who can I call if I feel upset or distressed later?

First Aid for Acute Psychosis

Facts on Acute Psychosis

A person who is experiencing psychosis has difficulty distinguishing what is real and what is not. Psychosis can occur as part of several mental disorders such as schizophrenia or bipolar disorder or when a person is intoxicated with a drug.

Acute psychosis may develop gradually over a few days or may seem to come on very suddenly. Acute psychosis can occur without an apparent reason or may be caused by something specific. Possible causes include extra stressors or life events (even positive life events such as a new job or holiday). Forgetting to take medication, or choosing not to, can also trigger a psychotic episode, which is one of the reasons that it is best for people to continue using their medication as prescribed. Some people experience acute psychosis only rarely, perhaps every few years; others experience it more frequently, and some may experience these states several times a year.

In acute psychosis, the person has severe symptoms, such as delusions, hallucinations, disorganized thinking, and odd behaviors. The person may be unable to care for themselves appropriately. The person's behavior may be disruptive or disturbing to others, prompting them to seek assistance for the person's symptoms.

How to Assist

In a crisis situation, remain as calm as possible. Assess the risks involved, such as whether the person will harm self or others. It is important to assess whether the person is at risk of suicide. If you believe the person is at risk, refer to *First Aid for Suicidal Thoughts and Behavior*.

When helping a young person experiencing psychosis, you should

- Communicate to the person in a clear and concise manner, and use short, simple sentences.

- Speak quietly in a nonthreatening tone of voice and at a moderate pace.

- Answer any questions calmly.

- Comply with reasonable requests, which give the person the opportunity to feel somewhat in control.

- Respect the person's culture by exhibiting verbal and physical behaviors that demonstrate this respect.

- If the young person has a safety or crisis plan, follow those instructions.

Assess whether it is safe for the person to be alone; if not, ensure that someone stays with them. Try to find out whether the young person has someone they trust (e.g., close friends or family) and try to enlist their help. If the young person says they have no one they trust, you may need to contact their parents or another caregiver against the young person's wishes. If this becomes necessary, tell the young person whom you are calling and explain that it is for their own safety and that you care about them.

Be aware that the young person might act on a delusion or hallucination. Remember that your primary task is to de-escalate the situation, and therefore do not do anything to further agitate the person. Try to maintain safety and protect the young person, yourself, and others from harm. Make sure you have access to an exit if you feel you are in danger.

You may not be able to de-escalate the situation, and if this is the case, be prepared to call for assistance. If the person is at risk of harming self or others, make sure an evaluation is done by a medical or mental health professional immediately. When the crisis staff arrives, you should convey specific, concise observations about the young person's behavior and symptoms. Explain to the young person who any unfamiliar helpers are, and describe how they are going to help. If your concerns about the person are dismissed by the services you contact, you should persevere in trying to seek support.

Emergency Help is Available in a Variety of Ways:[376]

- If the person is already getting professional help, then the person's current case manager, therapist, or counselor is a good first contact. Most mental health centers and clinics have 24-hour emergency numbers that may connect to a hotline, helpline or directly to a nearby hospital emergency room. Keep the emergency number handy so that it is easy to find in a time of crisis.

- If the person is not already receiving care, a local helpline or a hotline can be a good source of assistance.

- If the situation is very serious and no other help is available, call 911.

If you are not the young person's parent or caregiver, you will need to ensure that a parent or caregiver is informed about what has occurred. Do this in a calm and reassuring manner.

Self-Care

Assisting a young person who is experiencing psychosis can be a emotionally intense experience. It is important to pay attention to your own emotions and needs (such as proper diet and sleep). Seek and accept support from trusted colleagues, friends, and family. Allow yourself time for reflection and healing. If you talk to someone, remember to respect the young person's privacy; do not share the person's name or any personal details that might make them identifiable to the person you choose to share with.

Additional resources, information, and support can be found in *Mental Health First Aid for Youth and Young Adults* and *Psychosis in Young People* to help create a support network for the young person, their family, and you.

Self-Care

- Have I decided what I will do for self-care?

- Who can I speak with now?

- Who can I call if I feel upset or distressed later?

First Aid for a Medical Emergency Resulting From Alcohol Abuse

What Is Alcohol Intoxication, Alcohol Poisoning, Alcohol Withdrawal, and Binge Drinking?

- *Alcohol intoxication* refers to the high amount of alcohol in a person's blood stream, which substantially impairs thinking and behavior.

- *Alcohol poisoning* means the person has a toxic level of alcohol in the blood stream, which can lead to the person's death. The amount of alcohol that causes alcohol poisoning is different for every person.

- *Alcohol withdrawal* refers to the unpleasant symptoms a person experiences when the individual stops drinking or drinks substantially less than usual. Alcohol withdrawal, without the aid of medical attention, may lead to seizures.

- *Binge drinking* is defined as a pattern of heavy drinking. This pattern of drinking usually involves having five or more drinks on a single occasion for men or four or more drinks on a single occasion for women, generally within about two hours.[377]

How to Tell if a Young Person has Alcohol Intoxication

Common signs and symptoms of alcohol intoxication include

- Loss of coordination

- Slurred speech

- Staggering or falling over

- Loud, argumentative, or aggressive behavior

- Vomiting

- Drowsiness or sleepiness.

How to Assist

If the young person is intoxicated

›› STAY CALM

›› COMMUNICATE APPROPRIATELY
Talk with the young person in a respectful manner, and use simple, clear language. Do not laugh at, make fun of, or provoke the person.

›› MONITOR FOR DANGER
While intoxicated, the young person may engage in a wide range of risky activities (such as having unprotected sex, vandalizing property, or driving a car). Assess the situation for potential dangers, and ensure that you, the person, and others are safe. Monitor the young person and the environment to prevent tripping or falling. Ask the person if they have taken any medications or other drugs, in case the young person's condition deteriorates into a medical emergency.

›› ENSURE THE PERSON'S SAFETY

Stay with the young person or ensure they are not left alone. Be aware that the young person may be more intoxicated than they realize. Keep the young person away from machines and dangerous objects. If the young person attempts to drive (or ride a bike), try to discourage the behavior by telling them about the risks to self and others. Only prevent the person from driving if it is safe to do so. If it is unsafe, call law enforcement. Arrange for the young person to go to the hospital if you think they are at risk of self-harm; otherwise, organize a safe mode of transport to get the young person home. If you are not the young person's parent or caregiver, you will need to inform them about what has occurred. Do this in a calm and reassuring manner.

Alcohol intoxication, poisoning, and withdrawal may lead to medical emergencies.

Call 911 or seek medical help if the young person

- Cannot be awakened or is unconscious.

- Has irregular, shallow, or slow breathing.

- Has an irregular, weak, or slow pulse rate.

- Has cold, clammy, pale, or bluish-colored skin.

- Is continuously vomiting.

- Shows signs of a possible head injury (e.g., vomiting and/or talking incoherently).

- Has a seizure.

- Has *delirium tremens*, a state of confusion and visual hallucinations.

- Has *blackouts* (when the person forgets what happened during the drinking episode).

- May have consumed a spiked drink (*drink spiking* is the illegal act of placing a substance into a drink with the intention of causing harm to the drinker; in recent years, media reports have shown drink spiking to be on the rise).

Tips When Calling 911

- Do not be afraid to seek medical help for the young person, even if there may be legal implications.

- When you call 911 or call for an ambulance, it is important that you follow the emergency operator's instructions.

- When asked, describe the young person's symptoms and explain that the young person has been drinking alcohol.

- Give the address of where you are to the 911 operator, and stay with the person until the ambulance arrives.

- It is beneficial for a friend or family member to accompany the person to the hospital because they may be able to provide relevant information.

What to Do While Waiting for the EMTs or Ambulance

Ensure that

- The young person is not left alone.

- No food is given because the person may choke on it if they are not fully conscious.

- The person's airway, breathing, and circulation are monitored.

- If the person is vomiting and conscious, keep the person sitting. Alternatively put the person in the recovery position (see illustration on the next page).

- If the person is hard to wake, they should be placed in the recovery position (see illustration on the next page).

The Recovery Position

Any unconscious person needs **immediate medical attention**, and their **airway must be kept open**.

If an unconscious person is left lying on their back, they could suffocate on their vomit, or their tongue could block their airway. Putting the person in the recovery position will help to keep the airway open (see illustration below). Before placing the young person in the recovery position, check for sharp objects (e.g., broken glass or syringes on the ground). If necessary, clear the person's airway after they have vomited by using their own fingers to clear vomit from their mouth. Keep the person warm without allowing them to overheat. Do not use the recovery position if the person has a major injury, such as a back or neck injury.

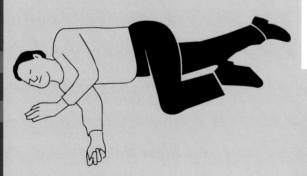

Can I help the young person sober up?

Only time will reverse the effects of intoxication. The body metabolizes approximately one standard drink of alcohol an hour. Drinking black coffee, sleeping, walking, and cold showers will not speed this process up.

What do I do if the intoxicated person becomes aggressive?

If this occurs, follow the advice in *First Aid for Aggressive Behaviors*.

Self-Care

Assisting a young person who is experiencing alcohol intoxication or alcohol poisoning can be an emotionally intense and draining experience. It is important to pay attention to your own emotions and needs (such as proper diet and sleep). Seek and accept support from trusted colleagues, friends, and family. Allow yourself time for reflection and healing. If you talk to someone, remember to respect the young person's privacy; do not share the individual's name or any personal details that might make them identifiable to the person you choose to share with.

Additional resources, information, and support can be found in *Mental Health First Aid for Youth and Young Adults* and *Substance Use and Substance Use Disorders in Young People* to help create a support network for the young person, the family, and you.

Self-Care

- Have I decided what I will do for self-care?

- Who can I speak with now?

- Who can I call if I feel upset or distressed later?

First Aid for Acute Effects of Alcohol and Drug Abuse or Misuse

This section focuses on how the first aider can assist a young person experiencing the acute effects of substance use. The information is relevant to both alcohol and drugs but will highlight drug use because the previous section focuses on alcohol abuse (see *First Aid for a Medical Emergency Resulting from Alcohol Abuse*). Illicit drugs can have varying effects because they are not manufactured in a controlled way. The incidence of prescription drug abuse is also high. It is often difficult to make a distinction between the effects of different drugs. The effects of alcohol and drugs on behavior can vary from person to person depending on how a young person abuses alcohol or on the type of drug used and the amount taken. *Overdose* refers to use of an amount of a drug, legal or illegal, that could cause death. Overdose can quickly lead to a loss of consciousness.

How to Tell Whether a Young Person is Experiencing Acute Effects from Drug Abuse or Misuse

- Some drugs have *stimulating effects* (uppers, such as cocaine and amphetamines), including making the person feel energetic and confident. Signs of more acute intoxication include becoming frustrated or angry, having a racing heart, overheating, or dehydration.

- Some drugs have *hallucinogenic effects* (trips, such as with mushrooms and LSD), including hallucinations, delusions, and strong feelings of affection for others. Signs of more acute intoxication include having more negative hallucinations and delusions and becoming fearful or paranoid.

- Some drugs have *depressant effects* (downers, such as marijuana and tranquilizers), including fatigue, slurred speech, and slowed reflexes. Signs of more acute intoxication include feelings of having trouble moving, vomiting, and loss of consciousness.

Some drugs (e.g., ecstasy and marijuana) may have multiple effects, which is why it can be hard to tell what sort of drug has been used.

How to Assist

If the person is in a substance-affected state,

›› STAY CALM

›› COMMUNICATE APPROPRIATELY
Talk with the young person in a respectful manner, and use simple, clear language. Repeat simple requests and instructions because the person may find it difficult to comprehend what has been said. Do not speak in an angry manner. Do not laugh at, make fun of, or provoke the person.

›› MONITOR FOR DANGER
While in a substance-affected state, the person may engage in a wide range of risky activities (such as having unprotected sex, vandalizing property, or driving a car). Assess the situation for potential dangers, and ensure that you, the person, and others are safe. Monitor the person and environment to prevent tripping or falling.

›› ENSURE THE PERSON'S SAFETY
Substance use can lead to a range of medical emergencies. Stay with the young person or ensure they are not left alone. Be aware that

the young person may be more affected than they realize.

>> Encourage the person to tell someone if they start to feel sick or uneasy and to call emergency services if they have an adverse reaction.

>> Keep the person away from machines and dangerous objects. If the person attempts to drive a vehicle (or ride a bike), you should discourage them (e.g., by telling the young person about the risks to both self and others). Only prevent the person from driving if it is safe for you to do so. If it is unsafe, call the police or 911.

>> Arrange for the person to go to a hospital if you think the person is a risk to self; otherwise, organize a safe mode of transport to get the person home.

>> If you are not the young person's parent or caregiver, you will need to ensure that a parent or caregiver is informed of what has occurred. Do this in a calm and reassuring manner.

When to Call 911 or an Ambulance

Call 911 or seek medical help if the young person

- Is unconscious or cannot be awakened.

- Has irregular, shallow, or slow breathing.

- Has an irregular, weak, or slow pulse rate.

- Has cold, clammy, pale, or bluish-colored skin.

- Vomits continuously.

- Shows signs of a possible head injury (e.g., vomiting and/or talking incoherently).

- Has a seizure.

- Appears delirious or confused.

- Has hallucinations.

- Is overheated or dehydrated.

Tips When Calling 911 or an Ambulance

- Do not be afraid to seek medical help for the person, even if there may be legal implications for the person. Be aware that EMTs, paramedics, and hospital staff are there to help the person and not to enforce the law. When abuse is suspected, mandatory reporting varies from state to state, but in all states, territories, and the District of Columbia, any person is permitted to report.

- Follow the operator's instructions.

- When asked, describe the young person's symptoms and explain that the person has been using alcohol or drugs. Try to get detailed information about what substances the person has taken by either asking the person and their friends or visually scanning the environment for clues.

- Give the address of where you are to the 911 operator, and stay with the person until the ambulance arrives.

- It is beneficial for a friend or family member to accompany the person to the hospital because they may be able to provide relevant information.

What to Do While Waiting for EMTs or an Ambulance

Ensure that

- The young person is not left alone.

- No food is given to the person because the person may choke on it if they are not fully conscious.

- The person's airway, breathing, and circulation are monitored.

- If the person is hard to wake, put them in the recovery position (see *Helping an unconscious person*).

- Give first aid for any overheating or dehydration (see *Helping a person who is overheating or dehydrated*).

Helping an Unconscious Person

Any unconscious person needs **immediate medical attention**, and their **airway must be kept open**. If left lying on their back, the person could suffocate on vomit or the tongue could block the airway. Putting the young person in the recovery position will help to keep the airway open. Before placing the person in the recovery position, check for sharp objects (e.g., broken glass or syringes on the ground). If necessary, clear the person's airway after they have vomited by using the person's own fingers to clear vomit from the mouth. Keep the person warm without allowing them to overheat. Do not use the recovery position if the person has a major injury, such as back or neck injury.

The Recovery Position

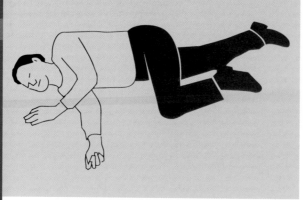

Helping a Person Who is Overheating or Dehydrated

Overheating or dehydration from drug misuse can lead to a medical emergency. Prolonged dancing in a hot environment while on some drugs (e.g., ecstasy) without adequate water intake can cause the person's body temperature to rise to dangerous levels.

Symptoms of overheating or dehydration include

- Feeling hot, exhausted, and weak.
- Persistent headache.
- Pale, cool, clammy skin.
- Rapid breathing and shortness of breath.
- Fatigue, thirst, and nausea.
- Giddiness and feeling faint.

If the young person is showing symptoms of overheating or dehydration, keep them calm and seek medical help immediately. Encourage the young person to stop the physical activity, such as dancing, and to rest in a place that is quiet and cool. While waiting for help to arrive, gradually reduce the young person's body temperature. Loosen any restrictive clothing, remove any additional layers, and encourage the person to sip nonalcoholic fluids (e.g., water and soft drinks). Prevent the young person from drinking too much water at once because it may lead to a coma or death. Do not allow the young person to drink any alcohol because it will further dehydrate them.

Helping a Person Who has Been Sniffing a Substance

If the young person has been using inhalants, you may notice items such as glue, lighter fluid, spray paint, gasoline, or shoe polish nearby and a strong smell of fumes. The person may be euphoric, dizzy, slurring speech, or uncommunicative. Stay with the person, or make sure they stay somewhere safe until the effects have worn off. Medical help should be sought if the effects are not wearing off after the person has stopped sniffing.

The use of inhalants can be fatal, as a result of either long-term use or "sudden sniffing death." Using inhalants can destroy the cells in the brain, the liver, and the kidneys. The person's heart and breathing are affected, and sudden exercise or a shock can cause the heart to stop. To reduce the risk of sudden sniffing death, do not threaten or chase the young person, and inform other people around that it is dangerous to chase or overexcite the person.

Also, the risk that inhalants may catch on fire and cause severe burns is high. Keep the young person away from anything that could cause inhalants to catch on fire (e.g., a lit cigarette, a cigarette lighter, or a campfire).

Try to create a calm environment for the young person by asking any onlookers to move. If possible, move the young person to a safe place with plenty of fresh air, or open any doors and windows. If the young person is not willing to hand over the inhalants, try to keep the young person talking or encourage the young person to do something with both hands so the young person is not actively sniffing.

What do I do if the young person becomes aggressive?

If this occurs, follow the advice in *First Aid for Aggressive Behaviors.*

Self-Care

Assisting a young person who is experiencing acute affects from any substance abuse can be an emotionally intense and draining experience. It is important to pay attention to your own emotions and needs (such as proper diet and sleep). Seek and accept support from trusted colleagues, friends, and family. Allow yourself time for reflection and healing. If you talk to someone, remember to respect the young person's privacy; do not share the young person's name or any personal details that might make them identifiable to the person you choose to share with.

Additional resources, information, and support can be found in *Mental Health First Aid for Youth and Young Adults* and *2.5 Substance Use and Substance Use Disorders in Young People* to help create a support network for the young person, their family, and you.

Self-Care

- Have I decided what I will do for self-care?

- Who can I speak with now?

- Who can I call if I feel upset or distressed later?

First Aid for Aggressive Behaviors

Facts on Aggressive Behaviors

Most people with mental health challenges or mental health disorders are not dangerous to others. Only a small portion (approximately 10 percent) of violence in society results from mental illness.[378, 379, 380] Depression and anxiety disorders rarely result in violent behavior toward others. However, the risk of violence is increased for people who have substance use disorders, personality disorders, or psychosis.[381] The use of alcohol or other drugs has a stronger association with violence than do mental disorders. Many crimes are committed by people who are intoxicated with alcohol or other drugs.

Youth and children may also exhibit challenging behaviors, which may include aggression. A child or youth may not be able to explain that the aggressive behavior is related to a mental health challenge, disorder, or severe emotional distress. Children with traumatic stress generally have difficulty regulating their behaviors and emotions. They may be clingy and fearful of new situations, easily frightened, difficult to console, aggressive and impulsive, or all of these.[382]

Aggressive, negative, defiant, destructive, or hostile behavior may also be symptoms of ADHD co-occurring with disruptive behavior disorders, such as oppositional defiant disorder or conduct disorder.[383]

How to Tell Whether a Young Person is Exhibiting Aggressive Behavior

Aggression has different components: verbal (e.g., insults or threats), behavioral (e.g., pounding, throwing things, or violating personal space), and emotional (e.g., raised voice or looks angry). What is seen as aggression can vary between individuals and across cultures. Aggressive behaviors may also be a response to fear. It is best to prevent aggression; therefore, as soon as you see it, take action to de-escalate the behavior. If you are concerned that a young person is becoming aggressive, you need to take steps to protect yourself and others.

How to Assist

■ Ensure your own safety. You should never put yourself at risk, and you must always ensure you have access to an exit.

■ If you are frightened, seek outside help immediately. Similarly, if the person's aggression escalates out of control at any time, you should remove yourself from the situation and call for emergency assistance (e.g., 911 or the police).

■ Take any threats or warnings seriously, particularly if the person believes they are being persecuted.

■ Remain as calm as possible, and try to de-escalate the situation.

How to De-escalate the Situation

■ Speak slowly and confidently with a gentle, caring tone of voice.

■ Avoid raising your voice or talking too fast.

■ Do not respond in a hostile, disciplinary, or challenging manner.

■ Do not argue with or threaten the young person, because it may increase fear or prompt aggressive behavior.

■ Use positive words (such as "Stay calm") instead of negative words (such as "Don't fight"). Ask

"What's happened?" rather than "What's wrong with you?"

- Avoid nervous behavior (e.g., shuffling your feet, fidgeting, or making abrupt movements).

- Do not restrict the young person's movement (e.g., if they want to pace up and down the room).

- Keep your distance from the youth, carefully calculated for their cultural comfort.

- Remain aware that certain acts, such as involving the police, might exacerbate the situation.

- Consider taking a break from the conversation to allow the young person a chance to calm down.

- Invite the young person to sit down if they are standing.

- If the young person is responsive, ask them if they have a safety or crisis plan in place, and work with them to follow the plan as well as you can.

For youth, how you behave during a challenging situation is important in de-escalating the behavior. You are modeling the emotions and behaviors you want them to show. Keep your composure, your body language relaxed (your arms at your sides), and your distance from the youth carefully calculated for cultural comfort and safety.

Depending on the situation, calling 911 may include arrival of the police, especially if the situation becomes unsafe. When calling 911 or the police, describe the person's behaviors rather than try to make a diagnosis of your own. If you suspect the person's aggression is related to a mental health problem, tell law enforcement that you need their help to obtain medical or mental health responders. If the young person is intoxicated, tell them that you believe the young person is intoxicated and what substances you believe they have used. In either case, you should tell the police whether you believe the person may have a weapon of any kind (e.g., knife, gun, any sharp object).

Although important, consider the effect involving law enforcement may have on the youth. According to the National Federation of Families for Children's Mental Health *Law Enforcement and Children's Mental Health Roundtable Discussion, Executive Summary*,

Law enforcement officers are generally trained to be action oriented, aiming to solve problems quickly. When called to respond to a situation, they have a certain amount of information and a particular set of tools at their disposal. They also have federal, state, local, and/or tribal regulations, laws, and policies that guide and mandate their actions. Children and youth with mental health challenges and their families have been impacted by the stigma surrounding mental health and are often isolated. Police arriving at their door likely means more negative attention from the community, fear of losing control of their family's situation, and even more distrust and anger at the systems, which have failed to help them…. And, the stigma may result in some police officers not knowing that mental health challenges in children and youth are real and are not the fault of their parents.[384]

Become familiar with helpful resources in your community. Some areas have specialized services such as mobile crisis units that can respond immediately.[385] Be aware that critical mental health resources do not exist in every community, especially in rural areas. If you have an ongoing relationship with the youth, it may be helpful for you to work with the youth, their family, other mental health professionals, and informal supports to develop a safety plan for the youth. The *safety plan* lays out clear steps for the youth and others to take should the youth feel that they may become aggressive. Some of these strategies may include complementary and alternative practices.

Self-Care

■ Have I decided what I will do for self-care?

■ Who can I speak with now?

■ Who can I call if I feel upset or distressed later?

Self-Care

Assisting a youth or young adult who is experiencing an aggressive episode can be an emotionally intense and draining experience. It is important to pay attention to your own emotions and needs (such as proper diet and sleep). Seek and accept support from trusted colleagues, friends, and family. Allow yourself time for reflection and healing. If you talk to someone, remember to respect the young person's privacy; do not share the young person's name or any personal details that might make them identifiable to the person you choose to share with.

Additional resources, information, and support are listed in *Mental Health First Aid for Youth and Young Adults* to help create a support network for the young person, the family, and you.

APPENDICES

APPENDIX 1:

Mandatory Reporters of Child Abuse and Neglect: Summary of State Laws[386]

Series: State Statutes
Author(s): Child Welfare Information Gateway
Year Published: 2010
Current Through April 2010

This brief introduction summarizes how states address this topic in statute. To access the statutes for a specific state or territory, visit the State Statutes Search at http://www.childwelfare.gov/systemwide/laws_policies/state/

All states, the District of Columbia, American Samoa, Guam, the Northern Mariana Islands, Puerto Rico, and the U.S. Virgin Islands have statutes identifying persons who are required to report child maltreatment under specific circumstances.

Professionals Required to Report

Approximately 48 states, the District of Columbia, American Samoa, Guam, the Northern Mariana Islands, Puerto Rico, and the Virgin Islands designate professions whose members are mandated by law to report child maltreatment.[1] Individuals designated as mandatory reporters typically have frequent contact with children. Such individuals may include:

- Social workers

- Teachers and other school personnel

- Physicians and other health-care workers

- Mental health professionals

- Child care providers

- Medical examiners or coroners

- Law enforcement officers

Some other professions frequently mandated across the states include commercial film or photograph processors (in 11 states, Guam, and Puerto Rico), substance abuse counselors (in 14 states), and probation or parole officers (in 17 States).[2] Seven States and the District of Columbia include domestic violence workers on the list of mandated reporters, while seven states and the District of Columbia include animal control or humane officers.[3] Court-appointed special advocates are mandatory reporters in nine states.[4] Members of the clergy now are required to report in 26 states.[5]

Reporting by Other Persons

In approximately 18 states and Puerto Rico, any person who suspects child abuse or neglect is required to report. Of these 18 states, 16 states and Puerto Rico specify certain professionals who must report but also require all persons to report suspected abuse or neglect, regardless of profession.[6] New Jersey and Wyoming require all persons to report without specifying any professions. In all other states, territories, and the District of Columbia, any person is permitted to report. These voluntary reporters of abuse are often referred to as "permissive reporters."

Standards for Making a Report

The circumstances under which a mandatory report must be made vary from state to state. Typically, a report must be made when the reporter, in their official capacity, *suspects or has reasons to believe* that a child has been abused or neglected. Another standard frequently used is when the reporter has knowledge of, or observes a child being subjected to, conditions that would reasonably result in harm to the child. Permissive reporters follow the same standards when electing to make a report.

Privileged Communications

Mandatory reporting statutes also may specify when a communication is privileged. "Privileged communications" is the statutory recognition of the right to maintain confidential communications between professionals and their clients, patients, or congregants. To enable states to provide protection to maltreated children, the reporting laws in most states and territories restrict this privilege for mandated reporters. All but three states and Puerto Rico currently address the issue of privileged communications within their reporting laws, either affirming the privilege or denying it (i.e., not allowing privilege to be grounds for failing to report).[7] For instance:

- The physician-patient and husband-wife privileges are the most common to be denied by states.

- The attorney-client privilege is most commonly affirmed.

- The clergy-penitent privilege is also widely affirmed, although that privilege usually is limited to confessional communications and, in some states, denied altogether.[8]

Inclusion of the Reporter's Name in the Report

Most states maintain toll-free telephone numbers for receiving reports of abuse or neglect.[9] Reports may be made anonymously to most of these reporting numbers, but states find it helpful to their investigations to know the identity of reporters. Approximately 18 states, the District of Columbia, American Samoa, Guam, and the Virgin Islands currently require mandatory reporters to provide their names and contact information, either at the time of the initial oral report or as part of a written report.[10] The laws in Connecticut, Delaware, and Washington allow child protection workers to request the name of the reporter. In Wyoming, the reporter does not have to provide their identity as part of the written report, but if the person takes and submits photographs or x rays of the child, the reporter's name must be provided.

Disclosure of the Reporter's Identity

All jurisdictions have provisions in statute to maintain the confidentiality of abuse and neglect records. The identity of the reporter is specifically protected from disclosure to the alleged perpetrator in 39 states, the District of Columbia, Puerto Rico, American Samoa, Guam, Puerto Rico, and the Northern Mariana Islands.[11] This protection is maintained even when other information from the report may be disclosed.

Release of the reporter's identity is allowed in some jurisdictions under specific circumstances or to specific departments or officials. For example, disclosure of the reporter's identity can be ordered by the court when there is a compelling reason to disclose (California, Mississippi, Tennessee, Texas, and Guam) or upon a finding that the reporter knowingly made a false report (Alabama, Arkansas, Connecticut, Kentucky, Louisiana, Minnesota, South Dakota, Vermont, and Virginia). In some jurisdictions (California, Florida, Minnesota, Tennessee, Texas, Vermont, the District of Columbia, and Guam), the reporter can waive confidentiality and give consent to the release of their name.

APPENDIX 1:

Endnotes

1   The word *approximately* is used to stress the fact that states frequently amend their laws. This information is current through April 2010. At that time, New Jersey and Wyoming were the

only two states that did not enumerate specific professional groups as mandated reporters but required all persons to report.

2   Film processors are mandated reporters in Alaska, California, Colorado, Georgia, Illinois, Iowa, Louisiana, Maine, Missouri, Oklahoma, and South Carolina. Substance abuse counselors are required to report in Alaska, California, Connecticut, Illinois, Iowa, Kansas, Massachusetts, Nevada, New York, North Dakota, Oregon, South Carolina, South Dakota, and Wisconsin. Probation or parole officers are mandated reporters in Arkansas, California, Colorado, Connecticut, Hawaii, Illinois, Louisiana, Massachusetts, Minnesota, Missouri, Nevada, North Dakota, South Dakota, Texas, Vermont, Virginia, and Washington.

3   Domestic violence workers are mandated reporters in Alaska, Arizona, Arkansas, Connecticut, Illinois, Maine, and South Dakota. Humane officers are mandated reporters in California, Colorado, Illinois, Maine, Ohio, Virginia, and West Virginia.

4   Arkansas, California, Louisiana, Maine, Montana, Oregon, Virginia, Washington, and Wisconsin.

5   Alabama, Arizona, Arkansas, California, Colorado, Connecticut, Illinois, Louisiana, Maine, Massachusetts, Michigan, Minnesota, Mississippi, Missouri, Montana, Nevada, New Hampshire, New Mexico, North Dakota, Ohio, Oregon, Pennsylvania, South Carolina, Vermont, West Virginia, and Wisconsin. For more information, see Child Welfare Information Gateway's *Clergy as Mandatory Reporters of Child Abuse and Neglect* at www.childwelfare.gov/ systemwide/laws_policies/statutes/ clergymandated.cfm.

6   Delaware, Florida, Idaho, Indiana, Kentucky, Maryland, Mississippi, Nebraska, New Hampshire, New Mexico, North Carolina, Oklahoma, Rhode Island, Tennessee, Texas, and Utah.

7   Connecticut, Mississippi, and New Jersey do not currently address the issue of privileged communications within their reporting laws. The issue of privilege may be addressed elsewhere in the statutes of these states, such as rules of evidence.

8   New Hampshire, North Carolina, Oklahoma, Rhode Island, Texas, and West Virginia disallow the use of the clergy-penitent privilege as grounds for failing to report suspected child abuse or neglect. For a more complete discussion of the requirement for clergy to report child abuse and neglect, see the Information Gateway's *Clergy as Mandatory Reporters of Child Abuse and Neglect* at www.childwelfare.gov/systemwide/laws_policies/ statutes/clergymandated.cfm.

9   For state-specific information about these hotlines, see Information Gateway's *Child Abuse Reporting Numbers* at www.childwelfare.gov/pubs/reslist/ rl_dsp.cfm?rs_id=5&rate_chno=11-11172.

10   California, Colorado, Florida, Illinois, Indiana, Iowa, Louisiana, Maine, Massachusetts, Minnesota, Mississippi, Missouri, Nebraska, New Mexico, New York, North Carolina, Pennsylvania, and Vermont have this requirement.

11   The statutes in Alaska, Arizona, Delaware, Idaho, Maryland, Massachusetts, New Hampshire, Oklahoma, Rhode Island, West Virginia, Wyoming, and the Virgin Islands do not specifically protect reporter identity but do provide for confidentiality of records in general.

This publication is a product of the State Statutes Series prepared by Child Welfare Information Gateway. While every attempt has been made to be as complete as possible, additional information on these topics may be in other sections of a State's code as well as agency regulations, case law, and informal practices and procedures.

APPENDIX 2:
Glossary of Terms

This glossary includes a list of treatment approaches, interventions, services, and supports in children's mental health. Although the list is not exhaustive, this glossary includes many terms used throughout this manual. Five major resources were used and adapted for this glossary:

- National Association of State Mental Health Program Directors; www.nasmhpd.org/glossary.cfm

- Statewide Children's Wraparound Initiative Glossary and Acronym List; www.oregon.gov/OHA/amh/wraparound/glossary.pdf

- IMPACT's (system of care in Ingham County, Michigan) Glossary of Terms; www.impactsystemofcare.org/glossary-of-terms.html

- Burns and Hoagwood's (2002) *Community Treatment for Youth* and the National Center for Trauma-Informed Care; www.samhsa.gov/nctic/trauma.asp

Alternative therapies are treatments for mental health challenges other than the traditional mental health, hospitalization, and institutional care options (e.g., biofeedback, yoga, therapeutic massage, light therapy).

Assertive case management is a form of case management intended to increase daily-task functioning, residential stability, and independence; reduce hospitalizations and inpatient service use; and promote continuity of outpatient care.

Assertive Community Treatment (ACT), sometimes referred to as *Program of Assertive Community Treatment (PACT)*, is a team-based approach to care in which the care of the person is managed by a team of health professionals, such as a psychiatrist, nurse, psychologist, and social worker. Care is available 24 hours a day and is tailored to the person's individual needs. Support is provided to family members as well.

Behavioral health care includes assessment and treatment of both mental and substance use or abuse disorders.

Case management is a treatment approach that links a variety of formal and informal services and supports.

Community-based treatment focuses on community- and home-based services so individuals can remain with family, in school, and in the community.

Community mental health services are public mental health services and supports provided directly to those in need of assistance in their home communities.

Comprehensive service or resource centers are "one-stop-shopping" service centers in which services (e.g., case management, financial, mental health, health) are all located in the same place.

Consumer-operated programs are services that are controlled and operated by consumers and that emphasize peer support and self-help as their operational approach.

Continuum of care describes the entire service array, including institutional and community mental health services, social support groups, and volunteer services that can be customized to meet the individual's needs.

Crisis intervention teams are specialized teams skilled in de-escalating potentially volatile situations (e.g., attempted suicides, nonfatal aggressive acts), gathering relevant history, and assessing health information and the individual's social support system.

Crisis residential treatment services are short-term, around-the-clock treatment provided in an unlocked, nonhospital setting during a crisis. The purpose of this treatment is to avoid hospitalization, stabilize the young person, and determine the next steps.

Cross-training is the implementation of a training program to educate individuals across disciplines (e.g., juvenile justice, mental health, child welfare, education, primary health) on the issues and concerns to help develop a more coordinated approach to the needs of individuals with behavioral health challenges.

Cultural competence is recognition of and response to cultural concerns of ethnic and racial groups, including their histories, traditions, beliefs, and value systems to help child and family service systems and professionals create better services for diverse populations. Cultural competence entails a set of behaviors, attitudes, and policies that enable a system, agency, or professionals to work effectively in cross-cultural situations.

Day treatment refers to nonresidential mental health services that allow the youth to return home at night.

Developmental disability is a substantial handicap in mental or physical functioning, with onset before age 18 and of indefinite duration (e.g., autism, cerebral palsy, uncontrolled epilepsy, mental retardation).

Diversion programs are treatment programs that address the specific needs of a person with a mental health challenge who has been diverted from the criminal justice system either before arrest or before trial.

Drop-in centers are peer-run programs that are housed at a central location and focus on social skills development and support in an informal setting.

Early intervention refers to recognizing warning signs that a youth is at risk for mental health problems and taking early action to address the problems. Early intervention can help youth get better more quickly and prevent problems from becoming worse.

Eligibility criteria refer to guidelines for determining whether a child is qualified to receive services from an agency. These guidelines usually include age, disability, and income but can also cover where the family resides, gender of the child, and availability of medical insurance.

Evaluation is a process that begins with a professional assessment and results in an opinion about a child's mental and emotional state. It may include recommendations about treatment or placement.

Evidence-based practices are interventions for which consistent scientific evidence has shown that they improve individual outcomes.

Family education and support are activities that provide information and education regarding mental disorders and their treatment and related topics to families and significant others. This activity is often led by parents.

Home-based services refer to short-term services provided in the home to help a family deal with a youth's mental health problems.

Individualized education program (IEP) refers to a written plan that describes a student's individual needs and the special education services that will be provided.

Initial referral or intake is a process used by an agency to determine whether a child and family are eligible to receive services.

Inpatient facilities are medical facilities—usually a hospital—where individuals stay for a period of time to receive treatment. Most mental health systems differentiate between acute care (short-term) facilities and long-term care facilities.

Inpatient hospitalization refers to around-the-clock mental health treatment in a hospital setting. The purpose of inpatient hospitalization is to stabilize and treat a youth in crisis and to prevent harm to the youth and to others.

Integrated services are delivery of treatment for both primary and mental health care in a single setting. Integrated services may also refer to treatment for co-occurring mental illness and substance abuse disorders offered by a single agency.

Intermediate care facility for the mentally retarded is a public or private facility, the primary purpose of which is to provide health or rehabilitative services to individuals with mental retardation or related conditions (e.g., cerebral palsy).

Mentoring is where a nonprofessional with good youth relationship skills helps youth to increase their engagement and functioning in school and community.

Mobile crisis teams are mental health service professionals who provide on-scene responses in mental health emergencies.

Multisystemic therapy is a treatment approach in which a clinician or clinical team work with parents in the home and neighborhood around management of youth problems as needed (e.g., daily basis, weekly basis) for a limited period of time.

Outpatient treatment is any professional care that takes place when a person is not admitted to a hospital or inpatient setting, such as a residential care facility. This treatment can include diagnosis, assessment, and family and individual counseling.

Parent advocates are individuals who have been trained to help families get the services and supports they need. Typically, parent advocates are family members who have raised a child with a behavioral or emotional problem and have worked with many of the agencies and providers in the community.

Peer services and supports is a generic reference to services that are provided by individuals who have experience in accessing services for themselves or their children (e.g., family to family, youth to youth).

Psychiatrists are medical doctors specializing in emotional, behavioral, and mental disorders. Qualified to prescribe medication and admit to hospitals.

Psychological evaluation is an assessment that tests a child's intelligence, aptitudes and abilities, social skills, emotional development, and thinking skills.

Psychologists are mental health professionals with advanced training who can administer psychological tests and evaluate and treat emotional disorders.

A psychologist is not a medical doctor and cannot prescribe medications.

Psychopharmacologists are psychiatrists who specialize in treating mental health disorders with medications.

Psychosocial treatment refers to interventions that target the psychological and social aspects of the mental disorder or mental health challenge.

Residential services refer to treatment in a setting that provides educational instruction and 24-hour care for youth who require continuous supervision and care.

Respite care is a temporary service whereby someone else takes care of the young person for a few hours or a few days so the family can have a short break. Respite care can be provided in the child's home, at the care provider's home, at a special facility, or at other community locations.

Screening is a preliminary assessment for mental health challenges done by a health or mental health professional.

Service planning teams (child and family teams) are a group of individuals selected by the parents to help develop a young person's service plan. The team can include family members, professionals, friends, experts, and support people.

Service plans are written documents describing all the services and supports the youth and family will receive. Typically, plans include information about the youth's and family's strengths, problems, and needs and spell out what the services and supports are designed to accomplish and how progress will be assessed.

Support services are the care provided that are not strictly medical but are nonetheless considered to be necessary to the recovery and treatment process (e.g., supports to maintain independent housing, education, employment, or other activities associated with community integration).

System of Care is a spectrum of effective, community-based services and supports for children and youth with or at risk for mental or other challenges and their families, that is organized into a coordinated network, builds meaningful partnerships with families and youth, and addresses their cultural and linguistic needs, in order to help them function better at home, in school, in the community, and throughout life.

Telemedicine or telepsychiatry is the delivery of health care or psychiatry via telecommunications (typically special medical computers) by a qualified mental health professional.

Therapeutic foster care is a home with trained foster parents where a youth with an emotional disturbance lives and has access to other support services.

Therapeutic group homes are community-based, homelike settings providing intensive treatment services with 24-hour supervision. Services offered in this setting try both to avoid inpatient hospitalization and to move the youth to a less restrictive living situation.

Transition refers to the process of moving to another setting. Transition can also mean moving to another activity, such as from evening to bedtime.

Transitional services are services that help youth move into adulthood or into the adult mental health system. These services include mental health care, supported housing, and vocational services.

Trauma-focused cognitive behavioral therapy is a treatment model that incorporates elements of cognitive behavioral, attachment, humanistic, empowerment, and family therapy models for traumatized children.

Trauma-informed care refers to when every part of an agency's organization, management, and service delivery system includes a basic understanding of how trauma affects the life of an individual seeking services. Trauma-informed organizations, programs, and services understand the vulnerabilities or triggers of trauma

survivors, so these services and programs can be more supportive and avoid retraumatization.

Trauma-specific treatment is designed specifically to address the consequences of trauma on the individual and to facilitate healing.

Treatment foster care is a service provided by foster parents with professional training who are supervised to work with children with mental health challenges living in foster care homes.

Vocational rehabilitation is a term that covers a wide range of services designed to assist individuals with disabilities in regaining skills needed to function in the workplace, generally delivered under the auspices of a state department of vocational rehabilitation.

Wraparound is a team approach that involves all individuals who are relevant to the well-being of the young person (such as family members, teachers, and social service providers) in setting goals with the young person, and developing an individualized set of services and supports. Wraparound services and supports are usually provided in the young person's home or community.

ENDNOTES: REFERENCES

1   Kitchener, B.A., Jorm, A.F. (2002). Mental health first aid training for the public: Evaluation of effects on knowledge, attitudes and helping behavior. *BMC*, 2: 10.

2   Kitchener, B.A., Jorm, A.F. (2004). Mental health first aid training in a workplace setting: A randomized controlled trial [ISRCTN13249129]. *BMC Psychiatry*, 4: 23.

3   Jorm, A. F., Kitchener, B. A., O'Kearney, R., & Dear, K.B.G. (2004). Mental health first aid training of the public in a rural area: A cluster randomized trial [ISRCTN53887541]. *BMC Psychiatry*, 4: 33.

4   Jorm, A.F., Kitchener, B.A., & Mugford, S.K. (2005). Experiences in applying skills learned in a mental health first aid training course: A qualitative study of participants' stories. *BMC Psychiatry*, 5: 43.

5   Hossain, D., Gorman, D., & Eley, R. (2009). Enhancing the knowledge and skills of advisory and extension agents in mental health issues of farmers. *Australasian Psychiatry*, 17: 116 - 20.

6   Sartore, G.M., Kelly, B., Stain, H.J., Fuller, J., Fragar, L., & Tonna, A. (2008). Improving mental health capacity in rural communities: Mental health first aid delivery in drought-affected rural New South Wales. *Australian Journal of Rural Health*, 16: 313-8.

7   York Consulting. (2004). *Evaluation of Mental Health First Aid Pilot Project in Scotland.* Edinburgh: Scottish Development Centre for Mental Health.

8   Kilpatrick, D.G., & Saunders, B.E. (1997). *Prevalence and consequences of child victimization: Results from the National Survey of Adolescents.* National Crime Victims Research and Treatment Center, Medical University of South Carolina.

9   Jennings, A. (2004). *The damaging consequences of violence and trauma.* Alexandria, VA: National Technical Assistance Center for State Mental Health Planning, National Association of State Mental Health Program Directors, under contract with the Center for Mental Health Services, Substance Abuse and Mental Health Services Administration, U.S. Department of Health and Human Services.

10 Kessler, R.C., Chiu, W.T., Demler, O. & Walters, E.E. (2005). Prevalence, severity, and comorbidity of twelve-month DSM-IV disorders in the National Comorbidity Survey Replication (NCS-R). *Archives of General Psychiatry*, 62, 617-627.

11 Kessler, R.C., Berglund, P.A., Demler, O., Jin, R. & Walters, E.E. (2005). Lifetime prevalence and age-of-onset distributions of DSM-IV Disorders in the National Comorbidity Survey Replication (NCS-R). *Archives of General Psychiatry*, 62, 593-602.

12 Cassels, C. (2010). First National Prevalence Data of Mental Disorders in American Youth released. *Journal of the American Academy of Child and Adolescent Psychiatry*, 49:980-989.

13 U.S. Public Health Service. (2000). *Report of the Surgeon General's Conference on Children's Mental Health: A National Action Agenda.* Washington, DC: Department of Health and Human Services.

14 New Freedom Commission on Mental Health. (2003). *Achieving the Promise: Transforming Mental Health Care in America: Final Report* (DHHS Pub. No. SMA-03-3832). Rockville, MD.

15 New Freedom Commission on Mental Health. (2003). *Achieving the Promise: Transforming Mental Health Care in America: Final Report* (DHHS Pub. No. SMA-03-3832), p. 5. Rockville, MD.

16 Friesen, B. J. (2005) *Frequently Asked Questions about Resilience and Recovery.* Portland, OR: Research & Training Center on Family Support and Children's Mental Health, Portland State University.

17 World Health Organization. (2007). *Mental Health: Strengthening Mental Health Promotion (Fact Sheet No. 220),* p. 1. Geneva: WHO.

18 Miles, J., Espiritu, R.C., Horen, N., Sebian, J., & Waetzig, E. (2010). *A Public Health Approach to Children's Mental Health: A Conceptual Framework.* Washington, DC: Georgetown University Center for Child and Human Development, National Technical Assistance Center for Children's Mental Health: 20.

19 Miles, J., Espiritu, R.C., Horen, N., Sebian, J., & Waetzig, E. (2010). *A Public Health Approach to Children's Mental Health: A Conceptual Framework.* Washington, DC: Georgetown University Center for Child and Human Development, National Technical Assistance Center for Children's Mental Health: 20.

20 Miles, J., Espiritu, R.C., Horen, N., Sebian, J., & Waetzig, E. (2010). *A Public Health Approach to Children's Mental Health: A Conceptual Framework.* Washington, DC: Georgetown University Center for Child and Human Development, National Technical Assistance Center for Children's Mental Health.

21 U.S. Public Health Service. (2000). *Report of the Surgeon General's Conference on Children's Mental Health: A National Action Agenda.* Washington, DC: Department of Health and Human Services.

22 American Psychiatric Association (APA). (2000). *Diagnostic and Statistical Manual of Mental Disorders, Fourth Edition, Text Revision (DSM-IV-TR).* Washington DC: APA.

23 The Main Place. (n.d.). *Mental Health Challenges.* http://www.themainplace.org/mentalchallenges.html, accessed February 18, 2011.

24 Center for Substance Abuse Treatment. (2007). *Definitions and Terms Relating to Co-Occurring Disorders.* COCE Overview Paper 1. DHHS Publication No. (SMA) 07-4163, p. 2. Rockville, MD: Substance Abuse and Mental Health Services Administration, Center for Mental Health Services: 266.

25 Center for Substance Abuse Treatment. (2007). *Definitions and Terms Relating to Co-Occurring Disorders.* COCE Overview Paper 1. DHHS Publication No. (SMA) 07-4163, p. 2. Rockville, MD: Substance Abuse and Mental Health Services Administration, Center for Mental Health Services: 265.

26 National Institutes of Health Medline Plus. *Dual Diagnosis.* http://www.nlm.nih.gov/medlineplus/dualdiagnosis.html accessed February 18, 2011.

27 Substance Abuse and Mental Health Services Administration. (2015). Results from the 2014 National Survey on Drug Use and Health: Mental health findings (NSDUH Series H-49, HHS Publication No. (SMA) 14-4887). Rockville, MD: Substance Abuse and Mental Health Services Administration.

28 *Breslau, J., Aguilar-Gaxiola, S., Kendler, K.S., Su, M., Williams, D., & Kessler, R.C. (2006).* Specifying race-ethnic differences in risk for psychiatric disorder in a USA national sample. Psychol Med. 36(1):57-68.

29 Merikangas, K.R., He, J., Bursteink, M., Swanson, S.A., Avenevoli, S., Cui, L., Benjet, C., Georgiades, K., & Swendsen, J. (2010, October). Lifetime prevalence of mental disorders in U.S. adolescents: Results from the National Comorbidity Study-Adolescent Supplement (NCS-A). *Journal of the American Academy of Child and Adolescent Psychiatry,* 49(10):980-989.

30 National Institutes of Mental Health Statistics. http://www.nimh.nih.gov/health/topics/child-and-adolescent-mental-health/index.shtml accessed February 18, 2011.

31   Child Mind Institute. (2015). Children's Mental Health Report. http://speakup.childmind.org.

32   Santoro, K., & Murphy, B. (2010, February). *Improving Early Identification & Treatment of Adolescent Depression: Considerations & Strategies for Health Plans: NIHCM Issue Brief.* Washington, DC: National Institute for Health Care Management.

33   Kaufman, R., & Cohen, E. (2000, May). *Early Childhood Mental Health Consultation.* Washington, DC: Georgetown University Center for Child and Human Development.

34   National Institute of Mental Health. (2005, June 6). *NIMH Press Release: Mental Illness Exacts Heavy Toll, Beginning in Youth.* Available at http://www.nimh.nih.gov/science-news/2005/mental-illness-exacts-heavy-toll-beginning-in-youth.shtml accessed February 18, 2011.

35   Santoro, K., & Murphy, B. (2010, February). *Improving Early Identification & Treatment of Adolescent Depression: Considerations & Strategies for Health Plans: NIHCM Issue Brief.* Washington, DC: National Institute for Health Care Management.

36   The World Health Organization. (2008). *The Global Burden of Disease: 2004 Update, Table A2: Burden of Disease in DALYs by Cause, Sex and Income Group in WHO Regions, Estimates for 2004.* Geneva, Switzerland: WHO.

37   Stouthard, M.E.A., Essink-Bot, M.L., Bonsel, G.J., Barendregt, J.J., Kramer, P.G., vande Water, H.P.A., Gunning-Schepers, L.J., & van der Maas, P.J. (1997). *Disability Weights for Diseases in the Netherlands.* Rotterdam: Erasmus University.

38   World Health Organization. (1996). *Diagnostic and Management Guidelines for Mental Disorders in Primary Care: ICD-10.* Chapter V Primary Care Version. Geneva: WHO.

39   Portland Research and Training Center on Family Support and Children's Mental Health. (2005, Summer). *Focal Point: Resilience and Recovery.* Vol. 19, No. 1. Portland, OR: Portland State University.

40   Jorm, A.F., Wright, A., & Morgan, A.J. (2007). Where to seek help for a mental disorder? National survey of the beliefs of Australian youth and their parents. *Medical Journal of Australia,* 187: 556-60.

41   Substance Abuse and Mental Health Administration. *National Registry of Evidence-based Programs and Practices.* http://nrepp.samhsa.gov accessed June 20, 2011.

42   Burns, B.J., & Hoagwood, K. (2002). *Community Treatment for Youth: Evidence-Based Intervention for Severe Emotional and Behavioral Disorders.* New York: Oxford University Press, Inc.

43   Zeltner, B. (2010, July 6). Mental health practitioners slowly turning to holistic practices. *The Plain Dealer.* http://www.cleveland.com/healthfit/index.ssf/2010/07/mental_health_practitioners_sl.html accessed April 4, 2011.

44   Public Information Office. (2011, March 24). *2010 Census Shows America's Diversity.* U.S. Census Bureau: Washington, DC. http://2010.census.gov/news/releases/operations/cb11-cn125.html accessed May 13, 2011.

45   Frey, W.H. (2011, April). *America's Diverse Future: Initial Glimpses at the U.S. Child Population from the 2010 Census.* The Brookings Institution: Washington, DC.

46   The Pew Forum on Religion and Public Life. *U.S. Religious Landscape Survey.* http://religions.pewforum.org/reports accessed Feb. 18, 2011.

47   U.S. Department of Health and Human Services. (2001). *Mental Health: Culture, Race, and Ethnicity —A Supplement to Mental Health: A Report of the Surgeon General.* Rockville, MD: U.S. Department of Health and Human Services, Substance Abuse and

Mental Health Services Administration, Center for Mental Health Services.

48 Russell, S.T., & Joyner, K. (2001). Adolescent sexual orientation and suicide risk: Evidence from a national study. *American Journal of Public Health,* 91:1276-1281.

49 Gibbs, J.T. (2001). African American adolescents. In J.T. Gibbs, L.N. Huang and Associates *Children of Color: Psychological Interventions with Culturally Diverse Youth.* Jossey-Bass Publishers: San Francisco: 203.

50 Sawyer, D., Gale, J., & Lambert, D. (2006). *Rural and Frontier Mental and Behavioral Health Care: Barriers, Effective Policy Strategies, Best Practices.* Waite Park, MN: National Association for Rural Mental Health.

51 Centers for Medicare and Medicaid. *Medicaid Eligibility.* https://www.cms.gov/Medicaid Eligibility/ accessed February 18, 2011.

52 Centers for Medicare and Medicaid. *Medicaid Eligibility.* https://www.cms.gov/Medicaid Eligibility/downloads/ListStateMedicaid Websites.pdf accessed February 18, 2011.

53 American Academy of Child and Adolescent Psychiatry. *Facts for Families: Normal Adolescent Development Part I.* http://aacap.org/cs/root/ facts_for_families/normal_adolescent_ development_part_i accessed April 5, 2011.

54 MedHelp. *Adolescent Development: Information, Symptoms, Treatments, and Resources.* http:// www.medhelp.org/medical-information/ show/5457/Adolescent-development?page=2 accessed April 5, 2011.

55 IBID.

56 National Institutes of Health Medline Plus. *Puberty.* http://www.nlm.nih.gov/medlineplus/ puberty.html accessed April 5, 2011.

57 American Academy of Child and Adolescent Psychiatry. *Facts for Families: Normal Adolescent Development Part I.* http://aacap.org/cs/root/ facts_for_families/normal_adolescent_ development_part_i accessed April 5, 2011.

58 American Academy of Child and Adolescent Psychiatry. *Facts for Families: Normal Adolescent Development Part I.* http://aacap.org/cs/root/ facts_for_families/normal_adolescent_ development_part_i accessed April 5, 2011.

59 Safe Schools Coalition. *About 'GLBTQ' and GLBTQ Youth.* http://www.safeschoolscoalition.org/ RG-glbtyouth.html accessed April 11, 2011.

60 FamilyDoctor.org. *Understanding Your Teenager's Emotional Health.* http://familydoctor.org/ online/famdocen/home/children/parents/ parents-teens/590.printerview.html accessed April 5, 2011.

61 IBID.

62 American Academy of Child and Adolescent Psychiatry. *When to Seek Help for your Child.* http://aacap.org/cs/root/facts_for_families/ when_to_seek_help_for_your_child accessed April 5, 2011.

63 American Association of Intellectual and Developmental Disorders. (2011). *Definition of Intellectual Disability.* http://www.aaidd.org/ content_100.cfm?navID=21 accessed May 2, 2011.

64 Kessler, R. C., Berglund, P., Demler, O., Jin, R., Koretz, D., Merikangas, K. R., et al. (2003). The epidemiology of major depressive disorder: Results from the National Comorbidity Survey Replication NCS-R. *Journal of the American Medical Association,* 289: 3095–3105.

65 National Institute of Mental Health. (June 6, 2005). *NIMH Press Release: Mental Illness Exacts*

Heavy Toll, Beginning in Youth. Available at http://www.nimh.nih.gov/science-news/2005/mental-illness-exacts-heavy-toll-beginning-in-youth.shtml accessed February 18, 2011.

66   Lubman, D.I., Yucel, M., & Hall, W.D. (2007). Substance use and the adolescent brain: A toxic combination? *Journal of Psychopharmacology*, 21:792.

67   Center for Substance Abuse Treatment. (2006). *National Summit on Recovery: Conference Report*. Rockville, MD: Substance Abuse and Mental Health Services Administration.

68   Jacobson, N., & Greenley, D. (2001, April). What is recovery? A conceptual model and explication. *Psychiatric Services*, 52: 482-485.

69   Center for Substance Abuse Treatment. (2006). *National Summit on Recovery: Conference Report*. Rockville, MD: Substance Abuse and Mental Health Services Administration.

70   Australian Bureau of Statistics. (2008). *2007 National Survey of Mental Health and Wellbeing: Summary of Results*. (Document 4326.0). Canberra: ABS.

71   National Institute of Mental Health. (2005, June 6). *NIMH Press Release: Mental Illness Exacts Heavy Toll, Beginning in Youth*. Available at http://www.nimh.nih.gov/science-news/2005/mental-illness-exacts-heavy-toll-beginning-in-youth.shtml accessed February 18, 2011.

72   Merikangas, K.R., He, J., Bursteink, M., Swanson, S.A., Avenevoli, S., Cui, L., Benjet, C., Georgiades, K., & Swendsen, J. (2010, October). Lifetime prevalence of mental disorders in U.S. adolescents: Results from the National Comorbidity Study-Adolescent Supplement (NCS-A). *Journal of the American Academy of Child and Adolescent Psychiatry*, 49(10):980-989.

73   Wright, A., Harris, M.G., Wiggers, J.H., Jorm, A.F., Cotton, S.M., Harrigan, S.M., et al. (2005). Recognition of depression and psychosis by young Australians and their beliefs about treatment. *Medical Journal of Australia*, 183: 18-23.

74   Jorm, A.F., Wright, A., & Morgan, A.J. (2007). Where to seek help for a mental disorder? National survey of the beliefs of Australian youth and their parents. *Medical Journal of Australia*, 187: 556-60.

75   Kitchener, B.A., & Jorm, A.F. (2002). Mental health first aid training for the public: Evaluation of effects on knowledge, attitudes and helping behavior. *BMC Psychiatry*, 2: 10.

76   Kitchener, B.A. & Jorm, A.F. (2004). Mental health first aid training in a workplace setting: A randomized controlled trial [ISRCTN13249129]. *BMC Psychiatry*, 4: 23.

77   Jorm, A.F., Kitchener, B.A., O'Kearney, R., & Dear, K.B.G. (2004). Mental health first aid training of the public in a rural area: A cluster randomized trial [ISRCTN53887541]. *BMC Psychiatry*, 4: 33.

78   Jorm, A.F., & Kitchener, B.A., Mugford, S.K (2005). Experiences in applying skills learned in a mental health first aid training course: A qualitative study of participants' stories. *BMC Psychiatry*, 5: 43.

79   Sylvia Rivera Law Project. *Your Healthcare Rights*. http://srlp.org/resources/pubs/healthcare_adult accessed April 5, 2011.

80   Gibbs, J.T., Huang, L. N., et al. (2001). *Children of Color: Psychological Interventions with Culturally Diverse Youth*. San Francisco: Jossey-Bass Publishers.

81   Williams, R. (n.d.). Cultural Safety: What Does It Mean for Our Work Practice?, p. 2. *Australia and New Zealand Journal of Public Health*. Vol. 123(2). http://www.ruralhealth.utas.edu.au/indigenous-health/RevisedCulturalSafetyPaper-pha.pdf accessed May 9, 2011.

82 Fox, K., Becker-Green, J., Gault, J., & Simmons, D. (2005). Native American youth in transition: The path from adolescence to adulthood in two Native American communities. Portland, OR: National Indian Child Welfare Association.

83 Nebelkopf, E. and Phillips, M. (Eds.). (2004). *Healing and Mental Health for Native Americans: Speaking in Red.* Walnut Creek, CA: AltaMira Press.

84 National Child Traumatic Stress Network. (2003). *Review of Child and Adolescent Refugee Mental Health: White Paper from the National Child Traumatic Stress Network Refugee Trauma Task Force.* Boston, MA: Funded by the Substance Abuse and Mental Health Services Administration, U.S. Department of Health and Human Services.

85 National Institute of Mental Health. Bipolar Disorder Among Children. http://www.nimh.nih.gov/health/statistics/prevalence/bipolar-disorder-among-children.shtml

86 Post, R.M. (1992). Transduction of psychosocial stress into the neurobiology of recurrent affective disorder. *American Journal of Psychiatry,* 149: 999-1010.

87 U.S. Food and Drug Administration. (2007, May). *Questions and Answers on Antidepressant Use in Children, Adolescents, and Adults.* http://www.fda.gov/Drugs/DrugSafety/Informationby DrugClass/ucm096321.htm accessed April 20, 2011.

88 Teesson, M., Slade, T., & Mills, K. (2009). Comorbidity in Australia: findings of the 2007 National Survey of Mental Health and Wellbeing. *Australian and New Zealand Journal of Psychiatry,* 43: 606-14.

89 Swanson, S. A., Crow, S. J., Le Grange, D., Swendsen, J., & Merikangas, K. R. (2011). Prevalence and correlates of eating disorders in adolescents: Results from the National Comorbidity Survey Replication Adolescent Supplement. Arch Gen Psychiatry. 68 (7): 714-723.

90 Kelly, C.M., Kitchener, B.A., & Jorm, A.F. (2010). *Youth Mental Health First Aid: A manual for adults assisting young people.* 2nd ed. Melbourne, Australia: Orygen Youth Health Research Centre.

91 National Institute of Mental Health. *What Are the Signs and Symptoms of Depression?.* http://www.nimh.nih.gov/health/publications/depression/what-are-the-signs-and-symptoms-of-depression.shtml accessed April 5, 2011.

92 Cash, R. (2004). *Depression in Young Children: Information for Parents and Educators.* Bethesda, MD: National Association of School Psychologists.

93 Depression and Bipolar Support Alliance. *About Mood Disorders.* http://www.dbsalliance.org accessed April 5, 2011.

94 West, A.E. & Pavuluri, M.N. (2009). Psychosocial treatments for childhood and adolescent bipolar disorder. *Child and Adolescent Psychiatric Clinics of North America,* 18: 471-82.

95 Marshall, M., Lewis, S., Lockwood, A., Drake, R., Jones, P., & Croudace, T. (2005). Association between duration of untreated psychosis and outcome in cohorts of first-episode patients: A systematic review. *Archives of General Psychiatry,* 62: 975-83.

96 Joyce, P.R. (2000). Epidemiology of mood disorders. In M.G. Gelder, J.J. Lopez-Ibor, N. Andreasen (eds.). *New Oxford Textbook of Psychiatry.* Oxford: Oxford University Press: 695-701.

97 Souery, D., Blairy, S., & Mendlewicz, J. (2000). Genetic and social aetiology of mood disorders In M.G. Gelder, J.J. Lopez-Ibor, N. Andreasen (eds.). *New Oxford Textbook of Psychiatry.* Oxford: Oxford University Press: 701-11.

98 Zahn-Waxler, C., Shirtcliff, E.A., & Marceau, K. (2008). Disorders of childhood and adolescence: gender and psychopathology. *Annual Review of Clinical Psychology,* 4: 275-303.

99 The American Academy of Child and Adolescent Psychiatry. (2011, March). *Facts for Families: Bullying.* http://www.aacap.org/cs/root/facts_for_families/bullying accessed June 20, 2011.

100 U.S. Department of Health and Human Services, Health Research and Services Administration. (2011). *Stop Bullying Now.* http://www.stop bullying.gov/community/tip_sheets/mental_health_professionals_bullied.pdf accessed July 1, 2011.

101 American Psychiatric Association. (2000). *Diagnostic and Statistical Manual of Mental Disorders, fourth edition, Text Revision (DSM-IV-TR).* Washington, DC: American Psychiatric Association.

102 Rubinow, D.R., Schmidt, P.J., & Roca, C.A. (1998). Estrogen-serotonin interactions: Implications for affective regulation. *Biological Psychiatry,* 44(9): 839-850.

103 Zahn-Waxler, C., Shirtcliff, E.A., & Marceau, K. (2008). Disorders of childhood and adolescence: Gender and psychopathology. *Annual Review of Clinical Psychology,* 4: 275-303.

104 Mourning, P.W. (1998). Melancholia and masculinity: Recognizing and treating depression in men. In W. Pollack & R. Levant (eds.). *New Psychotherapy for Men.* New York: Wiley: 147-166.

105 Cochran, S.V. & Rabinowitz, F.E. (2000). *Men and Depression: Clinical and Empirical Perspectives.* San Diego: Academic Press.

106 Tsuchiya, K.J., Byrne, M., & Mortensen, P.B. (2003). Risk factors in relation to an emergence of bipolar disorder: A systematic review. *Bipolar Disorders,* 5: 231-42.

107 Rao, U., & Chen, L.A. (2009). Characteristics, correlates, and outcomes of childhood and adolescent depressive disorders. *Dialogues in Clinical Neuroscience,* 11: 45-62.

108 Kelly, C.M., Jorm, A.F., Kitchener, B.A., & Langlands, R.L. (2008). Development of mental health first aid guidelines for suicidal ideation and behaviour: A Delphi study. *BMC Psychiatry,* 8:17.

109 Langlands, R.L., Jorm, A.F., Kelly, C.M., & Kitchener, B.A. (2008). First aid for depression: A Delphi consensus study with consumers, carers and clinicians. *Journal of Affective Disorders,* 105: 157-65.

110 U.S. Public Health Service. (2001). *National strategy for suicide prevention: Goals and objectives for action.* Washington, DC: Department of Health and Human Services.

111 Jacobson, C.M., & Gould, M. (2007). The epidemiology and phenomenology of non-suicidal self injurious behavior among adolescents: A critical review of the literature. *Archives of Suicide Research,* 11: 129-47.

112 Heath, N.L., Ross, S., Toste, J.R., Charlebois, A., & Nedecheva, T. (2009). Retrospective analysis of social factors and nonsuicidal self-injury among young adults. *Canadian Journal of Behavioural Science/Revue Canadienne des Sciences du Comportement,* 41: 180-6.

113 Scottish Executive NHS. (2005). *Scotland's Mental Health First Aid Manual.* Edinburgh: NHS Health Scotland.

114 Lazear, K.J., Pires, S.A., Isaacs, M.R., Chaulk, P. & Huang, L. (2008). Depression among Low-Income Women of Color: Qualitative Findings from Cross-Cultural Focus Groups. *Journal of Immigrant and Minority Health,* 10:127–133.

115 Substance Abuse and Mental Health Services Administration (SAMHSA), Center for Behavioral Health Statistics and Quality. (2011, April 28).

The NSDUH Report: Major Depressive Episode and Treatment among Adolescents: 2009. Rockville, MD: SAMHSA.

116   Klein, J.B., Jacobs, R.H., & Reinecke, M.A. (2007). Cognitive behavioral therapy for adolescent depression: A meta-analytic investigation of changes in effect-size estimates. *Journal of the American Academy of Child and Adolescent Psychiatry,* 46: 1403-13.

117   Weissman, M.M. (2006). Recent non-medication trials of interpersonal psychotherapy for depression. *International Journal of Neuropsychopharmacology,*10:117-22.

118   Keitner, G.I., Archambault, R., Ryan, C.E., & Miller, I.W. (2003, August). Family therapy and chronic depression. *Journal of Clinical Psychology,*59(8):873-84.

119   Eskin, M., Ertekin, K., & Demir, H. (2008). Efficacy of a problem-solving therapy for depression and suicide potential in adolescents and young adults. *Cognitive Therapy and Research,* 32: 227-45.

120   National Institute of Mental Health. *Antidepressant Medications for Children and Adolescents: Information for Parents and Caregivers.* http://nimh.nih.gov/health/topics/child-and-adolescent-mental-health/antidepressant-medications-for-children-and-adolescents-information-for-parents-and-caregivers.shtml accessed June 13, 2011.

121   Hetrick, S.E., Merry, S.N., McKenzie, J., & Sindahl, P. (2007). Selective serotonin reuptake inhibitors (SSRIs) for depressive disorders in children and adolescents. *Cochrane Database of Systematic Reviews,* 3: CD004851.

122   Yatham, L.N., Kennedy, S.H., Kennedy, C.D., Parikh, S., MacQueen, G., McIntyre, R., et al. (2005). Canadian Network for Mood and Anxiety Treatments (CANMAT) guidelines for the management of patients with bipolar disorder: Consensus and controversies. *Bipolar Disorders,* 7: S5-69.

123   Nandagopal, J.J., DelBello, M.P., & Kowatch, R. (2009). Pharmacologic treatment of pediatric bipolar disorder. *Child and Adolescent Psychiatric Clinics of North America,* 18: 455-69.

124   West, A.E., & Pavuluri, M.N. (2009). Psychosocial treatments for childhood and adolescent bipolar disorder. *Child and Adolescent Psychiatric Clinics of North America,* 18: 471-82.

125   West, A.E., & Pavuluri, M.N. (2009). Psychosocial treatments for childhood and adolescent bipolar disorder. *Child and Adolescent Psychiatric Clinics of North America,* 18: 471-82.

126   Frank, E., Swartz, H.A., & Kupfer, D.J. (2000). Interpersonal and social rhythm therapy: Managing the chaos of bipolar disorder. *Biological Psychiatry, 48*(6), 593-604.

127   West, A.E., & Pavuluri, M.N. (2009). Psychosocial treatments for childhood and adolescent bipolar disorder. *Child and Adolescent Psychiatric Clinics of North America,* 18: 471-82.

128   National Assembly on School-Based Care (NASBC). *Bringing Health Care to Schools for Student Success.* Washington, DC: NASBC. http://ww2.nasbhc.org/RoadMap/Public/MH_list_risk_factors.pdf accessed June 30, 2011.

129   Keitner, G.I., Ryan, C.E., Miller, I.W., Kohn, R., Bishop, D.S., & Epstein, N.B. (1995). Role of the family in recovery and major depression. *American Journal of Psychiatry,* 152: 1002-8.

130   Jorm, A.F., Morgan, A.J., & Wright, A. (2008). Interventions that are helpful for depression and anxiety in young people: A comparison of clinicians' beliefs with those of youth and

their parents. *Journal of Affective Disorders,* 111: 227-34.

131 Sánchez-Villegas, A., Delgado-Rodríguez, M., Alonso, A., Schlatter, J., Lahortiga, F., Majem, L.S., et al. (2009, October). Association of the Mediterranean dietary pattern with the incidence of depression: The Seguimiento Universidad de Navarra/University of Navarra follow-up (SUN) cohort. *Archives of General Psychiatry,* 66(10): 1090-8.

132 Hou, W.H., Chiang, P.T., Hsu, T.Y., Chiu, S.Y., & Yen, Y.C. (2010). Treatment effects of massage therapy in depressed people: A meta-analysis. *Journal of Clinical Psychology.* 71:894-901.

133 Golden, R.N., Gaynes, B.N., Ekstrom, R.D., Hamer, R.M., Jacobsen, F.M., Suppes, T., Wisner, K.L., & Nemeroff, C.B. (2005, April). The efficacy of light therapy in the treatment of mood disorders: A review and meta-analysis of the evidence. *American Journal of Psychiatry.* 162(4):656-62.

134 Costello, E. J., Angold, A., Burns, B. J., Stangl, D. K., Tweed, D. L., Erkanli, A., & Worthman, C. M. (1996). The Great Smoky Mountains Study of Youth. Goals, design, methods, and the prevalence of DSM-III-R disorders. *Archives of General Psychiatry,* 53, 1129–1136.

135 Kessler, R.C., Berglund, P.A., Demler, O., Jin R., & Walters, E.E. (2005). Lifetime prevalence and age-of-onset distributions of DSM-IV disorders in the National Comorbidity Survey Replication (NCS-R). Archives of General Psychiatry, 62, 593-602.

136 From, M., Kessler, R.C., Chiu, W.T., Demler, O., & Walters, E.E. (2005, June). Prevalence, severity, and comorbidity of twelve-month DSM-IV disorders in the National Comorbidity Survey Replication (NCS-R). *Archives of General Psychiatry,* 62(6): 617-27.

137 National Institutes of Mental Health. *Statistics.* http://www.nimh.nih.gov/statistics/index.shtml accessed April 6, 2011.

138 Kashani, J.H. & Orvaschel, H. (1990). A community study of anxiety in children and adolescents. *American Journal of Psychiatry,* 147: 313-8.

139 American Psychiatric Association. (2000). *Diagnostic and Statistical Manual of Mental Disorders, fourth edition, Text Revision (DSM-IV-TR).* Washington, DC: American Psychiatric Association.

140 Kendler, K.S., Neale, M.C., Kessler, R.C., et al. (1992). Generalized anxiety disorder in women. A population-based twin study. *Archives of General Psychiatry,* 49(4): 267-72.

141 Kessler, R.C., Chiu, W.T., Jin, R., Ruscio, A.M., Shear, K., Walters, E.E. (2006). The epidemiology of panic attacks, panic disorder, and agoraphobia in the National Comorbidity Survey Replication. *Archives of General Psychiatry,* 63: 415-24.

142 Robins, L.N., Regier, D.A., (eds.). (1991). *Psychiatric disorders in America: The Epidemiologic Catchment Area Study.* New York: The Free Press.

143 National Institutes of Mental Health. *Social Phobia (Social Anxiety Disorder).* http://www.nimh.nih.gov/health/publications/anxiety-disorders/social-phobia-social-anxiety-disorder.shtml accessed April 6, 2011.

144 Woodward, L.J., Fergusson, D.M. (2001). Life course outcomes of young people with anxiety disorders in adolescence. *Journal of the American Academy of Child & Adolescent Psychiatry,* 40: 1086-93.

145 National Institutes of Mental Health. *Post-Traumatic Stress Disorder.* http://www.nimh.nih.gov/health/publications/anxiety-disorders/post-traumatic-stress-disorder.shtml accessed April 6, 2011.

146 National Institutes of Mental Health. *Obsessive-Compulsive Disorder.* http://www.nimh.nih.gov/

health/publications/anxiety-disorders/ obsessive-compulsive-disorder.shtml accessed April 6, 2011.

147 Kushner, M.G., Sher, K.J., & Beitman, B.D. (1990). The relation between alcohol problems and the anxiety disorders. *American Journal of Psychiatry,* 147(6): 685-95.

148 Smith, J.P., & Book, S.W. (2010, January). Comorbidity of Generalized Anxiety Disorder and Alcohol Use Disorders among Individuals Seeking Outpatient Substance Abuse Treatment. *Addictive Behaviors,* 35(1): 42–45.

149 Woodward, L.J., & Fergusson, D.M. (2001). Life course outcomes of young people with anxiety disorders in adolescence. *Journal of the American Academy of Child & Adolescent Psychiatry,* 40: 1086-93.

150 Canadian Psychiatric Association. (2006).Clinical practice guidelines: Management of anxiety disorders: 2. *Canadian Journal of Psychiatry,* 51(Suppl 2): 1S-92S.

151 American Psychiatric Association. (2000). *Diagnostic and Statistical Manual of Mental Disorders, fourth edition, Text Revision (DSM-IV-TR).* Washington, DC: American Psychiatric Association.

152 Whitbeck, L.B., Adams, G.W., Hoyt, D.R., & Chen, X. (2004, June). Conceptualizing and measuring historical trauma among American Indian people. American Journal of Community Psychology,33 (3-4):119-30.

153 Anxiety Disorders Association of America. *Living with Anxiety: Children and Teens.* http://www. adaa.org/living-with-anxiety/children accessed April 6, 2011.

154 Arsenault-Lapierre, G., Kim, C., & Turecki, G. (2004). Psychiatric diagnoses in 3275 suicides: A meta-analysis. *BMC Psychiatry,* 4:37.

155 Jacobson, C.M. & Gould, M. (2007). The epidemiology and phenomenology of non-suicidal self injurious behavior among adolescents: A critical review of the literature. *Archives of Suicide Research,* 11: 129-47.

156 Soler, J.A., & Weatherall, R. (2005). Cognitive behavioural therapy for anxiety disorders in children and adolescents. *Cochrane Database of Systematic Reviews,* 4: CD004690.

157 O'Kearney, R.T., Anstey, K., & von Sanden, C. (2006). Behavioural and cognitive behavioural therapy for obsessive compulsive disorder in children and adolescents. *Cochrane Database of Systematic Reviews,* 4: CD004856.

158 de Arellano, M. A., Ko, S. J., Danielson, C. K., & Sprague, C. M. (2008). *Trauma-informed interventions: Clinical and research evidence and culture-specific information project.* Los Angeles, CA & Durham, NC: National Center for Child Traumatic Stress.

159 Ipser, J.C., Stein, D.J., Hawkridge, S., & Hoppe, L. (2009). Pharmacotherapy for anxiety disorders in children and adolescents. *Cochrane Database of Systematic Reviews,*CD005170.

160 Jorm, A.F., Wright, A., & Morgan, A.J. (2007). Where to seek help for a mental disorder? National survey of the beliefs of Australian youth and their parents. *Medical Journal of Australia,* 187: 556-60.

161 National Assembly on School-Based Care (NASBC). *Bringing Health Care to Schools for Student Success.* Washington, DC: NASBC. http://ww2.nasbhc.org/RoadMap/Public/MH_ list_risk_factors.pdf accessed June 30, 2011.

162 Jorm, A.F., Wright, A., & Morgan, A.J. (2007). Where to seek help for a mental disorder? National survey of the beliefs of Australian youth and their parents. *Medical Journal of Australia,* 187: 556-60.

163 Jorm, A.F., Morgan, A.J., & Wright A. (2008). Interventions that are helpful for depression and anxiety in young people: A comparison of clinicians' belief with those of youth and their parents. *Journal of Affective Disorders,* 111: 227-34.

164 Esch, T., Fricchione, G.L., & Stefano, G.B. (2003, February 26). The therapeutic use of the relaxation response in stress-related diseases. *Medical Science Monitor,* 9(2):RA23-34.

165 Parslow, R., Morgan, A.J., Allen, N.B., Jorm, A.F., O'Donnell, C.P., & Purcell, R. (2008). Effectiveness of complementary and self-help treatments for anxiety in children and adolescents. *Medical Journal of Australia,*188: 355-9.

166 Anxieties Disorders Association of America. *Complementary and Alternative Treatments.* http://www.adaa.org/finding-help/treatment/complementary-alternative-treatment accessed June 1, 2011.

166 National Child Traumatic Stress Network. *Understanding Child Traumatic Stress.* www.nctsn.org/resources/audience/parent-caregivers/understanding-child-traumatic-stress accessed June 1, 2011.

167 Fairburn, C.G., & Harrison, P.J. (2003). Eating disorders. *Lancet,* 361: 407-16.

168 Story, M., French, S.A., Neumark-Sztainer, D., Downes, B., Resnick, M.D., & Blum, R.W. (1997, April). Psychosocial and behavioral correlates of dieting and purging in Native American adolescents. *Pediatrics,* 99(4): 8.

169 Kilpatrick, M., Ohannessian, C., & Bartholomew, J. B. (1999). Adolescent weight management and perceptions: An analysis of the National Longitudinal Study of Adolescent Health. *Journal of School Health,* 69(4), 148-152.

170 Robinson, T.N., Killen, J.D., Litt, I.F., Hammer, L.D., Wilson, D.M, Haydel, K.F., Hayward, C., & Taylor, C.B. (1996, December). Ethnicity and body dissatisfaction: Are Hispanic and Asian girls at increased risk for eating disorders? *Journal of Adolescent Health,*19(4),384-393.

171 Eating Disorders Resources. *Eating Disorder Statistics.* http://www.bulimia.com/client/client_pages/eatingdisorderstats.cfm accessed March 2, 2011.

172 National Institute of Mental Health. (2007). *Eating Disorders.* Bethesda, MD: U.S. Department of Human Services, National Institutes of Health.

173 National Institute of Mental Health. *Eating Disorders.* http://www.nimh.nih.gov/health/publications/eating-disorders/complete-index.shtml#pub3 accessed March 2, 2011.

174 American Psychiatric Association. (2005). *Let's Talk Facts About Eating Disorders.* Arlington, VA: APA.

175 American Psychiatric Association (APA). (2005). *Let's Talk Facts About Eating Disorders.* Washington DC: APA.

176 Women'shealth.gov. *Anorexia Nervosa Fact Sheet.* http://www.womenshealth.gov/faq/anorexia-nervosa.cfm#a accessed March 2, 2011.

177 Wade, T.D., Reski-Rahkonen A., & Hudson J. (2011). Epidemiology of eating disorders. In M. Tsuang and M. Tohen (Eds.), Textbook in psychiatric epidemiology: Third Edition, 343-360. New York: Wiley.

178 National Association of Anorexia Nervosa and Associated Disorders. http://www.anad.org/get-information/about-eating-disorders/eating-disorders-statistics/

179 Women'shealth.gov. *Bulimia Nervosa Fact Sheet.* http://www.womenshealth.gov/faq/bulimia-nervosa.cfm accessed March 2, 2011.

180 National Institute of Mental Health. (2007). *Eating Disorders*. Bethesda, MD: U.S. Department of Human Services, National Institutes of Health.

181 American Psychiatric Association. (2000). *Diagnostic and Statistical Manual of Mental Disorders, fourth edition, Text Revision (DSM-IV-TR)*. Washington DC: American Psychiatric Association.

182 Crow, S.J., Peterson, C.B., Swanson, S.A., Raymond, N.C., Specker, S., Eckert, E.D., Mitchell, J.E. (2009) Increased mortality in bulimia nervosa and other eating disorders. *American Journal of Psychiatry* 166, 1342-1346.

183 Women'shealth.gov. *Binge Eating Disorder Fact Sheet*. http://www.womenshealth.gov/faq/binge-eating-disorder.cfm accessed March 2, 2011.

184 Hudson, J.I., Hiripi, E., Pope, H. G., & Kessler, R.C. (2007). The prevalence and correlates of eating disorders in the National Comorbidity Survey Replication. *Biological Psychiatry, 61,* 348-358.

185 American Psychiatric Association (APA). (2005). *Let's Talk Facts About Eating Disorders*. Washington, DC: APA.

186 National Institute of Mental Health. (2007). *Eating Disorders*. Bethesda, MD: U.S. Department of Human Services, National Institutes of Health.

187 National Eating Disorders Association. (2005). www.NationalEatingDisorders.org accessed March 2, 2011.

188 Kempa, M. L. & Thomas, A. J. (2000). Culturally sensitive assessment and treatment of eating disorders. *Eating Disorders, 8,* 17-30.

189 Gilbert, S. C. (2006). Eating disorders in women of color. *Clinical Psychology. Science and Practice,* 10, 444-455.

190 Grigg, M., Bowman, J., & Redman, S. (1996). Disordered eating and unhealthy weight reduction practices among adolescent females. *Preventive Medicine,* 25: 748-56.

191 Patton, G.C., Carlin, J.B., Shao, Q., Hibbert, M.E.,Rosier, M., Selzer, R., et al. (1997). Adolescent dieting: Healthy weight control or borderline eating disorder? *Journal of Child Psychology and Psychiatry,* 38: 299-306.

192 Patton, G.C., Selzer, R., Coffey, C., Carlin, J.B., & Wolfe, R. (1999). Onset of adolescent eating disorders: Population based cohort study over 3 years. *British Medical Journal,* 318: 765-8.

193 Center for Disease Control. (2013). Trends in the prevalence of obesity, dietary behaviors, and weight control practices: National YRBS 1991-2013. http://www.cdc.gov/healthyyouth/data/yrbs/pdf/trends/us_obesity_trend_yrbs.pdf

194 Wilson, G. T., Grilo. C. M., & Vitousek, K. M. (2007). Psychological treatment of eating disorders. *American Psychologist,* 62, 199-216.

195 Wilson, G. T., Grilo. C. M., & Vitousek, K. M. (2007). Psychological treatment of eating disorders. *American Psychologist,* 62, 199-216.

196 National Institute of Mental Health. (2007). *Eating Disorders*. Bethesda, MD: U.S. Department of Human Services, National Institutes of Health.

197 Patton, G.C., Coffey, C., & Sawyer, S.M. (2003). The outcome of adolescent eating disorders: Findings from the Victorian Adolescent Health Cohort Study. *European Child and Adolescent Psychiatry,* 12: S25-9.

198 Mental Health First Aid Training and Research Program.(2009). *Eating Disorders: First Aid Guidelines*. Melbourne: ORYGEN Research Centre, University of Melbourne. Available from: www.mhfa.com.au/Guidelines.shtml.

199 Nielsen, S. (2003). Standardised mortality ratio in bulimia nervosa. *Archives of General Psychiatry,* 60: 851.

200 Sullivan, P.F. (1995). Mortality in anorexia nervosa. *American Journal of Psychiatry,* 152: 1073-4.

201 Klonsky, E.D., & Muehlenkamp, J.J. (2007). Self-injury: A research review for the practitioner. *Journal of Clinical Psychology,* 63: 1045-56.

202 Kitchener, B.A., Jorm, A.F., & Kelly, C.M. (2009). *Mental Health First Aid USA.* Maryland Department of Health and Mental Hygiene, Missouri Department of Mental Health, and National Council for Community Behavioral Healthcare.

203 Kitchener, B.A., Jorm, A.F., & Kelly, C.M. (2009). *Mental Health First Aid USA.* Maryland Department of Health and Mental Hygiene, Missouri Department of Mental Health, and National Council for Community Behavioral Healthcare.

204 Wilson, G.T., Grilo, C.M., & Vitousek, K.M. (2007). Psychological treatment of eating disorders. *American Psychologist,* 62: 199-216.

205 Hay, P.J., Bacaltchuk, J., & Stefano, S. (2004). Psychotherapy for bulimia nervosa and bingeing. *Cochrane Database Systematic Reviews,* 3: CD000562.

206 Le Grange D, & Schmidt U. (2005). The treatment of adolescents with bulimia nervosa. *Journal of Mental Health,* 14: 587-97.

207 Perkins, S.J., Murphy, R., Schmidt, U., & Williams, C. (2006). Self-help and guided self-help for eating disorders. *Cochrane Database Systematic Reviews,* 3: CD004191.

208 Lock, J., & Gowers,S. (2005). Effective interventions for adolescents with anorexia nervosa. *Journal of Mental Health,* 14: 599-610.

209 Croll, J. Neumark-Sztainer, D., Story, M., & Ireland, M. (2002, August). Prevalence and risk and protective factors related to disordered eating behaviors among adolescents: Relationship to gender and ethnicity. *Journal of Adolescent Health.* 31(2). http://www.ncbi.nlm.nih.gov/pubmed/12127387 accessed June 30, 2011.

210 Perkins, S.J., Murphy, R., Schmidt, U., Williams, C. (2006). Self-help and guided self-help for eating disorders. *Cochrane Database Systematic Reviews,* 3: CD004191.

211 Kelly, C.M., Kitchener, B.A., & Jorm, A.F. (2010). *Youth Mental Health First Aid: A manual for adults assisting young people.* 2nd ed. Melbourne, Australia: Orygen Youth Health Research Centre.

212 Kitchener, B.A., Jorm, A.F., & Kelly, C.M. (2009). *Mental Health First Aid USA.* Maryland Department of Health and Mental Hygiene, Missouri Department of Mental Health and National Council for Community Behavioral Healthcare.

213 PubMedHealth. *Psychosis.* http://www.ncbi.nlm. nih.gov/pubmedhealth/PMH0002520/ accessed April 5, 2011.

214 Yale School of Medicine. *Specialized Treatment Early in Psychosis (STEP).* New Haven, CT: Step Program. www.step.yale.edu/psychosis/phasis.aspx accessed April 5, 2011.

215 Saha, S., Chant, D., Welham, J., & McGrath, J. (2005). A systematic review of the prevalence of schizophrenia. *PLoS Medicine,* 2: 413.

216 Duckworth, K. (July 2010). *Early Onset Schizophrenia.* Arlington, VA: National Alliance on Mental Illness. http://www.nami.org/Content/ContentGroups/ Helpline1/Early_Onset_Schizophrenia.htm accessed March, 2011.

217 Mental Health America. *Schizophrenia in Children.* www.mentalhealthamerica.net/go/information/

get-info/schizophrenia/schizophrenia-in-children accessed March 11, 2011.

218 National Institutes of Mental Health. *When Does Schizophrenia Start and Who Gets It?* http://www.nimh.nih.gov/health/publications/schizophrenia/when-does-schizophrenia-start-and-who-gets-it.shtml accessed March 11, 2011.

219 Nicolson, R., Lenane, M., Hamburger, S.D., Fernandez, T., Bedwell, J., & Rapoport, J.L. (2000). Lessons from childhood-onset schizophrenia. *Brain Research Review,* 31(2-3):147-156.

220 Masi, G., Mucci, M., & Pari, C. (2006). Children with schizophrenia: Clinical picture and pharmacological treatment. *CNS Drugs,* 20(10):841-866.

221 National Institutes of Mental Health. *What Are the Symptoms of Schizophrenia?* http://www.nimh.nih.gov/health/publications/schizophrenia/what-are-the-symptoms-of-schizophrenia.shtml accessed March 11, 2011.

222 American Psychiatric Association. (2000). *Diagnostic and Statistical Manual of Mental Disorders, fourth edition, Text Revision (DSM-IV-TR).* Washington DC: American Psychiatric Association.

223 Cannon, T.D., Cadenhead, K., Cornblatt, B., Woods, S.W., Addington, J., Walker, E., Seidman, L.J., Perkins, D., Tsuang, M., McGlashan, T., & Heinssen, R. (2008, January). Prediction of psychosis in high-risk youth: A multi-site longitudinal study in North America. *Archives of General Psychiatry.* 65(1):28-37.

224 Tandon, R., Keshavan, M.S., & Nasrallah, H.A. (2008). Schizophrenia, "Just the Facts": What we know in 2008. Part 2: Epidemiology and Etiology. *Schizophrenia Research,* 102: 1-18.

225 Bender, E. (2006, October 20). Data Confirm MH Crisis Growing in U.S. Prisons. *Psychiatric News.* American Psychiatric Association. 41(20): 17.

226 Crystal Meth Addition.org. *Crystal Meth Effects and Symptoms.* http://www.crystalmeth addiction.org/Crystal_Meth_Effects.htm accessed June 1, 2011.

227 Schizophrenia.com. *The Causes of Schizophrenia.* http://www.schizophrenia.com/hypo.php#child accessed June 29, 2011.

228 Marshall, M., Lewis, S., Lockwood, A., Drake, R., Jones, P., & Croudace, T. (2005). Association between duration of untreated psychosis and outcome in cohorts of first-episode patients: a systematic review. *Archives of General Psychiatry,* 62: 975-83.

229 Edwards, J., & McGorry, P.D. (2002). *Implementing Early Intervention in Psychosis: A Guide to Establishing Early Psychosis Services.* London: Martin Dunitz.

230 Palmer, B.A., Pankratz, V.S., & Bostwick, J.M. (2005). The lifetime risk of suicide in schizophrenia: A reexamination. *Archives of General Psychiatry,* 62: 247-53.

231 Simpson, S.G., & Jamison, K.R. (1999). The risk of suicide in patients with bipolar disorders. *Journal of Clinical Psychiatry,* 60: 53-6.

232 Simpson, S.G., & Jamison, K.R. (1999). The risk of suicide in patients with bipolar disorders. *Journal of Clinical Psychiatry,* 60: 53-6.

233 Hawton, K., Sutton, L., Haw, C., Sinclair, J., & Deeks, J.J. (2005). Schizophrenia and suicide: Systematic review of risk factors. *British Journal of Psychiatry,* 187: 9-20.

234 Wallace, C., Mullen, P., Burgess, P., Palmer, S., Ruschena, D., & Browne, C. (1998). Serious criminal

offending and mental disorder: Case linkage study. *British Journal of Psychiatry,* 172: 477-84.

235 Noffsinger, S.G., & Resnick, P.J. (1999). Violence and mental illness. *Current Opinion in Psychiatry,*12: 683-7.

236 Walsh, E., Buchanan, A., & Fahy, T. (2002). Violence and schizophrenia: Examining the evidence. *British Journal of Psychiatry,* 80: 490-5.

237 Tandon, R., Keshavan, M.S., & Nasrallah, H.A. (2008). Schizophrenia, "Just the Facts": What we know in 2008. Part 2: Epidemiology and Etiology. *Schizophrenia Research,* 100: 4-19.

238 National Institutes of Mental Health. *What Causes Schizophrenia?* http://www.nimh.nih.gov/health/publications/schizophrenia/what-causes-schizophrenia.shtml accessed March 11, 2011.

239 National Assembly on School-Based Care (NASBC). *Bringing Health Care to Schools for Student Success.* Washington, DC: NASBC. http://ww2.nasbhc.org/RoadMap/Public/MH_list_risk_factors.pdf accessed June 30, 2011.

240 McGorry, P., Killackey, E., Elkins, K., Lambert, M., & Lambert, T. (2003). Summary Australian and New Zealand clinical practice guideline for the treatment of schizophrenia. *Australian & New Zealand Psychiatry,* 11: 136-47.

241 Pharoah, F.M., Rathbone, J., Mari, J.J., & Streiner, D. (2003). Family intervention for Schizophrenia. *Cochrane Database of Systematic Reviews,* 3: CD000088.

242 West, A.E., & Pavuluri, M.N. (2009). Psychosocial treatments for childhood and adolescent bipolar disorder. *Child and Adolescent Psychiatric Clinics of North America,* 18: 471-82.

243 Daniels, A., Grant, E., Filson, B., Powell, I., Fricks, L., & Goodale, L. (Eds.). (2010, January). *Pillars of Peer Support: Transforming Mental Health Systems of Care Through Peer Support Services.* Available at: www.pillarsofpeersupport.org.

244 Phillips, P., & Johnson, S. (2001). How does drug and alcohol misuse develop among people with psychotic illness? A literature review. *Social Psychiatry and Psychiatric Epidemiology,* 36: 269-76.

245 Linszen, D.H., Dingemans, M.P.,& Lenior, M,E. (1994). Cannabis abuse and the course of recent onset schizophrenic disorders. *Archives of General Psychiatry,* 51: 273-9.

246 Lubman, D.I., Hides, L., Yücel, M., & Toumbourou, J.W. (2007). Intervening early to reduce developmentally harmful substance use among youth populations. *Medical Journal of Australia,* 187(Suppl 7): S22-5.

247 American Psychiatric Association. (2000). *Diagnostic and Statistical Manual of Mental Disorders, fourth edition, Text Revision (DSM-IV-TR).* Washington DC: American Psychiatric Association.

248 American Psychiatric Association. (2000). *Diagnostic and Statistical Manual of Mental Disorders, fourth edition,* Text Revision (DSM-IV-TR). Washington DC: American Psychiatric Association.

249 http://www.oas.samhsa.gov/CoD/Cod.htm

250 Center for Mental Health Services. (2001). *Mental Health Care for Youth: A National Assessment, Annual/Final Progress Report - January 2001-December 2001.* Rockville, MD: Substance Abuse and Mental Health Services Administration.

251 Brown, S.A. (Undated). *Comorbidity.* http://www.drugstrategies.com/teens/research.html accessed May 28,2011.

252 Center for Disease Control. (2014). Youth risk behavior surveillance - United States, 2013. MMWR, Surveillance Summaries. 63(4). http://www.cdc.gov/mmwr/pdf/ss/ss6304.pdf

253 Centers for Disease Control and Prevention. Youth Risk Behavior Surveillance—United States, 2007 [Online]. (2009). National Center for Chronic Disease Prevention and Health Promotion (producer). [Cited 2009 Nov 6].

254 Naimi, T.S., Brewer, R.D., Mokdad, A., Denny, C., Serdula, M.K., & Marks, J.S. (2003). Binge drinking among U.S. adults. *Journal of the American Medical Association,* 289: 70-75.

255 U.S. Department of Health and Human Services. (2007). *The Surgeon General's Call to Action to Prevent and Reduce Underage Drinking.* Rockville, MD: U.S. Department of Health and Human Services, Office of the Surgeon General.

256 Center for Disease Control. (2014). Youth risk behavior surveillance - United States, 2013. MMWR, Surveillance Summaries. 63(4). http://www.cdc.gov/mmwr/pdf/ss/ss6304.pdf

257 Center for Behavioral Health Statistics and Quality. (2015). Behavioral health trends in the United States: Results from the 2014 National Survey on Drug Use and Health. (HHS Publication No. SMA 15-4927, NSDUH Series H-50). Retrieved from http://www.samhsa.gov/data/sites/ default/files/NSDUH-FRR1-2014/NSDUH-FRR1-2014.htm#idtextanchor057

258 Centers for Disease Control and Prevention. (2010). Youth Risk Behavior Surveillance - United States, 2009. *Morbidity & Mortality Weekly Report,* 59 (No.SS-5):1-142.

259 Grant, B.F., & Dawson, D.A. (1998). Age at onset of drug use and its association with DSM–IV drug abuse and dependence: Results from the National Longitudinal Alcohol Epidemiologic Survey. *Journal of Substance Abuse,* 10:163–173.

260 Center for Behavioral Health Statistics and Quality. (2015). Behavioral health trends in the United States: Results from the 2014 National Survey on Drug Use and Health. (HHS Publication No. SMA 15-4927, NSDUH Series H-50). Retrieved from http://www.samhsa.gov/data/sites/ default/files/NSDUH-FRR1-2014/NSDUH-FRR1-2014.htm#idtextanchor057

261 Substance Abuse and Mental Health Services Administration, *Results from the 2010 National Survey on Drug Use and Health: Summary of National Findings,* NSDUH Series H-41, HHS Publication No. (SMA) 11-4658. Rockville, MD: Substance Abuse and Mental Health Services Administration, 2011.

262 Kitchener, B.A., Jorm, A.F., & Kelly, C.M. (2009). *Mental Health First Aid USA.* Maryland Department of Health and Mental Hygiene, Missouri Department of Mental Health, and National Council for Community Behavioral Healthcare.

263 Yucel, M., Solowij, N., Respondek, C., Whittle, S., Fornito, A., Pantelis, C., et al. (2008). Regional, brain abnormalities associated with longterm heavy cannabis use. *Archives of General Psychiatry,* 65: 694-701.

264 Center for Behavioral Health Statistics and Quality. (2015). Behavioral health trends in the United States: Results from the 2014 National Survey on Drug Use and Health. (HHS Publication No. SMA 15-4927, NSDUH Series H-50). Retrieved from http://www.samhsa.gov/data/sites/ default/files/NSDUH-FRR1-2014/NSDUH-FRR1-2014.htm#idtextanchor057

265 Arseneault, L., Cannon, M., Witton, J., Murray, R.M. (2004). Causal association between cannabis and psychosis: Examination of the evidence. *British Journal of Psychiatry,* 184: 110-7.

266 Center for Behavioral Health Statistics and Quality. (2015). Behavioral health trends in the United States: Results from the 2014 National Survey on Drug Use and Health. (HHS Publication No. SMA 15-4927, NSDUH Series H-50). Retrieved

from http://www.samhsa.gov/data/sites/default/ files/NSDUH-FRR1-2014/NSDUH-FRR1-2014. htm#idtextanchor057

267 Center for Disease Control. (2014). Youth risk behavior surveillance - United States, 2013. MMWR, Surveillance Summaries. 63(4). http://www.cdc.gov/ mmwr/pdf/ss/ss6304.pdf

268 Substance Abuse and Mental Health Services Administration (SAMHSA). (2007). *Results from the 2006 National Survey on Drug Use and Health: National Findings.* Applied Studies, NSDUH Series H-32, DHHS Publication No. SMA 07-4293. Rockville, MD: SAMHSA.

269 Substance Abuse and Mental Health Services Administration (SAMHSA). (2008). *Misuse of Over-the-Counter Cough and Cold Medications among Persons Aged 12 – 25.* Rockville, MD: SAMHSA.

270 Center for Behavioral Health Statistics and Quality. (2015). Behavioral health trends in the United States: Results from the 2014 National Survey on Drug Use and Health. (HHS Publication No. SMA 15-4927, NSDUH Series H-50). Retrieved from http://www.samhsa.gov/data/sites/ default/files/NSDUH-FRR1-2014/NSDUH-FRR1-2014.htm#idtextanchor057

271 National Institute on Drug Abuse (NIDA). (2010, March). *NIDA InfoFACTS: Methamphetamine.* Available at http://www.nida.nih.gov/infofacts/ methamphetamine.html.

272 Bureau of Indian Affairs. *Summary of the Office of Justice Services.* http://www.bia.gov/WhoWeAre/ BIA/OJS/index.htm accessed March 10, 2011.

273 Kelleher, J.B. (2007, June 10). Meth adds scourge to trouble Native American lands. *Washington Post.* Available at: http://www.washingtonpost. com/wp-dyn/content/article/2007/06/10/ AR2007061001182.html.

274 Center for Disease Control. (2014). Youth risk behavior surveillance - United States, 2013. MMWR, Surveillance Summaries. 63(4). http://www.cdc. gov/mmwr/pdf/ss/ss6304.pdf

275 de Win, M.M., Jager, G., Booij, J., Reneman, L., Schilt, T., Lavini, C., et al. (2008). Neurotoxic effects of ecstasy on the thalamus. *British Journal of Psychiatry,* 193: 289-96.

276 Parrott, A.C. (2002). Recreational ecstasy/MDMA, the serotonin syndrome, and serotonergic neurotoxicity. *Pharmacology Biochemistry and Behavior,* 71: 837-44.

277 Center for Disease Control. (2014). Youth risk behavior surveillance - United States, 2013. MMWR, Surveillance Summaries. 63(4). http://www.cdc. gov/mmwr/pdf/ss/ss6304.pdf

278 NIDA for Teens. *Inhalants: What Are They?* http:// teens.drugabuse.gov/facts/facts_inhale1. php#street_names accessed March 20, 2011.

279 Center for Disease Control. (2014). Youth risk behavior surveillance - United States, 2013. MMWR, Surveillance Summaries. 63(4). http://www.cdc. gov/mmwr/pdf/ss/ss6304.pdf

280 Center for Behavioral Health Statistics and Quality. (2015). Behavioral health trends in the United States: Results from the 2014 National Survey on Drug Use and Health. (HHS Publication No. SMA 15-4927, NSDUH Series H-50). Retrieved from http:// www.samhsa.gov/data/sites/default/files/NSDUH-FRR1-2014/NSDUH-FRR1-2014.htm#idtextanchor057

281 American Cancer Society (ACS). (2010). *Child and Teen Tobacco Use.* http://www.cancer.org/Cancer/ CancerCauses/TobaccoCancer/ChildandTeen TobaccoUse/child-and-teen-tobacco-use-facts-and-stats accessed March 20, 2011.

282 Lasser, K., Boyd, J.W., Woolhandler, S., Himmelstein, D., McCormick, D., & Bor, D. (2000). Smoking and mental illness: A population based prevalence

study. *Journal of the American Medical Association,* 284: 2606-10.

283 De Leon, J., & Diaz, F.J. (2005). A meta-analysis of worldwide studies demonstrates an association between schizophrenia and tobacco smoking behaviors. *Schizophrenia Research,* 76: 135-57.

284 Orygen Youth Health Research Centre. (2010). *Parenting Guidelines for Adolescent Alcohol Use.* Melbourne: Orygen Youth Health Research Centre, University of Melbourne. Available from: www.mhfa.com.au/Guidelines.shtml.

285 American Psychological Association. *Understanding Alcohol Use Disorders and their Treatment.* www.apa.org/helpcenter/alcohol-disorders.aspx accessed March 20, 2011.

286 Negrete, J.C. (2000). Aetiology of alcohol problems. In Gelder. M.G., Lopez-Ibor, J.J., Andreasen, N. (eds.). *New Oxford Textbook of Psychiatry.* Oxford: Oxford University Press: 477-82.

287 Substance Abuse and Mental Health Services Administration. (2009). *Designing a Recovery-Oriented Care Model for Adolescents and Transition Age Youth with Substance Use or Cooccurring Mental Health Disorders.* Rockville, MD: U.S. Department of Health and Human Services.

288 Lubman, D.I., Yucel, M., & Hall, W.D. (2007). Substance use and the adolescent brain: A toxic combination? *Journal of Psychopharmacology,* 21:792.

289 McArdle, P. (2008). Use and misuse of drugs and alcohol in adolescence. *British Medical Journal,* 008; 337:a306.

290 American Medical Association. *Harmful Consequences of Alcohol Use on the Brains of Children, Adolescents, and College Students.* Available at: www.ama-assn.org/ama1/pub/upload/mm/388/harmful_consequences.pdf.

291 National Institute on Drug Abuse. *Marijuana Abuse: How Does Marijuana Use Affect Your Brain and Body.* http://www.nida.nih.gov/Research Reports/marijuana/Marijuana3.html accessed June 15, 2011.

292 Teesson, M., Slade, T., & Mills, K. (2009). Comorbidity in Australia: Findings of the 2007 National Survey of Mental Health and Wellbeing. *Australian and New Zealand Journal of Psychiatry,* 43: 606-14.

293 National Health and Medical Research Council (NHMRC). (2009). *Australian Guidelines to Reduce Health Risks from Drinking Alcohol.* Canberra: NHMRC.

294 Yung, A., & Cosgrove, E. (2006, March 10). Cigarettes and alcohol: Youth at risk. *Australian Doctor:* 27-34.

295 Arseneault, L., Moffitt, T.E., Caspi, A., Taylor, P.J., & Silva, P.A. (2000). Mental disorders and violence in a total birth cohort: Results from the Dunedin study. *Archives of General Psychiatry,* 57: 979-86.

296 Arsenault-Lapierre, G., Kim, C., & Turecki, G. (2004). Psychiatric diagnoses in 3275 suicides: A meta-analysis. *BMC Psychiatry,* 4:37.

297 Enoch, M.A., & Goldman D. (2002). Problem drinking and alcoholism: Diagnosis and treatment. *American Family Physician,* 65: 441-54.

298 Pilling, S., Strang, J., & Gerada, C. (2007). Psychosocial interventions and opioid detoxification for drug misuse: Summary of NICE guidance. *British Medical Journal,* 335: 203-5.

299 Minkoff, K., & Cline, C.A. (2007). *Co-Occurring Disorder Resource Bibliography.* Available at: http://www.kenminkoff.com/resource.html accessed June 1, 2011.

300 Kanary, P. (2011, May 19). *Webinar: Designing a Recovery-Oriented Care Model for Adolescents and Transition Age Youth with Co-Occurring Substance Use and Mental Health Disorders*. Washington, DC: Georgetown University National Technical Assistance Center for Children's Mental Health. Powerpoint available at: http://gucchdtacenter. georgetown.edu/resources/2011calls.html.

301 National Assembly on School-Based Care (NASBC). *Bringing Health Care to Schools for Student Success*. Washington, DC: NASBC. http:// ww2.nasbhc.org/RoadMap/Public/MH_list_risk_ factors.pdf accessed June 30, 2011.

302 Croll, J., Neumark-Sztainer, D., Story, M., & Ireland, M. (2002, August). Prevalence and risk and protective factors related to disordered eating behaviors among adolescents: Relationship to gender and ethnicity. *Journal of Adolescent Health. 31(2)*. http://www.ncbi.nlm.nih.gov/ pubmed/12127387 accessed June 30, 2011.

303 American Psychiatric Association (APA). (2000). *Diagnostic and Statistical Manual of Mental Disorders, Fourth Edition, Text Revision (DSM-IV-TR)*. Washington DC: APA.

304 American Psychiatric Association (APA). (2000). *Diagnostic and Statistical Manual of Mental Disorders, Fourth Edition, Text Revision (DSM-IV-TR)*. Washington, DC: APA.

305 Waslick, B., & Greenhill, L. (1997). Attention-deficit/ hyperactivity disorder. In J. M. Weiner (Ed.), *Textbook of child and adolescent psychiatry* (2nd ed.). Washington, DC: American Academy of Child & Adolescent Psychiatry, American Psychiatric Press: 389–410.

306 PubMed Health. *Attention Deficit Hyperactivity Disorder*. http://www.ncbi.nlm.nih.gov/ pubmedhealth/PMH0002518/accessed June 20, 2011.

307 Grizenko, N., & Pawliuk, M. (1994). Risk and protective factors for disruptive behavior disorders in children. *American Journal of Orthopsychiatry, 64(4)*: 534-544. doi:10.1037/h0079566.

308 National Institute of Mental Health. *ADHD: What Efforts are Underway to Improve Treatment*. http:// www.nimh.nih.gov/health/publications/attention- deficit-hyperactivity-disorder/what-efforts-are- under-way-to-improve-treatment.shtml accessed June 13, 2011.

309 ADHD Issues. *What Are the Risk Factors and Causes of Attention Deficit Hyperactivity Disorder (ADHD)?* http://www.adhdissues.com/ms/guides/adhd_ risk_factors/main.html accessed July 1, 2011.

310 Sciberras, E., Ukoumunne, O.C., & Efron, D. (2011, April). Predictors of parent-reported attention- deficit/hyperactivity disorder in children aged 6-7 years: A national longitudinal study. *Journal of Abnormal Child Psychology*. [ePub ahead of print. Available at: http://www.ncbi.nlm.nih.gov/ pubmed/21468666?dopt=Abstract.

311 Loeber, R., & Stouthamer-Loeber, M. (1986). Family factors as correlates and predictors of juvenile conduct problems and delinquency. In M. Tonry, & N. Morris (Eds.), *Crime and Justice,* Vol. 7. Chicago: University of Chicago Press: 29-147.

312 Sampson, R.J., & Laub, J.H. (1993). *Crime in the Making Pathways and Turning Points Through Life*. Cambridge, MA: Harvard University Press.

313 Mayo Clinic. (2009, December 19). *Risk factors for oppositional defiant disorders*. http://www. mayoclinic.com/health/oppositional-defiant- disorder/DS00630/DSECTION=risk-factors accessed July 1, 2011.

314 Children and Adults with Attention Deficit Hyperactivity Disorder (CHADD). http://www.chadd.org.

315 Shaffer, D., Fisher, P., Dulcan, M., Davies, M., Piacentini, J., Schwab-Stone, M., Lahey, B., Bourdon, K., Jensen, P., Bird, H., & Canino, G.R.D. (1996). The second version of the NIMH Diagnostic Interview Schedule for Children (DISC–2). *Journal of the American Academy of Child and Adolescent Psychiatry,* 35: 865–877.

316 National Institute of Mental Health. *Do Teens with ADHD Have Special Needs?* http://www.nimh.nih.gov/health/publications/attention-deficit-hyperactivity-disorder/do-teens-with-adhd-have-special-needs.shtml accessed June 13, 2011.

317 National Institute of Mental Health. *ADHD: Psychotherapy.* Adapted from http://www.nimh.nih.gov/health/publications/attention-deficit-hyperactivity-disorder/psychotherapy.shtml accessed June 13, 2011.

318 National Institute of Mental Health. *How is ADHD Treated?* http://www.nimh.nih.gov/health/publications/attention-deficit-hyperactivity-disorder/how-is-adhd-treated.shtml accessed June 13, 2011.

319 American Academy of Child and Adolescent Psychiatry. (2010). *FAQ's on Oppositional Defiant Disorder.* http://www.aacap.org/cs/resource_center/odd_faqs accessed July 1, 2011.

320 National Institute of Mental Health. *ADHD: Medications.* http://www.nimh.nih.gov/health/publications/attention-deficit-hyperactivity-disorder/medications.shtml accessed June 13, 2011.

321 Burns, B.J., & Hoagwood, K. (2002). *Community Treatment for Youth: Evidence-Based Intervention for Severe Emotional and Behavioral Disorders.* Oxford University Press.

322 U.S. Public Health Service. (2000). *Report of the Surgeon General's Conference on Children's Mental Health: A National Action Agenda.* Washington, DC: Department of Health and Human Services.

323 Johnson, D.L., & Breckenridge, J.N. (1982). The Houston Parent-Child Development Center and primary prevention of behavior problems in young children. *American Journal of Community Psychology,* 10: 305-316.

324 Huss, M. (2008, June). Attention-deficit hyperactivity disorder: risk factors, protective factors, health supply, quality of life. A brief review. *Bundesgesundheitsblatt Gesundheitsforschung Gesundheitsschutz,* 51(6): 602-5. Available at: http://www.ncbi.nlm.nih.gov/pubmed/18446300.

325 Hennis Rhoads, L. K. (2006, December). The link between attention-deficit/hyperactivity disorder and oppositional defiant disorder: Risk and protective factors. The University of North Carolina at Greensboro. Available at: http://libres.uncg.edu/ir/listing.aspx?id=1059.

326 Treatment Improvement Protocol (TIP) Series. (2009, March 4). *Addressing Suicidal Thoughts and Behaviors – Part 3: A Review of the Literature.* Rockville, MD: U.S. Department of Health and Human Services, Substance Abuse and Mental Health Services Administration, Center for Substance Abuse Treatment. www.kap.samhsa.gov/products/Manuals/tips/pdf/TIP50_LitRev.pdf.

327 National Assembly on School-Based Care (NASBC). *Bringing Health Care to Schools for Student Success.* Washington, DC: NASBC. http://ww2.nasbhc.org/RoadMap/Public/MH_list_risk_factors.pdf accessed June 30, 2011.

328 Center for Disease Control and Prevention. 10 leading causes of death by age group, United States - 2014. National Center for Injury Prevention and Control.

329 Centers for Disease Control and Prevention. (2011). *Web-based Injury Statistics Query and Reporting System (WISQARS): Leading Causes of Death.* Retrieved from http://webappa.cdc.gov/sasweb/ncipc/leadcaus10.html.

330 Centers for Disease Control and Prevention. (2011). *Web-based Injury Statistics Query and Reporting System (WISQARS): Leading Causes of Death.* Retrieved from http://webappa.cdc.gov/sasweb/ncipc/leadcaus10.html.

331 U.S. Department of Health and Human Services. (2010). Youth Risk Behavior Surveillance-United States, 2009. *MMWR*, 59(SS-5).

332 Centers for Disease Control and Prevention. (2011). *Web-based Injury Statistics Query and Reporting System (WISQARS): Leading Causes of Death.* Retrieved from http://webappa.cdc.gov/sasweb/ncipc/leadcaus10.html.

333 Suicide Prevention Resource Center. (2008). *Suicide Risk and Prevention for Lesbian, Gay, Bisexual, and Transgender Youth.* Newton, MA: Education Development Center, Inc.

334 Bontempo, D. E., & D'Augelli, A. R. (2002). Effects of at-school victimization and sexual orientation on lesbian, gay, or bisexual youths' health risk behavior. *Journal of Adolescent Health, 30*(5): 364–374.

335 Russell, S.T., & Joyner, K. (2001). Adolescent sexual orientation and suicide risk: Evidence from a national study. *American Journal of Public Health, 91*: 1276-1281.

336 O'Donnell, L., O'Donnell, C., Wardlaw, D. M., & Stueve, A. (2004). Risk factors influencing suicidality among urban African American and Latino youth. *American Journal of Community Psychology, 33*(1/2): 37-49.

337 Rudd, M.D., Berman, A.L., Joiner, Jr., T.E., Nock, M.K., Silverman, M.M., Mandrusiak, M., et al. (2006). Warning signs for suicide: Theory, research, and clinical applications. *Suicide and Life- Threatening Behavior*, 36: 255-62.

338 Nemours. *Warning Signs of Suicide.* http://kidshealth.org/teen/your_mind/friends/talking_about_suicide.html# accessed May 13, 2011.

339 Medline Plus. *Suicide.* http://www.nlm.nih.gov/medlineplus/suicide.html accessed May 13, 2011.

340 Nemours. *Warning Signs of Suicide.* http://kidshealth.org/teen/your_mind/friends/talking_about_suicide.html# accessed May 13, 2011.

341 Kitchener, B.A., Jorm, A.F., & Kelly, C.M. (2009). *Mental Health First Aid USA.* Maryland Department of Health and Mental Hygiene, Missouri Department of Mental Health and National Council for Community Behavioral Healthcare.

342 American Foundation for Suicide Prevention. *When You Fear Someone May Take Their Life.* http://www.afsp.org/index.cfm?page_id=F2F25092-7E90-9BD4-C4658F1D2B5D19A0 accessed May 13, 2011.

343 Youth Suicide Prevention Program. *Talking with Your Child About Suicide.* http://www.yspp.org/parents/talkwithyourchild.htm accessed May 13, 2011.

344 National Suicide Prevention Lifeline. *What if Someone I Know Needs Help?* http://www.suicideprevention lifeline.org/GetHelp/WhatIfSomeoneIKnow NeedsHelp.aspx accessed May 13, 2011.

345 National Suicide Prevention Lifeline. *What Are The Warning Signs For Suicide?* http://www.suicide preventionlifeline.org/GetHelp/SuicideWarning Signs.aspx accessed May 13, 2011.

346 National Alliance for the Mentally Ill (NAMI). (Undated). *Taking Care of Yourself and Your Family After an Attempt: Family Guide for Your Relative in the Emergency Department.* Arlington, VA: NAMI.

Available at: http://www.suicidology.org/c/ document_library/get_file?folderId=229&name =DLFE-98.pdf.

347 Whitlock, J., Eckenrode, J., & Silverman, D. (2006). Self injurious behaviors in a college population. *Pediatrics,* 117: 1939-48.

348 American Academy of Child and Adolescent Psychiatry. *Facts for Family: Self-Injury in Adolescents.* http://aacap.org/page.ww?name= Self-Injury+in+Adolescents&section=Facts+for+ Families accessed June 3, 2011.

349 Barrocas, A. L., Hankin, B. L., Young, J. F., and Abela, J. R. (2012). Rates of nonsuicidal self-injury in youth: Age, sex, and behavioral methods in a community sample. Pediatrics, 130(1): 39-45.

350 American Academy of Child and Adolescent Psychiatry. *Facts for Family: Self-Injury in Adolescents.* http://aacap.org/page.ww?name= Self-Injury+in+Adolescents&section=Facts+for+ Families accessed June 3, 2011.

351 Klonsky, E.D., & Muehlenkamp J.J. (2007). Self-injury: A research review for the practitioner. *Journal of Clinical Psychology,* 63: 1045-56.

352 Kessler, R.C., Chiu, W.T., Jin, R., Ruscio, A.M., Shear, K., & Walters, E.E. (2006). The epidemiology of panic attacks, panic disorder, and agoraphobia in the National Comorbidity Survey Replication. *Archives of General Psychiatry,* 63: 415-24.

353 Barlow, D.H. (1988). *Anxiety and its disorders.* New York: Guilford.

354 Klerman, G.L., Weissman, M.M., Ouellette, R., Johnson, J., & Greenwald, S. (1991). Panic attacks in the community. Social morbidity and health care utilization. *The Journal of the American Medical Association,* 265:742–746.

355 American Psychiatric Association. (1998). Practice guidelines for the treatment of patients with panic disorder. *American Journal of Psychiatry,* 155 (Suppl. 12): 1–34.

356 U.S. Department of Health and Human Services. (1999). *Mental Health: A Report of the Surgeon General—Chapter 4 – Adults and Mental Health.* Rockville, MD: U.S. Department of Health and Human Services, Substance Abuse and Mental Health Services Administration, Center for Mental Health Services, National Institutes of Health, National Institute of Mental Health. http://www. surgeongeneral.gov/library/mentalhealth/ chapter4/sec2.html.

357 American Psychiatric Association. (2000). *Diagnostic and Statistical Manual of Mental Disorders, fourth edition, Text Revision (DSM-IV-TR).* Washington DC: American Psychiatric Association.

358 Cure Panic Attacks in Children: You Can Help Your Child. *Resources.* http://curepanicattacksin children.com/resources/ accessed June 1, 2011.

359 U.S. Department of Health and Human Services. (1999). *Mental Health: A Report of the Surgeon General—Chapter 4 – Adults and Mental Health.* Rockville, MD: U.S. Department of Health and Human Services, Substance Abuse and Mental Health Services Administration, Center for Mental Health Services, National Institutes of Health, National Institute of Mental Health. http://www. surgeongeneral.gov/library/mentalhealth/ chapter4/sec2.html.

360 Salkovskis, P.M., Clark, D..M, & Gelder, M.G. (1996). Cognition-behaviour links in the persistence of panic. *Behaviour Research and Therapy,* 34: 453-8.

361 National Child Traumatic Stress Network. *Understanding Child Traumatic Stress.* www.nctsn.org/resources/audience/parent-caregivers/understanding-child-traumatic-stress accessed June 1, 2011.

362 National Child Traumatic Stress Network. *Early Childhood Trauma.* http://www.nctsnet.org/trauma-types/early-childhood-trauma accessed June 1, 2011.

363 National Child Traumatic Stress Network. *Understanding Child Traumatic Stress.* www.nctsn.org/resources/audience/parent-caregivers/understanding-child-traumatic-stress accessed June 1, 2011.

364 Araújo, B., & Borrell, L. (2006). Understanding the link between discrimination, life chances and mental health outcomes among Latino/as. *Hispanic Journal of Behavioral Sciences, 28*(2): 245-266.

365 The Chadwick Center. (Undated). *Communication and Linguistic Competence: Latino Adaptation Guidelines.* Available at: http://www.chadwick center.org/Documents/WALS/Adaptation%20 Guidelines%20-%20Communication%20and%20 Linguistic%20Competence%20Priority%20Area.pdf.

366 Alim, T.N., Graves, E., Mellman, T.A., Aigbogun, N., Gray, E., Lawson, W., & Charney, D.S. (2006, October). Trauma exposure, posttraumatic stress disorder and depression in an African-American primary care population. *Journal of the National Medical Association, 98*(10): 1630–1636.

367 2008 Presidential Task Force on Posttraumatic Stress Disorder and Trauma in Children and Adolescents. (2008). *Children and Trauma: Update for Mental Health Professionals.* Washington, DC: American Psychological Association. Available at: http://www.apa.org/pi/families/resources/children-trauma-update.aspx.

368 National Child Traumatic Stress Network (NCTSN) Refugee Trauma Task Force. (2005). *Mental Health Interventions for Refugee Children in Resettlement: White Paper 2.* Los Angeles, CA and Durham, NC: NCTSN. Available at: http://www.nctsnet.org/sites/ default/files/assets/pdfs/MH_Interventions_for_ Refugee_Children.pdf.

369 Poirier, J. M., Francis, K. B., Fisher, S. K., Williams-Washington, K., Goode, T. D., & Jackson, V. H. (2008). *Practice Brief 1: Providing Services and Supports for Youth Who Are Lesbian, Gay, Bisexual, Transgender, Questioning, Intersex, or Two-Spirit.* Washington, DC: National Center for Cultural Competence, Georgetown University Center for Child and Human Development. Available at: http://nccc.georgetown.edu/documents/lgbtqi2s.pdf.

370 DeBruyn, L., M. Chino, et al. (2001). Child maltreatment in American Indian and Alaska Native communities: Integrating culture, history, and public health for intervention and prevention. *Child Maltreatment, 6*(2): 89-102.

371 American Medical Association (AMA). (2005). *Management of Public Health Emergencies: A Resource Guide for Physicians and Other Community Responders:* Section 9 - Meeting the Mental Health Needs of Victims, Families, and Responders. Chicago, IL: AMA. Available at: http://www.ama-assn.org/resources/doc/cphpdr/09_ mentalhealth.pdf.

372 American Academy of Child and Adolescent Psychiatry. (2008, December). *Helping Children After A Disaster.* http://aacap.org/page.ww?name= Helping+Children+After+a+Disaster&section=Facts +for+Families accessed June 1, 2011.

373 Kelly, C.M., Jorm, A.F., & Kitchener, B.A. (2010). Development of Mental Health First Aid Guide-lines on How A Member of the Public Can Support a Person Affected by a Traumatic Event: A Delphi Study. *BMC Psychiatry.* Available at: http://www. medscape.com/viewarticle/725637.

374 M.I.S.S. Foundation. *Vicarious Trauma and Caregivers.* http://www.missfoundation.org/pro/ articles/VicariousTrauma.pdf accessed June 1, 2011.

375 M.I.S.S. Foundation. *Vicarious Trauma and Caregivers.* http://www.missfoundation.org/pro/articles/VicariousTrauma.pdf accessed June 1, 2011.

376 UNC School of Medicine, Department of Psychiatry. *What To Do If a Family Member or Friend Has Psychotic Symptoms.* http://www.med.unc.edu/psych/psychoticdisorders/about/what-to-do accessed June 1, 2011.

377 National Institute of Alcohol Abuse and Alcoholism (NIAAA). (2004). NIAAA council approves definition of binge drinking. *NIAAA Newsletter,* No. 3 Available at http://pubs.niaaa.nih.gov/publications/Newsletter/winter2004/Newsletter_Number3.pdf.

378 Wallace, C., Mullen, P., Burgess, P., Palmer, S., Ruschena, D., & Browne, C. (1998). Serious criminal offending and mental disorder: Case linkage study. *British Journal of Psychiatry,* 172: 477-84.

379 Noffsinger, S.G., & Resnick, P.J. (1999). Violence and mental illness. *Current Opinion in Psychiatry,* 12: 683-7.

380 Walsh, E., Buchanan, A., & Fahy, T. (2002). Violence and schizophrenia: Examining the Evidence. *British Journal of Psychiatry,* 180:490-5.

381 Arseneault, L., Moffitt, T.E., Caspi, A., Taylor, P.J., & Silva, P.A. (2000). Mental disorders and violence in a total birth cohort: Results from the Dunedin study. *Archives of General Psychiatry,* 57: 979-86.

382 National Child Traumatic Stress Network (NCTSN). *Symptoms and Behaviors Associated with Exposure to Trauma.* http://nctsnet.org/trauma-types/early-childhood-trauma/Symptoms-and-Behaviors-Associated-with-Exposure-to-Trauma accessed June 1, 2011.

383 National Alliance for the Mentally Ill. *ADHD and Coexisting Conditions.* www.nami.org/Template.cfm?Section=ADHD&Template=/ContentManagement/ContentDisplay.cfm&ContentID=106383 accessed June 1, 2011.

384 National Federation of Families for Children's Mental Health (FFCMH). (2007). *Law Enforcement and Children's Mental Health Roundtable Discussion: Executive Summary,* p. 5. Rockville, MD: FFCMH. http://ffcmh.org/wp-content/uploads/2009/pdffiles/LawEnforcement Roundtable.pdf.

385 National Federation of Families for Children's Mental Health (FFCMH). (2007). *Law Enforcement and Children's Mental Health Roundtable Discussion: Executive Summary.* Rockville, MD: FFCMH. http://ffcmh.org/wp-content/uploads/2009/pdffiles/LawEnforcement Roundtable.pdf.

386 Child Welfare Information Gateway. (2010). *Mandatory Reporters of Child Abuse and Neglect: Summary of State Laws. Administration for Children and Families.* Washington, DC: Administration for Children and Families, U.S. Department of Health and Human Services. http://www.childwelfare.gov/systemwide/laws_policies/statutes/manda.cfm accessed July 15, 2011.